Jason Webster was born in San Francisco in 1970 and grew up in England and Germany. After living for several years in Italy and Egypt, he went to Spain where he learnt flamenco guitar. He currently lives in Oxfordshire and Valencia. This is his first book. His new book *Andalus*, will be available soon from Doubleday.

Acclaim for *Duende*:

'Ever wanted to run away and join the gypsies? Don't. That way lies heartache, flame-haired temptresses (married, with gun-toting husbands and knife-wielding lovers) and lines of white powder laid on the bonnets of stolen BMWs at dawn. Hooked? You will be. If there's such a thing as literary *duende* – the word used in flamenco for what happens when everything goes right – Jason Webster has it in spades . . . it's unputdownable. The autobiography-as-travelogue that is also a rite of passage is a form which worked brilliantly for Laurie Lee and Bruce Chatwin – both novelists as well as seekers after the truth-behind-the-truth. Ladies and gentlemen, we have a new star of the genre: Jason Webster' *Daily Mail*

'*Duende* is a fascinating book, the most gripping I have read for years. I can't remember ever before having stuck my fingers in my ears to block out the wails of my children in order to finish a chapter.

The best travel writing is not about topography but people, and Webster's infiltration of this notoriously closed community makes for compulsive reading. Spain is so often described as a colourful place, but Webster does justice to the greys and blacks of it too: the street-corner junkies, the miserable flats, the lack of imagination. It's not all about driving over lemons.

The greatest strength of the book may be that it mimics, in its own structure, Webster's quest for duende. At the beginning the writing is as uncertain as the writer, but it gathers confidence and pace until, by the middle section, which deals with Madrid, it is exhilarating. This is the moment of hair-raising, spine-tingling, child-ignoring duende.

I know from my own experience living among Madrid's transvestites, poets and revolutionaries that Spain is the strangest place. It is disconcertingly easy to cross a line there and find yourself embroiled in events that seem bizarre when examined in the cold light of day . . . Jason Webster is an exceptional writer, and this is a great book' *Guardian*

'Webster quickly discovers the *compás*, or rhythm, of his narrative voice; the result is a compelling account of a culture closed to most *guiris* (foreigners) and infinitely darker and more dramatic than the colourful tourist spectacles would have them believe ... Webster has skilfully edited his experiences ... he resists the temptation to go into too many descriptive flights about the Spanish landscape, instead creating a sense of place through the conversations of the characters he meets and their immediate environments ... he has a talent for finding moments of humour in unlikely places without overplaying them. Perhaps his greatest achievement is to involve the reader so deeply in the narrator's diffuse quest that what the potential to be a fairly self-indulgent memoir instead becomes a page-turner. *Duende* is an intensely personal portrait of a country in the throes of modernisation, whose spirit still defies definition' *Observer*

'Here, flamenco is shown to stand for all that is wild, anti-establishment and passionate in Spain. It is, in Carmen's words, a bohemian child. This is a romantic view ... one that quickly seduces our traveller and us with him. For a first book, indeed for any book, Webster's writing has great assurance, and there are some superbly constructed moments ... an impressive début ... *Duende* sweeps along from one harmonious chord to the next and builds into a crescendo that is as rich in atmosphere and emotion as the world it seeks to portray ... what it does most successfully is describe a young man's rite of passage through a foreign culture, a journey from which he emerges with a greater understanding of his subject and considerably wiser about the nature of human relationships ... passionate and evocative' *Sunday Times*

'Duende is indefinable, (a know-it-when-you-experience-it thing), but it is when everything comes together perfectly. Luis Antonio de Vega said, "Flamenco is the means through which man reaches God without the intervention of the saints or angels". Real flamenco is exciting, alive, vibrant, and above all, passionate. Alive, vibrant and passionate are good words to describe Jason Webster's outstanding début book ... *Duende* is the most authentic and compelling account of flamenco in English, and one of the best books ever written about Spain' *Literary Review*

'Webster's Spain is remorselessly modern, urban and inhabited not merely by the standard *picaros gitanos* and colourful low-life of the traditional Hispanophile's lexicon, but also tourists, foreign residents and the Costa tackiness which J.G. Ballard evoked so effectively in his recent *Cocaine Nights* . . . thirty years ago this book would undoubtedly have been written as a first novel; it has the pace, crisp dialogue and narrative drama which characterized a certain type of male, heterosexual Anglo-Saxon fiction. The traditions of the Bildungsroman and the rites-of-passage novel have migrated into the travel genre' *Times Literary Supplement*

'Webster . . . has an exquisite nose for trouble, and it is the diversions on the road to flamenco that make such enjoyable reading . . . the mix of romance and determination that propels Webster through life is more than enough to bring the reader along too' *Irish Times*

'Webster became obsessed with *duende* while studying at Oxford, heading to Spain on graduation to learn flamenco guitar and find out more.

Underscoring this search is a more personal journey; the desire to slough off a lingering immaturity and transcend the emotionally repressed make-up of the typical Englishman through immersion in a culture more attuned to passion and its expression. The two themes – the search for *duende* and the search for self – harmonise perfectly.

Webster's experiences are skilfully edited and neatly shaped too, the selective dramatisations and insights into character lending the book the feel of a novel. In its unassuming way it contains multitudes – a young man's emotional growth, a history of flamenco, and a view of a very different Spain to the one we're accustomed to reading about and visiting. Music, passion, drugs, a "beakerful of the warm South" – who could resist all that in these dark days?' *Time Out*

'Webster seems to have encountered the weirdest set of Spaniards imaginable but treats all the ups and (many) downs of his unbelievable adventures with a wry sense of humour. He also manages to deliver an enjoyable beginner's guide to this truly Spanish musical form' *Metro*

'A travel story with a difference. Jason Webster went to Spain with a girlfriend and a guitar, lost the former, found the latter and eventually became obsessed with making music that captured the untranslatable word *duende* – the mixture of passion, pathos and sensuality that is the heart of flamenco. It's a raw story of gypsies, guitars, life on the rough side of Madrid, and always the music, singing, and dancing of flamenco in the background. Any musician will appreciate this book, but it's also a brightly textured description of an English person trying to get to grips with Spain' *Focus*

'What a rich, anecdotal story: clandestine sex, jealous husbands, car thieves, drug-taking. The vivid narrative almost obscures the flamenco knowledge inside it, yet there is real insider material here, and facts and informed opinions pattern the text. The flamenco underworld of Madrid gypsies rings true, including their opportunistic "use" of Webster, the *guiri* outsider. Ultimately, the meanings of flamenco remain elusive, but the book conveys the flamenco way of life, the way of thinking, the way of being.

Through Webster's *rite de passage* you become endeared to him – for his whole-hearted immersion in the lifestyle, the way he respected what he found and how he was accepted for the risks he took' *Songlines*

'One line into his true tale of running away to Spain to live, to really live the flamenco life, I decided I hated Jason Webster. Hated him for saying this: "Often we end up doing what we almost want to do because we lack the courage to do what we really want to do". Bastard. Not only has this 32-year-old newcomer written one of the great opening lines in recent reading but he saw in himself the above tragic portent a whole 10 years ago, when he was still young and reckless enough to head if off' *Herald Sun* (Melbourne)

'For anyone interested in Spain or flamenco, this book is a fascinating personal revelation of both. Mind you, its style and intensity make it attractive to a far wider audience too' *Brisbane News*

'The repressed Anglo-Saxon discovering something-or-other in sultry climes is almost a literary cliché. E.M. Forster scarcely departed from the theme over his entire writing life, while Ernest Hemingway gave it compelling, hairy-chested treatment and a specific location in Spain. Webster's book is distinguished by directness, a lack of pretension and a literary grace that give renewed life to a familiar story'
West Australian

'In many ways this is the best kind of travel book – a passage of self-discovery blended with a learning process and all set against a stirring background'   *Weekend Australian*

DUENDE

A Journey in Search of Flamenco

Jason Webster

BLACK SWAN

DUENDE
A BLACK SWAN BOOK: 0 552 99997 0

Originally published in Great Britain by Doubleday
a division of Transworld Publishers

PRINTING HISTORY
Doubleday edition published 2003
Black Swan edition published 2004

1 3 5 7 9 10 8 6 4 2

Set in 11/13pt Melior by
Falcon Oast Graphic Art Ltd.

Black Swan Books are published by Transworld Publishers,
61–63 Uxbridge Road, London W5 5SA,
a division of The Random House Group Ltd,
in Australia by Random House Australia (Pty) Ltd,
20 Alfred Street, Milsons Point, Sydney, NSW 2061, Australia,
in New Zealand by Random House New Zealand Ltd,
18 Poland Road, Glenfield, Auckland 10, New Zealand
and in South Africa by Random House (Pty) Ltd,
Endulini, 5a Jubilee Road, Parktown 2193, South Africa.

Printed and bound in Great Britain by
Cox & Wyman Ltd, Reading, Berkshire.

Papers used by Transworld Publishers are natural, recyclable products
made from wood grown in sustainable forests. The manufacturing
processes conform to the environmental regulations of the country of origin.

'Duende . . . *A mysterious power that everyone feels but that no philosopher has explained.*'
Goethe

'*Dismal Spanish wailings punctuated by the rattle of the castanets and the clashing harmonies of the guitar.*'
Aldous Huxley

'*The truth marries no-one.*'
Spanish proverb

For Rafa,
and the duende moments with him
that inspired me

To protect the identities of those involved, some of the names of people and places have been changed.

prologue

*O*ften we end up doing what we almost want to do because we lack the courage to do what we really want to do. For years I lived in Italy because I wanted to be in Spain.

As a teenager, Spain had captivated me. Touristy photo books showed a technicolour land of cathedral-like blue skies, dark, open-faced women with bright red carnations in their hair, and the delicate columns and lines of the Alhambra and the Great Mosque in Córdoba. It seemed ancient, mysterious, exotic; a mythical country of semi-madness where men in tight trousers fought deadly beasts and people spoke in earthy, guttural sentences that gave great philosophical importance to everyday tasks such as buying the milk. Outside my window, the Fens of East Anglia stretched an eternal grey in every direction; a flat, wet desert of inbred farmers and plump girls on bicycles, where the only possible excitement was trying to persuade

Blind Bob, the barman at the Red Lion, to give me a drink despite the fact that I was underage. In the books, Spain and its people were always beautiful and warm and passionate. It felt like a lost home. One day I felt sure I would go and live there.

But things got in the way: a chance to live in Italy and the beginning of a self-destructive relationship; university to study Arabic; a year living in Egypt eating beans and running away from over-zealous papyrus salesmen. In my ignorance I thought I was being drawn to the Mediterranean in general. I was wrong. I never found the human warmth and openness I sought and expected to find – the Italians were too busy worrying about how they looked, the Egyptians about the next meal. It was, and always had been, Spain.

Then a chance to remedy things came unexpectedly: after four dry, affectionless years, my Florentine girl-friend left me on the day of my last exam. Bound by the addictive ideas of first love, the plan had been for me to go and join her in Italy once my degree was over: after a relationship built on phone calls and holidays, we could finally be together. But after so much time spent dreaming of an end to our separation, the opportunity to make it real proved too much, and the self-destructive streak in her took control just as my time at university came to an end. No more girl, no more Italy, no more university, no more Middle East.

Suitably heartbroken, I realised that my chance to make a break for Spain had finally come. Loveless and eager for adventure, I was free to escape the mistakes I'd made and explore the passionate world that had inspired me as a teenager; a world I felt I should have been experiencing all along. Spain, I felt, was calling me. But I was keen not just to float around. I wanted something to do there.

'All that university stuff's self-indulgent crap!' a drunken busker assured me in a pub one evening after offering to rearrange my nose.

'I mean, what the fuck are you gonna do with your degree if you're ever up shit creek? You can't eat a degree. At least I can play "Streets of London" and earn a few quid that way.'

He hit a nerve. After four years' study, all I could offer were five different words for 'camel' and the classical Arabic term for masturbation. I desperately wanted a skill, to be able to do something with my hands after years of sitting in libraries concocting meaningless arguments to impress my tutors with. But bricklaying and plastering had only limited appeal. I wanted something more creative.

The busker took pity on me and asked me to buy him a drink.

'Tell you what,' he said as I handed over a large brandy and soda, 'you should take up the guitar, learn a few chords, like me.'

I had never been particularly musical, although the guitar had always appealed to me. But at the age of nine, inspired by a man in a pork-pie hat in a ska band on the television, I temporarily forgot my deep-felt ambition and took up the saxophone instead. It was a mistake from the start: the instrument was bigger than I was, then my teacher had a nervous breakdown and fled to a hippy commune in Scotland. Finally my saxophone was stolen by the school thief. I gave up music after that.

Playing an instrument, however, was precisely the kind of skill I wanted to learn now. I realised all the wrong choices I had made could be cancelled out at once. I was free to live in Spain and to pick up the instrument I had always intended to. All at once it became clear: I should learn flamenco guitar, the musical heart and essence of Spain. It was colourful, exciting and wild – everything my life wasn't. The decision itself was deceptively simple. With almost no idea about flamenco, or where it might lead me, I decided to start straight away.

It was a frightening thing to do, though – leaving everything, a structured life, the network of friends and comforts of an environment I knew well. University life was easy and sheltering. That was precisely why so many of those apparently wise and wrinkled old dons wandering around the quads seemed so childish once you got talking to them; bickering and flirting just like the post-adolescents they were teaching. At university you could live all the adventures you wanted in your head just by going to the library and reading about exotic places, while still enjoying cycling around town with a flowing scarf and snuggling by a fire with a pint in a warm pub in wintertime. I began to have doubts.

'You should think about staying on to do some research,' my tutor said when I saw him in the street. 'Whatever you do, don't just take off somewhere. Have you thought about a life in academia? I can just see you as a lecturer.'

I bought a ticket and a guitar and caught a plane the next day.

A journey and a quest lasting several years lay ahead of me, an experience that would change me for good. There was far more to flamenco – and to Spain – than I could ever have imagined.

18

chapter ONE

Por Fandangos

Yo como tú no encuentro ninguna,
mujer, con quien compararte;
sólo he visto, por fortuna,
a una en un estandarte
y a los pies lleva la luna.

I've found nobody
to compare to you, woman;
only one other seen, fortunately,
on a church banner
with the moon at her feet.

A large woman stands up at the back of the stage and approaches the audience as the guitars play on. Raising an arm above her head, she stamps her foot hard, sweeps her hand down sharply to the side and stares at us in defiance. The music stops and everyone falls silent.

Power emanates from her across the square. Breathing hard, legs rooted to the ground, chin raised, eyes bright, her face a vivid expression of pain. Everyone in the audience focuses on her as she stands motionless, leaning forward slightly, head thrust back, black hair falling loosely over her dark yellow dress. Stretching her arms down at her sides, she tenses her hands open, as though receiving or absorbing some invisible energy. For a moment I think she might never move, need never move even, so strong is the spell she has cast over us. Then, slowly, she lowers her head till it rests on her chest.

A sound begins from somewhere, low and deep: a human voice resonating with complex harmonies locked into a single note. I assume it is coming from the stage, but the song – if song it is – seems to be unprojected, effortlessly filling the space around us like water. It shocks me, as if some long-dormant, primitive, and troubled part of myself is being forced into wakefulness against its will. I have never felt anything like this before and struggle to comprehend as previously unfelt or forgotten emotions begin flowing through me, released by the trigger of the music. My eyes fixed ahead, I watch as the woman lifts her face once more, her mouth partly open, and I realise that the sound is coming from her.

She is singing. But there is no sweet voice, no pleasant melody, no recognisable tune at all. It is more like a scream, a cry, or a shout. Behind her the guitarists begin playing with short, rapid beats, fingers rippling over the strings in strange Moorish-sounding chords. The woman's voice lilts like a muezzin's call to prayer.

I am held by the music, as though any separation between myself and the rhythm has disappeared. A fat woman singing on stage, dancing in a way that seems as if she is barely moving, yet I feel she is stepping inside something and drawing me in with her. A chill, like a ripping sensation, moves up to my eyes. Tears begin to well up, while the cry from her lungs finds an echo within me, and makes me want to shout along with her. The hairs on my skin stand on end, blood drains to my feet. I am rooted to the spot, suspended between the emotion being drawn out of me, as though bypassing my mind, and the shame of what I am feeling.

The song continues and I become aware that others in the audience are experiencing the same. I can tell by the expressions on their faces, a certain look in their eyes, and simply feeling it sweep around us all in a second, like a trance. Then the cries begin as she finds the echo inside us: shouts of '*Ole*', '*Arsa*', '*Eso es*'. Some whisper under their breath, others shout, thick veins pulsating in their necks. The woman fills us, and the evening around us, with a sense of another space.

The song ends, and the audience breaks out into spontaneous, ecstatic applause. It is an emotional release, the greatest one might ever imagine. Pedro leans over to me.

'Did you feel it?' he asks.

The plane flew in over the dust-yellow land. Mountains like pieces of rock half-buried in the sand pushed their way up from the earth, casting long shadows over the landscape as the sun descended behind us. I stared down through the window at the empty space below: arid semi-desert banked by an azure sea, with a promise of balmy, jasmine-scented nights.

Pedro was my only contact in Spain and therefore, I reasoned, a natural starting point for my journey. A friend of a friend and a university lecturer in Arabic, he greeted me at the airport like a lost son, embracing me warmly in the arrivals hall, and quickly gave me a new name: *Mi querido Watson*. He said my surname reminded him of the old Sherlock Holmes films and the time he'd spent living on Baker Street as a youth. I couldn't see the similarity myself.

'Don't worry. Be *kh*appy,' he laughed.

He took me to his house just to the north of Alicante. His father had built it in the Fifties: a white rect-angular villa with bright green shutters, verandas and balconies. I was given the top floor and told I could stay as long as I needed. From the roof you could see the sea stretching across to Algeria. Africa seemed very close.

The garden was straight out of *A Thousand and One Nights*. Date palms stood next to pungent rosemary bushes in an oasis filled with fig trees, jasmine, delicate red and pink roses, pomegranate trees, and row upon row of lemon and orange trees. The jasmine had been trained over the years to create a covered sanctuary where we could sit away from the intense midday sun, half-intoxicated by the perfume circling around us. Pedro insisted we sit together, talking and drinking tea from bone china cups. At first I was happy to acclimatise in this leisurely fashion. After a few days, though, it was frustrating. I wanted to get going, to begin my flamenco adventure, but my host was a man who liked to take his time over any task at hand, always deliberate and careful in everything he did.

'You can't run away from your own feet,' he said, determined to hold me down there in his garden, to stop me from rushing around before I knew where to look.

He would talk non-stop, one story flowing into another in a constant stream of tales and anecdotes. I could hardly get a word in, and when he let me, it was only to fill in some detail, the name of a town, or a person we both knew. At first our conversation centred on Arabic, which we had both studied, but it soon moved on to other subjects. He talked of his love of England, the folklore of Alicante, astronomy, and recipes for chicken broth. He told me everything I would ever want to know about the ancient Roman settlement over the road, and how one of his cousins had been a Fascist and the other a Republican, but they never let politics interfere in family life. He spoke of the haunting beauty of the ancient statue of a woman's head that had been found in the nearby town of Elche.

'No-one knows who made her! The Greeks? The Phoenicians? The Iberians? It's a mystery.'

And of course, he talked about Arabic poetry, quoting verses of Ibn Hazm, Al-Russafi and Abu al-Hashash al-Munsafi. Dark would fall, the scent of the jasmine giving way to the *galán de noche*, the gentleman of the night, offering up its stronger more energetic scent, and we would still be there, tales of the Alhambra hanging in the night air.

'You will go there one day,' Pedro said, swapping in and out between English and Spanish as my ear grew used to his voice. 'You will see Granada, and it will change you for ever.' And he pursed his moustachioed lips momentarily before downing his camomile tea.

'Don't worry. Be *kh*appy.'

The exact origins of flamenco are uncertain. The eighteenth and nineteenth centuries are often cited as the period when it started to take shape, but the Roman poet Juvenal referred to Cádiz girls in Rome – *puellae gaditanae* – who performed dances with bronze castanets in the time of the emperor Trajan. For the poet and flamencologist Domingo Manfredi, writing in the 1960s, this was evidence enough to date flamenco back to classical times. Others have suggested a multiple origin, pointing to the rich mixture of cultures – Iberian, Phoenician, Visigothic, Greek, Roman, Arabic – that have flourished in Spain over the centuries. The composer Manuel de Falla specified the Moorish invasion in 711, the Spanish Church's adoption of the Byzantine liturgical chant, and the arrival of the Gypsies, bringing with them enharmonic influences from Indian songs, as the key factors in the development of flamenco.

The role of the Gypsies is crucial but perhaps the least understood. First, there is the question of when they actually arrived in Spain. There appear to have been at least two waves: one from North Africa during the Islamic period, and another from France in the years shortly before the fall of Granada in 1492. No-one doubts that they have played a major role in the development of flamenco; the question is, to what extent? Are they its sole creators? If so, why aren't there more obvious echoes in Gypsy music from other countries? Did they just take already existing folk-songs and transform them by playing them with their own interpretation and style? Some have tried to divide *palos* – the different styles and songs within flamenco – into those of supposedly Gypsy and non-Gypsy origin. But then others place some *palos* outside flamenco altogether. *Sevillanas*, the essence for most foreigners of 'typical Spanish' flamenco, with clacking castanets and dancers in long frilly dresses, would be classified by many aficionados as 'folklore', not as flamenco.

For most *flamencos*, though, these things are intuited, if thought about at all. Moorish or Jewish, Gypsy or Andalusian, there is an instinctive feel for flamenco, making it easy to recognise, if difficult to pin down. Part of it is to do with being away from the mainstream, or on the outside. For the past two hundred years at least, flamenco has been the music and dance of outcasts, people on the margins of

Spanish, and particularly Andalusian, society. From which, perhaps, stems the natural affinity with Gypsies, and accounts for the large number of songs about injustice or going to jail:

> *A las rejas de la cárcel*
> *no me vengas a llorá.*
> *Ya que no me quitas pena,*
> *no me la vengas a dá.*

> Don't come crying
> to the prison bars.
> Since you can't ease my pain,
> don't come here making it worse.

The only certainty about flamenco is that it began in Andalusia and remains to this day Andalusian, despite spreading across Spain and around the world. Madrid, and to a lesser extent Barcelona, have recently become flamenco centres, but only by importing southern communities and culture. Andalusia, with its poverty, arid heat and proximity to Africa, remains the eternal reference point and true source.

'Drink this, Watson. It will make you clean on the inside.'

We spent mornings at Pedro's house picking ripe figs, oranges and pomegranates from his orchard to make exotic juices for breakfast.

He had managed to create on a small scale what I imagined the great Arab gardens of the past had been like. The Moorish conquerors had a desert people's natural love of gardens and their irrigation systems had turned parts of the eastern coast into one of the most fertile areas in Europe. When Philip III had the last remaining Muslims thrown out of Valencia in a fit of pique at the beginning of the seventeenth century, the local economy collapsed, as the only people with the necessary gardening know-how – built up over nine hundred years – had been forced from their homes into exile. Some said the knowledge had never been fully recovered, but sitting in Pedro's garden, I was prepared to believe they were wrong. Here you could rest, a deep rest that saturated the entire body. And slowly I began to feel myself falling under the spell of the place, days with no beginning or end, my mission almost forgotten.

But then with a jolt it would return, like a violent itch. There were things to be done. I must be on the move. I wanted to start learning flamenco. Alicante, the home of my only contact, had seemed the obvious place to start, but on my few walks around town I had found no flamenco bars, no guitarists idling in the shade, no dancers practising their steps on the street, nothing. At that time I had only a vague idea that flamenco was to be found in Andalusia, and looking at the map, Alicante hadn't seemed that far away. Surely I would find evidence of it on every street corner? But as my limited searching led nowhere, I began to understand how ill-prepared I had been. I had no idea where to start or what to expect. Pedro would know what I needed to do.

No sooner had I found him, though, watering the date palms and feeding TV, his exquisite white-furred cat, than he distracted me with yet another story. The little local train – the *trenet* – passing next to the garden, jolted us out of our chatter as it thundered along its single track, belching out black diesel fumes.

'Ah, *mi querido Watson*,' said Pedro, as our lazy afternoon was shattered once again, '*qu'est-ce qu'on peut faire?*' And he shrugged his shoulders and pouted in a Gallic manner, a hangover from his student days in France. He liked to remind me that it was back in Paris that he had been given a part in the film of *What's New Pussycat?* – a token Spaniard at a fancy dress party.

'*Hombre*, they wanted me to take a bigger role, but I wasn't interested. I was too busy trying to get to know the girls at the Sorbonne.' His eyes twinkled.

For an erstwhile movie star and seducer of Parisian women, Pedro hardly looked the part. Age had taken its toll. Take away the belly and the grey hair and . . . maybe. But it required a leap of the imagination. Perhaps the girls were big on moustaches back then.

And so I spent these first days at Pedro's acclimatising as best I could to the new environment. Spanish was relatively easy to pick up – having already learned Italian and Arabic, it felt more like I was remembering it than learning it for the first time, and within a week English had all but disappeared. I learned how to cook *tortilla de patatas* and *cocido* (a type of stew), weeded the garden while Pedro gave his classes at the university, walked over dusty fields to the beach, and swam in the late summer sun. But all the while, at the back of my mind, a nagging, restless voice was pressing me to begin my search in earnest.

'So you want to know about flamenco?' Pedro asked one morning at breakfast. I heaved a sigh of relief. He stared into the sky and began to recite:

Empieza el llanto
de la guitarra.
Se rompen las copas
de la madrugada.
Empieza el llanto
de la guitarra.
Es inútil
callarla.

The cry of the guitar begins.
In the early morning,
wine glasses shatter.
The cry of the guitar begins.
Useless
to silence it.

It was Lorca, the flamenco poet. Pedro's eyes moistened as he kept his gaze on the darkening clouds above.

'Of course, I myself am also a poet. As we all are,' he said.

'Really?' I asked. 'I'd like to see some of your poetry.'

'*Hombre*, what makes you think I've written any?' There was a stern expression on his face. 'You do not have to write poetry to call yourself a poet. The two things are entirely separate.'

'I see,' I said.

'Flamenco,' he said. 'No-one even knows the origin of the word. Some say it was a term used by Spanish Jews for songs their relatives were allowed to sing after moving to Flanders, but which they themselves were forbidden by law to perform. Or perhaps you'd rather go for the Arabic version: that it comes from *felah manju*, or escaped peasant.' He screwed up his nose sceptically. 'If *felah manju*, why not *felah manghum* — melodious peasant? You can speculate for ever.'

I listened to him eagerly. I was finally getting somewhere.

'I can't help you much with flamenco, *mi querido Watson*,' he said eventually. 'I know nothing about it.'

My heart sank. I was relying on him. How could he not know anything about it? I felt sure he would be able to put me on the right track. He seemed to know so much about so many things. My mind raced forward, thinking about other opportunities, other places in Spain I could go to. I could even catch the bus tonight. No reason to stay here. I could manage on my own. Granada perhaps. Or Seville. Jerez?

Pedro's voice interrupted my feverish plan-making.

'Don't worry. I'm sure something will come up when the time is right.' And he smiled at me, a warm, genuine, childlike smile. For some reason I believed him.

'There's a performance this evening in the main square in town,' Pedro told me three days later. From the expression on his face I knew exactly what he meant.

'Dancing! Dancing!' he cried, and skipped his way into the house, clacking his fingers above his head.

It was midnight by the time we arrived. I thought we might have missed it.

'Don't worry,' said Pedro. 'They won't have started yet.'

I had already seen enough of Spaniards and their bizarre relationship with time to know he was right. The Spanish were Arab enough always to arrive late, but European enough to feel guilty about never being on time. It created a strange kind of neurosis.

We found the Plaza Mayor, an odd square with an elegant baroque town hall on one side, and ugly 1960s blocks on the other three. A stage had been set up in the middle of the square, and already the place was crowded. No seats, no tickets, everyone simply standing around waiting for it to start. Our late arrival meant we were unable to get a good view and it was impossible to squeeze through any closer to the stage. I stood on tiptoe, grateful that I was taller than most of the audience.

On the stage sat three men: two guitarists and an older man with a stick. Next to them sat three very large women. Were they going to dance? Without warning the music began. Simple chords at first, difficult to hear: there was no real attempt by the audience to quieten down. Women were chatting, children running around, babies crying.

One of the fat women stood up, the low hum-like song began, and the audience fell silent.

'Did you feel it?' Pedro asked again when the piece was over.

'Yes,' I said.

'No,' he said. 'Did you really *feel* it?'

I couldn't speak. The performance had filled me with something I had never felt before, and didn't know how to describe.

'That was *duende*,' he said.

The word only half-registered. *Duende*. It sounded familiar. Perhaps I had heard it before somewhere.

When the concert seemed to be winding down, I gestured to Pedro that we should go.

'Wait,' he said, moving closer to the stage. 'There's more.'

I looked up and saw a man helping up a fourth

31

dancer: a younger, slimmer woman with a head of wavy, dark red hair. She seemed reluctant to dance at first, as though needing encouragement from her friends. I watched her as she held back, using her weight against the numerous arms and hands that were pulling and pushing her onto the stage, while at the same time the expression on her face revealed she was glad of their attentions and had been expecting this. Finally she conceded, and gracefully walked to the centre of the stage, a long-fringed black silk shawl thrown over her raised shoulders, the blood-red dress swaying from side to side with each step, her hands held on her waist. I tried to see her face, but she had lowered her head, and wisps of red hair masked her eyes.

She began to dance, both arms raised, wrists arched, fingers extended and crooked, like flames. The guitars came in, and an old man started to sing in a high-pitched, strangely feminine voice. But something was wrong. She was dancing in rhythm, her body moving well with the music, but there was a confidence missing, as if she couldn't quite find her feet, as if she didn't belong there. The other dancers behind her could sense it, and began shouting encouragement, egging her on. She danced harder, beating the floor until the sweat shone on her brow, her arms rising and circling like storm clouds. As she danced, her hair came loose from the knot at the back of her head until it was flying in all directions, while her hips moved playfully and erotically from side to side.

But it was not to be. She slipped and fell forward, her feet folding beneath her. Her shoes couldn't grip the temporary stage and she almost crashed to the floor, just managing to save herself from falling flat on her face at the last minute. Recovering, she raised her arms defiantly with a flourish and stormed off in disgust. The guitarists quickly nose-dived to conclude the piece, and the concert ended abruptly.

There were cries from the audience, cheers, some jeering. Everyone seemed confused. There was a sense of anticlimax, but eventually the crowds began to move. Pedro and I looked at each other and shrugged. It was time to go.

'Pedro,' I asked as we walked back to the car, the narrow streets crawling with people as they headed off, 'what is *duende*?'

He didn't reply at first, but waited until we had emerged onto the esplanade.

'*Duende*,' he said. '*Duende* is *duende*. More than this you will have to find out for yourself, *mi querido Watson*. That is, after all, what you are here for.'

I urgently needed to earn some money, and the only simple way was to teach English. The *Yellow Pages* listed dozens of language schools with grandiose-sounding names like the Big Ben Academy, or the Cambridge College for English. After a few calls I quickly established that most of them had either gone bust, never existed in the first place, or had plenty of teachers, thank you, but would I like to re-apply next autumn? Pedro tried to help, but none of his contacts within the Spanish equivalent of the old-boy network – Augustinians, the Jesuits, or the Franciscans – managed to produce anything. Inwardly, I heaved a sigh of relief, not relishing the thought of working for monks. I went back to the *Yellow Pages* and did some more phoning. A couple of schools eventually invited me to come and look around, but they weren't promising anything.

First I went to the London School. It was opposite the old tobacco factory – a nineteenth-century building like a military barracks that exuded a terrific, all-pervading stink of cigars. I made my way up the stairwell. The 'school' was just a spare room in a flat. A small, fat, middle-aged man with greased-back greying hair and a moustache welcomed me with a yellow smile. Would I like a seat? A cigarette? I sat down. It was a small, dark room, with a few chairs and tables, and a blackboard on one wall. In the back of my mind I had already decided not to work here, but felt I should stay and hear him out for courtesy's sake. He said nothing, though, and simply looked at me with an uncomfortably intense gaze, a grin stuck to his face as though it had been cut out of card and glued there. Finally he lowered his head and began studying my CV.

'Of course, it is always an honour to be able to welcome someone from Oxford. But, you know, times are bad. These politicians are just thieves. Under Franco this never happened.'

I was thrown by this opening gambit and hesitated for a moment as I tried to work out what an English teaching job had to do with the odd little dictator. Close on two decades had passed since his death in 1975, and the country had made its successful leap into democracy, thanks largely to the king, Juan Carlos. But even after just a short time in Spain I had the strong sensation that you only had to scratch a little below the surface to find Franco staring you in the face. Frustrated-looking men in their fifties always seemed to be the most nostalgic for the good old days of Fascist rule.

'What never happened?' I asked, still trying to fathom his logic.

'All this! Corruption! These Socialists are syphoning off billions! Billions! Spain could be a great country with all its wealth, like Great Britain, or France.' There was a touch of hysteria in his voice. 'But instead these villains are holding us down in the Third World. We need a new Franco. A strong man who would make us great again. Not the bunch of criminals in charge at the moment. You wait, though. Our time will come!'

I looked at the man in front of me: the thin moustache, the stout build, small, mean eyes. He wasn't too dissimilar to the Generalísimo himself. He would probably do well as a small bureaucrat in a dictatorship, seated at an oversized desk, little legs swinging underneath his chair.

'You never saw any beggars on the streets in *his* time . . .' He was off again, but seemed to realise he was losing his audience.

'So, as you can see, things are tight,' he concluded. I began to feel annoyed. Had I come all this way just for a lecture on right-wing politics from a man who, before I'd even taught a single class, was trying to lower my salary?

'Of course, we can always come to an arrangement,' he added hurriedly. I was confused. He clicked his fingers like a character in a Bond film. The door behind him opened and a woman with peroxide blond hair and a low-cut, revealing dress appeared. She walked forward and stood next to the smiling man, rocking her hips suggestively and looking at me with a sweet, sickly smile of her own.

'If you help us,' said the man, 'we can help you. You understand me?' I looked in astonishment. The woman lifted her index finger, ending with a false red nail, to her over-painted lips and began sucking and nibbling at it. My forehead knotted as her eyes ran up and down me like a snake. I looked back at the man. He was still smiling. I was smiling, but feeling sick. At the other end of the room a fly was buzzing at the window, desperately trying to get out.

'My wife is very . . . er, demanding.'

I stood up suddenly. I was sure his wife was lots of things, but I didn't want to find out about any of them.

'You know, it has been lovely coming here and seeing your lovely school,' I stammered, walking backwards towards the door. 'And I hope you do find the teachers you need. But I don't think Alicante is the place for me. I think I really want to live in, er, Greece. Yes, Greece.' I reached behind me and found the doorknob.

'But *señor*,' the man interjected. The smile was fading now, on its way to a scowl of disappointment.

'I'm sorry,' I said, and 'Goodbye,' as I hurriedly passed through the door.

I stumbled down the stairs and out into the tobacco-thick air. Pedro was waiting for me, and seemed to have some intuition of what had happened.

'Come with me.' He grabbed my arm and dragged me quickly into a church on the other side of the road. We sat down on a pew and he made me repeat an Arabic verse.

'This is very good. It will cleanse you,' he said.

My head was spinning. Maybe I should go somewhere else after all. The only things Alicante had for me so far were unreconstructed Fascists who liked watching foreign men satisfying their wives, and romantics who recommended reciting Islamic prayers in Catholic churches. But there was still the other school to visit, a long way from here, on the other side of town.

They offered me two classes a week, starting at the end of the month. Things were not looking good. As I was leaving, one of the staff suggested another school in the centre of town: Escuela Uno. I had been told it was the best language centre in the city. This had put me off, as they were sure to be flush with teachers. But at this point there was nothing to lose.

The school was situated in a sidestreet. I climbed the bare, institutional stairs. The door was open and the lights were on, but it looked empty. A noise came from behind the tall desk in the reception area. I turned and a woman stood up. I noticed her dark red hair, engaging eyes, a look of defiance about her. It was the dancer who had nearly fallen at the flamenco performance a few nights before. The night of my first experience of *duende*.

She caught my hesitation. 'Well,' she snapped, 'I suppose you've come here looking for a job.'

'Yes,' I hit back. 'As a matter of fact I have.'

'Oh,' she responded, more softly. 'Well, you might be in luck then. One of the girls we hired has dropped out, so there's a vacancy. But you'll have to see my husband Vicente.' She spoke rapidly, pushing the words out forcefully. 'Where's your CV?'

I handed it over and she stared at it, looking down her long nose, her head poised, nostrils flared. There was a powerful energy about her that seemed out of place in the surroundings of a school. The silence was broken by the sound of footsteps. I turned to see a man with an air of authority striding over towards us. He looked like a thousand other moderately successful

Spaniards in their forties: neat beard with a few white hairs sprouting, combed-back, straight black hair, a thick aquiline nose, sports jacket and black trousers. The only difference was that instead of wearing Spanish shoes, he was sporting a pair of highly polished English brogues.

'Vicente, this young man wants a job,' the woman said coolly. He smiled and shook my hand, then placing his fingers in the small of my back, he propelled me towards an empty classroom.

'Providence has obviously brought you here.' He spoke in English in a deep, clipped voice. 'One of our teachers left us suddenly. She was pregnant.' There was only a hint of Spanish in his near-perfect accent, and I could tell from his reaction the moment I opened my mouth that I had made an impression. Vicente seemed to have a love for 'old-fashioned' England, and my accent was enough for me to fit in with his world view straight away. He gave me the job on the spot.

'Welcome,' he said warmly. 'Glad to have you aboard. Lola, my wife, will sort out the paperwork.' He steered me back to reception, but Lola had gone. For a moment Vicente's suave manner gave way to extreme irritation, and he swore under his breath. Then he turned around, smiling. Would I mind coming back tomorrow?

Pedro was not at home when I arrived at the house, so I went to the beach to pass the time. Children were splashing in the light-speckled, late-afternoon water, while men with felt hats read newspapers in the shade of palm trees. Three elderly women walked topless along the shore, their pendulous, darkened breasts heavy on their swollen bellies. No self-consciousness,

38

no attempts to change or hide their shape. Not showy, either. What would Franco have thought of this, I wondered.

Pedro came past, skipping like a boy on the hot sand to avoid burning his feet.

'Pedro, I've got a job!' I called out. He stopped, smiled, then put his finger to his pursed lips and walked away behind the rocks. A few moments later he returned, dripping wet. In the midday heat, the need for a swim had obviously been the most pressing thing on his mind.

'Come along, Watson,' he said. 'Let's go and celebrate.'

Within a week I had moved into an empty flat of Pedro's in the centre of the city. Palm trees caressed the bay windows, which looked out onto a wide open boulevard below. There was a curious Heath Robinson device used to open the main door, involving ropes and pulleys, which took half a day to master. I was on the second floor above a photography shop run by a skinny Algerian *pied noir* with bad eczema, a nagging Italian wife, and two enormous sons who helped him with the business. Their shop was dark and dingy and seemed to have virtually no customers.

'One day I'll open up an Italian restaurant here,' he would say. 'Or at least that's what *she* wants,' he added, gesturing towards his wife and smiling ruefully.

Next to our building was a café permanently inhabited by workmen knocking back enormous brandies, and beyond that, the city's main lottery shop. The place was always full, mostly with middle-aged housewives with harsh memories of the past,

39

hoping that today they would strike lucky. On the other side of the flat was an optician's fluorescent, flashing thermometer, which made patterns on my living-room wall – except when it rained, when the water invariably blew its circuits. Across the road was a tobacco shop run by an old woman; a left-over from the dictatorship, when Franco allocated these jobs to the nation's war widows.

The money earned from the school was just enough for me to live on. It turned out to be a friendly and lively place and, as I had suspected, was the best and most successful English school in the city. Classes were usually held in the late afternoons and evenings, leaving me the rest of the day free to wander. Most mornings I would walk down to the esplanade for breakfast, read the paper, and watch the sailboats come and go from the harbour. Then it was off to explore the castle, the old town, the beach, the red-light area, the Gypsy quarter, always looking in vain for some sign of flamenco: a bar, a concert hall, or even someone just playing it from an open window. There was nothing.

Ever since the night of the performance in the main square, I had been puzzling over the powerful experience it had produced in me. *Duende*. The dictionary merely defined it as 'goblin' or 'earth spirit', or, in a flamenco context, as 'soul'. But this was like nothing I had ever felt before, and far more intense than anything I had ever experienced listening to jazz or the blues. There was something mysterious about it too; Pedro's reluctance to tell me any more about it had made me curious, and I wanted to find out more. But I had yet to make any progress. The obvious option was to talk to the dancer at the school, to Lola. But the problem was how to approach her. Her sharp manner made conversation difficult. What should I say? 'Magnificent performance. Is your ankle better now?' She would probably never speak to me again. Most of the staff were daunted or even frightened by her no-nonsense, abrupt attitude. She appeared to be slightly less aggressive with me, but even so, her manner did not invite small-talk. I planned various strategies, determined not to lose this opportunity, waiting for the right moment. But as I prevaricated, I realised I was beginning to find her spiky aloofness attractive. She was fiery and passionate underneath, I convinced myself, and very *flamenca*. She possessed an intense spirit and an air of suppressed energy. I had seen it in her dance. Some of the looks she gave her husband would have destroyed a lesser man. I *had* to talk to her.

I spent a week procrastinating, thinking of ways of bringing up the topic in general conversation, but in the end it simply happened. It was late, the school was closing, and the other teachers had already left. Lola was alone in reception. Sensing that this was it, I grabbed my chance.

'You're a dancer, aren't you?' I said. 'Flamenco.'

She looked up from her desk and gave me a scrutinising look.

'*Te gusta el flamenco?* You like flamenco?' she asked.

Ten minutes later we were in the bar below the school. I told her of my interest, how I'd come to Spain looking to find out more. She sat listening, smoke from a Ducados cigarette curling up from her lips, and for the first time I saw the beginnings of a smile.

'Tell me, though,' she said. 'How did you know?'

41

'Know what?'

'How did you know about me, and flamenco . . .?'

I wanted to be able to say something about seeing it in her eyes, her hands, her body, but the courage escaped me.

'I saw you dance in the Plaza Mayor a few weeks ago,' I said nervously.

She burst out laughing, a low, rich, belly laugh rushing through her wide open mouth.

'Then you must know what a great dancer I am,' she said. She was smiling, her brown eyes now shining and warm. 'But what makes a *guiri* like you come all the way from England? Just flamenco? Or is there something else? I bet you've got yourself a nice little María tucked away somewhere. Eh?'

She was on the offensive again, and the way she called me *guiri* – a derogatory word for foreigner – had jarred.

'No. There's no-one. I only came here for flamenco.'

'Then why, for the love of God, did you come here? Alicante? It's hardly the place to be. You should be in Madrid, or Seville. Not here. There's nothing here. Nothing.' She spat the words out.

'You're here,' I said quietly.

She looked at me sharply. I realised the mistake.

'I mean, you love flamenco, and you seem to manage here,' I said.

'That's different. It's not the same for me. You're free.'

'But what about the concert,' I said. 'It was magnificent. How can you say . . .'

'It was a one off. You don't think we have that sort of thing here every night, do you? They aren't from around here. They're friends from Murcia. It's the first time in years we've had anything. You were lucky, that's all.'

'It was the best thing I've ever seen.'

'Really?' She was genuinely surprised. 'The best concert?' She laughed and looked away. 'You'll see better. This is only the beginning, remember? You wait. You'll see some of the greats: Cristina Hoyos, Paco de Lucía, Enrique Morente . . .' Her voice tailed off.

'And I thought you danced very well.'

'What?'

'No, really. There was tremendous spirit there. It was just unfortunate . . .'

'It was a cheap stage. The town hall paid for it. What can you expect? It was unfortunate. But – thank you.'

We were silent for a few moments. Remembering the fall seemed to annoy her. I wished I had never brought it up.

'Look,' she said. 'You won't find any big flamenco scene here. No *tablaos*, no flamenco bars. This is not Andalusia, or Madrid. People here don't like flamenco. It doesn't belong to them.'

I looked away.

'Listen to me.' She lowered her voice. 'I have a small group of friends – aficionados. Some of them play. We meet up every now and again to fool around, but it's nothing serious. It's all I can offer you. But you'd be better off leaving tomorrow and going somewhere else.'

It seemed she wanted me gone. But I already felt half-settled. I didn't want to be moving on again. Not now.

'No,' I said. 'I'm staying.'

She smiled and placed her hand on my arm. 'Wait

43

for me after class finishes tomorrow. I'll introduce you to the others.'

We drove out of the city in the failing autumn light, heading inland past olive groves planted in red earth and sharp-sweet smelling eucalyptus trees. The landscape was different here: greener, lusher, less barren than the area around the city. Blue-tiled church domes dotted the countryside like islands of water in a sea of dark, heavy green.

We wound up the deserted road then turned off onto a dirt track that seemed to lead us into a field. It was darker now, and I could see some lights ahead. We arrived at what seemed to be a small barn in the middle of nowhere. About a dozen people were milling around, carrying food and glasses inside.

The 'barn' was in fact some kind of house, like a shepherd's cottage. It was much colder here than down on the coast and a fire was burning in the hearth. On seeing Lola, there were genuine cries of delight, warm embraces, and a spontaneous and friendly energy filled the room. I was introduced as a new member of the club. Everyone came over to greet me with kisses and handshakes. They seemed like a very ordinary group of people. Not many of them were actually *flamencos*; most were simply there because of the company and to hear performances by those who could dance or play the guitar. I was taken to one side by a small, intense, wiry woman with bulging eyes, called Pilar. As she led me away, I turned back and saw Lola already surrounded by a group of men by the fire.

Pilar was firing off questions like an artillery barrage. How did I become interested in flamenco, where was I from, when did I arrive, how did I know Lola, what was I doing here in Alicante?

I told her I was looking for a guitar teacher.

'Oh! Then you must talk to Juan,' she said.

'Juan! Juan!' she called across the room, gripping my arm. A man seated by the table looked up from his beer.

'Juan,' Pilar said, 'he wants to learn to play.'

Juan lifted his arm and, with a simple flick of the fingers, beckoned me over. Pilar tagged along behind.

'Juan,' she panted, 'he said he likes the guitar. He's looking for a teacher.' Then to me she said, 'Juan used to teach the guitar, but he hasn't done so for years. Isn't that right?'

Juan nodded and then pointed to an empty chair next to him. There was no room for Pilar.

I looked at him. He was small, with white skin, black hair, and brilliant light blue eyes. There was something serious and melancholy about him.

The music had begun. A man on the other side of the room was playing a guitar, while four or five people clapped out a complicated rhythm. Lola began to dance.

'You know what this is?' Juan asked, turning to face me. I had the impression he didn't want to watch.

'No. I don't.'

'This is called *Bulerías*. It's one of the most difficult *palos* in flamenco. It's fast and frenetic. They say nobody can work it out unless it is explained to them. Only Gypsies used to know it. Now it's common property.'

'I feel I want to clap along,' I said. 'But I don't know how. Every time I try, it comes out wrong.'

'That's normal . . . at the beginning.'

45

'Can you teach me?'

He screwed his face up for a moment, eyes squinting, scrutinising me. 'I haven't taught for years.'

'I know, but . . .' I had to think of something. 'Everyone's told me what a wonderful guitarist you are.'

'Really?' He was suspicious. 'Who?'

'Oh, Pilar. Lola . . .'

'Lola?'

'Yes.'

He went silent for a while, turning his gaze back to the throng. Lola and another man were dancing together in the centre amid the rising din. She lifted her skirt in a handful at her waist, flirting with her eyes.

Juan took in a deep breath, and then without looking at me, beckoned me to copy him as he clapped.

'Twelve-beat rhythm,' he said. 'Listen to the stresses. Follow me.'

Some time later Lola came and bent over me, so that I could hear what she was saying. Her skin was damp with sweat, her face radiant.

'Are you enjoying it, *guiri*?' she asked breathlessly. I nodded.

'I see you've found yourself a teacher.' She flicked her head towards Juan. He didn't respond.

'Well, I hope so.'

'Good,' she said. 'Juan's the best there is.'

Juan stood up and went to get himself another drink. I looked around quickly. Pilar was nowhere to be seen.

'I hardly got a chance to speak to Juan,' I said. 'Your friend Pilar . . .'

'Oh, Pilar. You have to watch out for her. Doesn't know when to stop.'

And she walked back into the middle of the room, clapping her hands and shouting to one of the other dancers.

The music continued as the evening wore on. Juan returned and began to explain to me the different *palos*: *Tangos*, *Alegrías*, *Rumbas*, each with a different rhythm and feeling. And then later, as the drinking continued, other pieces: *Soleá*, *Seguiriya*, slow at first but often speeding up towards the end in a dramatic climax.

'*Compás* – rhythm,' he said, 'is the most important thing. Flamenco begins and ends with *compás*. Or at least most of it does. It depends.'

I was confused.

'I'm sure you'll get on fine,' Juan said. 'Fine.'

The guitar began again. Lola was back in the middle. She is beautiful, I thought. I leaned over to Juan.

'*Duende*,' I asked. 'What is *duende*?' He laughed.

'Have you ever been in love?' he asked.

I didn't reply.

'*Duende* is love,' he said. '*Duende* is being in love. It is being with people you love and care for.' He paused. 'Like now.'

chapter TWO

Por Rumba

No estamos locos,
que sabemos lo que queremos.
Vive la vida
igual que si fuera un sueño,
pero que nunca termina
que se pierde con el tiempo.
Y buscaré.

We're not mad, we know what we
want.
Live life as if dreaming,
a dream which never ends and is lost
in time.
And I will keep on searching.

Ketama

*F*lamenco is organic. A living thing that will become your life-force ... if you practise hard enough.'

It was late afternoon and I was sitting in Juan's red flat: red walls, red floors, red chairs, red table, red curtains hanging over red windows.

'Red is the colour of flamenco,' he would say. 'The colour of passion.'

He served coffee from a red pot into red cups and we stirred it with red-handled spoons. Everything, from the corridor to the bedroom to the bathroom, was red. The toilet paper, however, was pink.

'Yes,' he said, looking a little disappointed when I pointed this out.

The flat was a temple to flamenco. Pictures of past greats stared down at us from the walls: the singer La Niña de los Peines with her thinly pencilled eyebrows and heavy, bad-tempered face; the dancer La Argentinita, the flamenco muse of the 1920s and 30s who inspired Manuel de Falla to write his famous *El Amor Brujo*; and Ramón Montoya, the first *flamenco* to develop the guitar as a solo instrument – fat and immaculately dressed as the previous generation of *flamencos* always had been. Juan had old guitars placed in corners, or hanging from the walls, as if he needed a constant reminder of who he was. I couldn't be sure if it was reflected light, but I could have sworn some of them had a red tinge in the varnish.

Juan spent most of the first lessons guiding me through the array of flamenco objects dotted around his flat. It seemed to please him to have someone to show off his memorabilia to and for the time being I went along with it, happy to delay the serious business of starting to play in earnest. I told him I could barely hit a note and was coming to flamenco with hardly any musical knowledge; a plea, I suppose, for him not to expect too much. Despite his friendliness, I could sense there was a fierce temperament in him, and a moodiness that I wanted to avoid as much as possible.

Flamenco music played all the time. Juan had hundreds, possibly thousands, of records and CDs and an entire wall was taken up by a sophisticated stereo system, which was black: luckily there were no red ones on sale. He seemed to spend most of his time buying expensive pieces of kit to add on to it, producing some crucial improvement in the sound quality. I could never tell the difference, but he always swore by his gadgets. And when not playing the guitar, Juan was usually tapping out some complicated rhythm with his fingers, flicking them out one by one with amazing dexterity. Invariably as I walked into his house for a class, a new recording was blaring, while he rapped his knuckles in time on the counter like a typist.

'Have you heard this?' he would shout enthusiastically above the music. 'It's the latest from Carmen Linares. I met her once. Nice woman. I love her singing.' At this point I would put down the guitar and head to the kitchen to pour myself a glass of water.

'The cables for the speakers are new – made of gold,' he would shout through. 'It gives a purer sound. More heart. More love.' And he would pound the centre of his chest while looking up at the red ceiling.

The music only stopped for our lessons, when my fumbling on the guitar demanded silence and Juan's reluctant attention. For all his love of flamenco, he rarely seemed keen to teach me. He would rather spend the time talking – about a particular guitarist or singer, or mostly about new superfluous pieces of equipment. 'Hey, have a look at this electronic tuner. Fantastic. Tells you exactly when you're in tune.'

Each time it was a challenge just to get the lesson started. No longer childishly enthusiastic, he would, as I had half-suspected, become surly and moody.

'Look, boy. You're not even holding it properly. Concentrate.'

We started at the very beginning. In the posters on the walls the old guitarists sat mostly in the traditional posture, with the guitar resting on the left or right leg, pointing diagonally upwards to aid access for the left hand. The contemporary style was to cross the legs, right over left, and hug the guitar into the hip, tilting it away from the body, so that the fretboard was almost invisible and you relied on touch and familiarity alone. This put a strain on the muscles in the left arm at first, stretching them into a strange position, and the right hand constantly suffered from pins and needles as the forearm rested too heavily on the edge of the guitar. It took months to perfect.

'Work on it. You've got it totally wrong,' Juan barked. Then, in a rare moment of compassion, he added, 'It's worth it. It gives you a more relaxed feel. And more importantly' – he lowered his voice and I leaned forward to catch his words of wisdom – 'you look really cool.'

It was hard to feel cool while contorting my body into what seemed like the most unnatural position imaginable. Admittedly, it didn't look that difficult – as I gazed at myself in the full-length, red-framed mirror on the wall – but the strain on my arms and wrists was excruciating. I'm going to be permanently crippled at this rate, I thought. My body felt frozen in the act of playing; even outside the class my right hand would fall into a 'telephone' position: little finger sticking out for balance and thumb bent back, as though resting on the bottom string, middle fingers bent into the palm slightly. I took to shaking it like a rattle to try to loosen the muscles and tendons.

'Your hands are too stiff,' Juan would moan. 'Too hard. Relax that wrist. Here, feel my hand.'

It felt like a freshly killed chicken; warm, limp, not quite all there.

'Today we're looking at the *Bulería*,' he said one afternoon when I'd finally persuaded him to teach me something. *Bulería* was the *palo* he had first pointed out the night of the party. Flamenco, I was slowly realising, was far more than simply the energetic beat of the Gypsy Kings, or ornate singing and playing. It was a world in itself, with its own lexicon and rules. There were scores of different *palos*, each with a unique feeling based on variations in key, rhythm and pace. Regional styles created an extra level of complication, with differences between, say, a *Fandango de Málaga* and a *Fandango de Huelva*.

'*Bulería*. It comes from *burlar*. It means to joke around, make fun of someone. It captures something essential, the essence of flamenco. You listen to a good *Bulería*, and you feel like you hardly know where the rhythm is going next – they keep playing with it all the time. But they always stay religiously within the rules. It's a type of magic. Takes years to get to that stage.'

I had listened to him playing *Bulerías* and they fascinated me with their manic, restless beat, impossible to follow at this early stage unless he counted out loud, helping me understand the complicated rhythm. It had a Gypsy feel to it: anarchic, unpredictable, weaving in and out as though you might never catch hold of it.

'This is the real thing, boy: what we always play at *juergas* – flamenco parties,' Juan said. 'I suppose you expected to learn all that Gypsy Kings stuff, eh? Simple *Rumbas* to show off to the girls? Look, if you want to learn with me, we start with the most difficult things first. Got it?'

We sat opposite one another in the red haze. Juan was looking at me – how I sat, the positioning of the guitar. He seemed about to say something, a look of reproach on his face, but instead he checked himself and glanced down at his own guitar.

'You already know the rhythm.'

He played, his fingers moving with great speed, and a hypnotic sound filled the room. It seemed so effortless, I simply listened in amazement, my eyes and attention wandering over the faces on the posters around us. It still surprised me sometimes that I was here in Spain having lessons with a real flamenco guitar teacher. Only a couple of weeks previously I had thought I had made a disastrous choice in coming to Alicante to begin my search, but I had suddenly landed on my feet and now things were moving faster than I could take them in.

Juan stopped with a flourish. I stared. I had no idea what he had just done. But he was glaring at me.

'Come on!' he growled. 'Your turn!'

I felt a knot tightening in my guts. Do what, exactly?

'Umm . . .' I stammered.

'Concentrate, boy. If you're going to take this seriously, I expect you to watch *every* move I make like a hawk. I play, you watch, you learn. That's how it goes.'

I nodded in agreement, silently wishing I were somewhere else. Sweat began to trickle down my neck.

'Now watch! I'll do it again. But understand that I'm being nice to you. Don't expect me to play things twice for you in the future.'

This time I leaned forward over my guitar, straining my eyes in an attempt to follow his fingers as they danced over the strings. The problem was how to divide my attention; there was as much happening with his right hand as there was with his left, and try as I might, I couldn't watch them both at the same time. In the end, I concentrated on the left, reasoning that at least I might be able to get the chords. The right hand would have to come later.

Juan finished the piece and then stood up.

'OK, boy. Now you do it.'

He walked into the kitchen to light a cigarette – Marlboro, they had the reddest packets, he said – and started heating some water for coffee.

'And work on your right hand. The left will look after itself.'

Wrong again. I hunched desperately over the guitar. My fingers formed into what looked like an approximation of what I had seen him do. The forefinger was bent in some strange position covering two strings at the same time. I felt a shot of pain as it was forced back against itself while the strings underneath cut into my skin from the pressure. Wincing, I looked up. Juan's back was turned.

'Come on! I can't hear anything.'

I gritted my teeth and started strumming with my right hand. There was a horrible, dead sound. I readjusted my fingers on the fretboard, and the pain shot up my arm as the soft fingertips were sliced by the strings. Juan, now standing in the doorway, was looking at me sternly. I swallowed an urge to give up, and pressed on. There was a small improvement – sound now coming from at least three strings – but my fingers were raw and I let them drop.

'Eh! What are you doing? Come on! Next chord.'

I placed my hands back where they had been, hoping that they would automatically remember what came next. But they let me down. I sat, flustered, my mind blank, Juan's eyes burning into the top of my head as he stood over me. His foot was tapping, but I couldn't tell whether it was impatience or just another rhythm working its way through his mind. My face turned red, like everything else in the flat.

'Come on, boy.'

With my fingers slipping over the ebony board, I tried as hard as I could to remember how he had placed his hand. Like this? No, bring that finger down. One more fret. There. I struck down with my index finger and waited for the cacophony and the bark of reproach that would inevitably follow. I stopped. My head stayed bent over the guitar. There was silence for a minute, then finally Juan spoke.

'Well?' he said, cigarette hanging from his mouth. 'What are you waiting for? Do it again! Come on. *Compás!* Rhythm! One, two, THREE, four, five . . .'

I fumbled to catch up with his clapping, and then somehow I got it. I had caught the rhythm, even if the sound was still like a cat with a poker up its arse. But Juan was driving me on and I didn't want to lose it.

When not teaching English, I practised the guitar. I was lucky in that the flat directly below me was empty, and the girl who lived above was either at work or out with her friends, so I could make as much noise as I liked. As this was usually fairly discordant, it was no bad thing either. I was inspired by a scratched record of La Niña de los Peines that Pedro had lent me. Her singing made me feel like that first night at the concert in the Plaza Mayor – a feeling of exposure and emotional intensity that yielded a sharper sense of reality.

> *Hasta los limones saben*
> *que nos queremos los dos.*

> Even the lemons know
> We're in love.

I would hum along to her Moorish-sounding melodies, trying in vain to mimic her. But after a few days of singing like a foghorn on the blink I gave up, deciding it was impossible for my non-Spanish vocal chords to sing flamenco. Then I would pick up the guitar and try to copy at least the rhythm and chords of the recording. Was that a *Soleá*? Or perhaps a *Tango*? It was still a struggle to distinguish the various *palos*, and I would have to rely on Juan to explain.

'As far as you're concerned, boy, it's a *Bulería*,' he'd say. 'It's just that for the singer, it's a *Lorqueña* – she's singing a poem of Lorca's. But you don't have to worry about it. *No te preocupes.*'

Flamenco was one of those subjects where the more you found out, the more you realised how little you knew.

And so I sat at home, practising for hours, the skin on my fingertips slowly hardening as it grew used to the pressure of the strings.

'You must feel as though your fingers extend into the strings, are becoming one with the strings,' Juan told me. 'No division between you and the guitar. You must love your guitar.'

For now it was still a foreign object in my lap, no matter how long it sat there. My fingers struggled to find the right chords, never feeling as if they belonged. I had seen footage of professional guitarists – rock, jazz, classical and flamenco – and they all looked as though the guitar had become welded to them. One day, I promised myself, I would be like that.

My progress was erratic and I would often think about giving up. I blocked these thoughts out as best I could. Discipline was crucially important. I had come to Spain for this. There *was* nothing else as far as I was concerned at that time. And so, I would renew my determination to prove to myself I could master something difficult and worthwhile.

* * *

If I had a guitar lesson in the evening, Juan and I would often go to the local bar for a drink afterwards. It was a grubby place, where the smell of cheap bleach mixed with the acid sweat and antiperspirant of Ginés, the overweight owner. Juan always ordered red wine. Pilar, the goggle-eyed woman from the party, would often come, along with one or two others I recognised. The most regular was Rafael, a banker from Ciudad Real, who brought a curious stamp-collecting mentality to our conversations. There were usually about three or four of us, meeting for a drink and a chat before heading off to bed at the end of the day. Lola would show up from the school every once in a while, but rationed her appearances as if for greater impact. As a meeting place for friends to talk about a common interest, it was a peculiar choice of venue. We had to shout to make ourselves heard, as the room was full of old men playing dominoes, which often led to arguments and playing pieces being thrown to the sawdust-covered floor in bouts of rage. More than once I had to pick bits of woodchipping from my beer.

We talked about anything, as long as it had a flamenco connection: the latest records, memories of great concerts, regional differences in style (fast dying out, it seemed), the power of a particular singer. But most of all, eclipsing all other topics, was the question of flamenco itself – what it was and where it was going.

The history of flamenco was a series of evolutionary cycles in which it spiralled closer to popular culture and legitimacy before being taken over and being forced to reinvent itself to avoid assimilation and disappearing for good. Every time it seemed as if flamenco was about to be absorbed, a new movement would emerge from some quarter with a different sound or simply a raw vitality that reconnected it with its counter-culture origins. It had happened with the *cafés cantante* of the nineteenth century, which for years gave many performers the wherewithal to perform their art. But these popular venues began to limit and dictate the form as audiences shunned the harsher, more challenging sound of the *cante jondo*, or deep song, which is at the heart of flamenco.

'Back then we were saved by Lorca and Falla,' Rafael the banker told me authoritatively. 'They organised the *Concurso del Cante Jondo* contest in Granada in 1922. People came from miles around, some walking for weeks over the mountains to take part. It reignited flamenco, made it live again.'

The generation after this produced some of the greatest *flamencos* ever – La Niña de los Peines, the dancer Carmen Amaya. But even they began to lose momentum as Spain opened itself up and began to westernise, producing an anodyne watered-down version viewed by the authorities as acceptable for the tourists now flocking to the Costas.

Salvation came a second time round from the guitarists, who started to assert themselves at last, moving from being mere accompanists to taking centre stage. It started with Ramón Montoya, before Sabicas and El Niño Ricardo went a step further to make the guitar – the *toque* – as important, if not more important, than the song, the *cante*, and the dance, the *baile*. These men were the godfathers of the new sound – the *nuevo flamenco* we hear everywhere today.

The subject of *nuevo flamenco* was a common topic of conversation at the bar, with everyone stridently expressing their opinions. All except Juan, who kept quiet on the matter. From my observation of him in our lessons, he seemed to be something of an open-minded traditionalist, happy to appreciate new developments while sticking with what he knew best in his own playing. I would sometimes ask him why he didn't try playing the more modern stuff, but he was cagey and avoided answering.

There was, I suspected, a reason. One night after Juan had left us early, Pilar lowered her voice and told us the story of the great love of his life. Nobody ever knew who she was, or if the woman was still in Alicante, but for a time he had been a different man. They had all seen it, all known the reason, but he kept it quiet and nobody ever brought it up. When the love affair ended, he shrank away from them, disappearing from their company for over a year, until a chance meeting in the street had brought him back to the group.

'He never returned to how he was, though,' Pilar said. 'I used to say to the others, "Look at this guy – he's half-destroyed." And it was true. Whoever she was, she must have really hurt him. And now he can't get away from it. All smiles on top, but underneath . . . *oof*!'

I imagined him emotionally frozen in time, playing the same record over and over again, never moving on. There was certainly no indication of anyone else in his life. But he would never give anything away, he just kept playing and talking about love, how flamenco was all about love.

Despite my growing obsession with the guitar, I was still able to spend time exploring Alicante. I found a lightness and a sense of joy there that was uplifting and colourful after the greyness of the life I had left behind.

The most interesting part of the city was the old quarter – the *barrio* – built on the remains of the Arabic city. Here, there was a labyrinth of monasteries, churches, strip clubs, bars, neglected squares and once brightly painted houses, all linked together by dirty, narrow lanes that smelt of piss. You could walk down the ancient high street – now paved over – and call in at a chemist's with eighteenth-century murals of angels adorning the ceiling. Or else a working-man's drinking hole decorated with bullfighting para- phernalia. Further on was the town hall with its spiralling baroque columns, and behind it, a tiny square with a now-defunct water-pipe and streetlamps that still showed the mark: London, 1832. Further on was the church of Santa María, built on the site of the old mosque, half-remembered now in the horseshoe arches. Beneath it, in the walls facing the sea, there were still bullet holes from the Civil War. Alicante had been one of the last places to fall to the Fascists, and when the promised relief boats for the Republican refugees failed to arrive, scores of people had committed suicide in the harbour.

Standing further back, towards the beach, there was the 'Face of the Moor': the natural formation in the castle rock that looked like the profile of a man with a hooked nose and a turban. Some parts of the old town gave you the impression that the Arabs had never left. The area of tightly knit white houses nestling just below the castle had a very Andalusian feel to it, its tiny pathways littered with a thousand plants in rich terracotta pots. From here you could see much of the coastline and the rest of the city stretching out in all directions.

It was not so much the physical city that attracted me, however, as the people who lived in it. There was a simple pleasure in the company of others; in talking, chatting, spending time observing passers-by. People-watching was easy in Spain – everyone else did it, so there was rarely the threat of violence common in England. Spaniards simply stared back at you and walked on, aware that as soon as they had passed, your attention would turn to someone else. At first this had been disconcerting. An English wariness and suspicion would kick in: surely they wanted something, were trying to trick me, pull a fast one. Yet more quickly than I might have imagined, these conditioned responses fell away as the feared attack, con, or robbery failed to materialise, and I began to be able to see things around me without fear. Engaging with others was just a part of life, a social need. And as a need, it was dealt with, without self-consciousness.

One morning I found myself walking down a street near the beach. It was a clear day, with enough warmth to entice a few bodies onto the sand. In front of me stood a large woman in the doorway of her house, doing nothing. As I approached her I smiled – not previously a normal thing for me to do, but I was quickly adopting native ways. In return she stepped out, grabbed me by the shoulders and kissed me on each cheek, her face beaming with joy, then jabbered something about my blond hair. I beamed back. She grabbed me again and squeezed my arm, and I walked on with her joyful voice still ringing in my ears.

I realised that being friendly was the most normal way of having contact with other people, which meant that anything, from buying a loaf of bread to posting a letter, could become a social event. The bank clerk and I soon got to know one another, and as I was withdrawing money, he might enquire about how I was getting on settling down in his lovely city, or answer my questions on some point of grammar I hadn't quite mastered. The man at the meat stall in the covered market would tell me of the house he was building for himself and his family up the coast at San Juan, and pass on the best way to cook a chicken breast with a little oil and lemon. The lady at the flower stall explained how best to protect my skin from the sun: 'You see, I have a cousin from the north with white skin like yours . . .'

I met Eduardo one morning near the beach. He had a powerful confidence and easy wit that immediately captured me. He was a streetwise wideboy – a *chulo* – who had a natural gift for knowing all the right people and places for whatever situation he found himself in. Few realised, as I later discovered, that in fact he was an insecure man, a nail-biter and stutterer – this last trait only appeared when he let his guard down – and his charm was a mask, hard-won after years of struggling with himself. But he had emerged as an excellent journalist, an affable man with an under-lying sharpness that could winkle out the real story those he went after were trying to conceal. Not a month went by without a piece bearing his byline appearing in a local newspaper with another tale of corruption within local government.

We met in mid-winter, just as I was beginning to feel that everything was stagnating. The lessons with Juan were continuing, but I had reached a plateau in my playing. There were none of the rapid leaps in technique I had enjoyed at the beginning. I was practising hour after hour and felt I was getting worse. And our classes were becoming harder to bear. Now that I knew how to hold the guitar, it was simply a question of hammering out *palo* after *palo*, week after week, never managing to create the wonderful sound that he made when showing me what to do.

'*Por Dios!*' he would mutter as soon as I had started. 'Why the hell did I ever come out of retirement for a stupid *guiri* like this?'

I played on, scowling at him as my head leaned in concentration over the guitar. The reference to my foreignness smarted.

'I'll show him. I'll show him. Bastard.'

And I had had no luck in establishing a friendship with Lola either. We had barely talked for months. She hadn't been to the bar for a long time, and at the school her mood was so fierce I felt uncomfortable even looking at her.

As ever with Eduardo, our meeting and the subsequent friendship that quickly developed felt like the right person in the right place at the right time. He was passionate about *nuevo flamenco* and swore he had every recording since 1975, lovingly catalogued on his computer, complete with notes and observations.

'Of course, it all started with Paco and *Almoraima*,' he said one evening as we sat under the palm trees drinking *horchata* – tiger-nut milk – on the breezy esplanade. Never one to understate things, I had the impression he was about to pass down some important information.

'What started?' I asked tentatively.

'Paco de Lucía. 1976.'

I was puzzled.

'He brought out *Almoraima* in 1976 and that was it. Bam! He reinvented flamenco. It was dying, dead, before then.'

Paco was a big name; the father of the new sound. He had taken the ideas of players from the previous generation – Sabicas and El Niño Ricardo – and transformed them, introducing new elements from jazz and rock. Now probably the best-known *flamenco* on the planet, he had an ever-larger following outside Spain after his collaboration with John McLaughlin and Al di Meola in the 1980s. Almost every contemporary flamenco guitarist owed a debt to him in their playing, so great was the impact of the revolution he had spearheaded over the previous two decades. He had his critics – people who thought the music had been sacrificed for technique – but they were a minority. Most aficionados revered him, and his new records were always eagerly awaited to see if the great master was about to point out a new direction for the rest to follow.

'What do you mean, dead?' I retorted. 'What about all the people before him? Carlos Montoya . . .'

'Carlos Montoya? Don't make me laugh. Have you ever heard Carlos Montoya?'

'Yes, I . . .'

'*Ese no vale una mierda!* Crap. Can't play to save his life. You listen to his *compás*, it's all over the place. Can't keep the rhythm. I tell you, if he were playing today, he'd be laughed off the stage.'

'Oh, come on! You mean everyone who's playing now is better than him?'

'Yes.' His answer was so abrupt and confident it was impossible to argue.

'You need to be listening to a lot more stuff if you're

still on Carlos Montoya, son. Tomatito, Gerardo Núñez, Pepe Habichuela – these are the guys you've got to get hold of.'

I had to concede. I still knew too little about it all to start arguing with a real aficionado. Besides, it would be a sign of even greater weakness to admit I couldn't hear the supposed flaws.

'Listen, son, if you're as interested in flamenco as you say you are, you've got to learn everything about it. Got to turn yourself into an expert. You can't be ignorant all your life.'

I nodded.

'Anyway,' he said, 'you'll find out soon enough: flamenco does strange things to you.'

Over the following weeks I learned as much as I could from my new flamenco guru. Juan would teach me how to play, but it was Eduardo who would tell me all there was to know about the contemporary scene: who to listen to, who to avoid, why such-and-such a player was so important, the lesser-known guitarists some of the greats had taken their ideas from. From here, it was a full-on flamenco course. My day was taken up either playing the guitar with Juan, listening to tapes lent to me by Eduardo, or hearing him talking about it into the early hours. He would often come to the flat un-announced for a tutorial on his way to interview a local official, or we would meet at a café on the sea-front before moving to the late-night bars in the *barrio*. His obsession was far greater than anything I had come across amongst Lola's group of friends, who, I soon realised, were mere amateurs by comparison. Eduardo could talk endlessly, and loved nothing better than to have me as his disciple, a new convert to the cause in a world which, in his eyes, was appreciating real flamenco less and less.

'Paco may be the leader of the pack, but a lot's down to his dad. He had this plan to take over flamenco. Tried to turn all five kids into professional *flamencos*. Almost succeeded. His only failure is the second son – ended up working in a hotel in Madrid, or something.' He waved for two more beers. 'Don't get me wrong: Paco's a genius, greatest player of his time. But, well, has he gone too far? That's the question.'

'Too far in what?' I asked.

'Too jazzy, son, too jazzy. Here, how much flamenco are you listening to?

'Um . . .'

'It's just that his latest stuff's straying a bit too far for my liking. Some people love it. So do I. Love it. But is it still flamenco? I don't know. For me, well . . . it's his early stuff that's just brilliant, just brilliant. Of course, some say he just nicked all his ideas from others like El Niño Miguel. But you hear them playing, and you know, you can just tell, Paco's just storming. Amazing.'

'You can tell them apart, then?' Still drowning in ignorance, I took a punt on what sounded like a more educated question.

'Course, son. *Por supuesto*. Much earthier sound, not all there. But he didn't have the contacts. Not like Paco. No wonder he never made it big. He's poor and forgotten now.'

There was another 'great' in modern flamenco, though, and Eduardo revered him even more than Paco.

'Camarón de la Isla.' His voice would go all soft and wobbly just at the name. I found it hard to get enthusiastic about someone called the 'Shrimp of the Island'.

'The greatest singer there's ever been. Anywhere. Other singers can do it sometimes, but he, he . . .' His eyes would go all strange at this point, mad and staring.

'Do what?'

'It. *Duende.*'

I sat up. Yes, what did *duende* mean to Eduardo? What was it?

From the look he gave me I might as well have asked him if he suffered from haemorrhoids. Slowly he pulled a tape from his pocket and handed it to me.

'Go home and listen to this.'

Back in the flat I put the tape on. Camarón had a much higher voice than I'd expected from the photo on the front cover: a light-haired man with a saurian face and bright, emotional eyes. But as soon as the music began, I could understand Eduardo's devotion. He had a unique voice that conveyed a gut-twisting, tragic sorrow. Even when singing happier pieces – an *Alegría* for example – there was an unmistakable melancholy and agony in his voice. And from what Eduardo told me, he was an explosive character: a Gypsy and the 'hard man' of flamenco whose life reflected the passion of his art. It was widely suspected that he was an alcoholic and drug addict. And predictably, perhaps, he had died young of a mysterious illness. People thought it might have been AIDS, but nobody was sure, only that they had lost the greatest *flamenco* of their generation, a man who had now been immortalised.

'A man like that only comes once every hundred years,' Eduardo told me when I handed the tape back.

'There might never be another one like him. This is a Golden Age, a Golden Age, I tell you. Catch it, because it's going to end soon.'

chapter THREE

Por Sevillanas

Me dió unos zapatitos
del ala de mi sombrero.
Muy fino y muy flamenquito,
que es muy flamenco,
mi zapatero.

He made me some shoes
from the brim of my hat.
He's very proper and 'flamenco',
my cobbler.

Camarón de la Isla

'This is a classy newspaper. Bloody bible for most people out here.'

The *Costa Gazette* was based 30 miles or so up the coast in the tourist mecca of Benidorm, formerly an attractive fishing village that had quickly lost its essential character after the discovery of its special 'microclimate' and the beginning of the tourism boom. With the Fifties came the town planners, and the village's three elegant bays were soon draped in concrete and dissected by arrow-straight roads.

Foreigners were thin on the ground in Alicante and I enjoyed the genuinely Spanish life there. Going to Benidorm would feel like I was letting myself down, almost like returning to England itself. But Eduardo was urging me on to try my hand at journalism. I needed to get out more, he said, broaden myself. Learning the guitar wasn't enough on its own.

Eduardo had met Barry, the editor of the *Costa Gazette*, a handful of times. The paper frequently rewrote material from local Spanish-language news-papers, translating and summarising to fill its own news pages, so there was something of a debt owed. We planned simply to turn up and take it from there. Picking up a copy of the paper from a newsagent, though, I began to wonder if the whole thing was really such a good idea. It was a bizarre hybrid of local news, results from the amateur bowling league and soft porn. Not a world I expected to slot into easily. But I was beginning to understand something of Eduardo's intention. In his view, becoming a *flamenco* was all a question of being able to slot into anything at any time, if possible. Working as a journalist would be part of the course.

'Each *palo* is different, has a different feel,' he said, 'and every time you play it, it's different. As a guitarist you are going to have to be able to move in and out of each one, bringing whatever is necessary at each moment to bring out the best performance in those around you – the dancers and singers – and even to lift yourself as well.'

It seemed odd to think that working on a local ex-pat rag might help me develop as a *flamenco*, but my guru had spoken and I dutifully followed, led, not least, by a degree of curiosity.

We decided to make a day of it, travelling up on the ancient, smog-bellowing *trenet* – which chugged up and down the coast so slowly it was surprising when it actually reached anywhere. We were surrounded by Germans, Swedes, Dutch and English, all soaking up the much-needed winter light. The low, white sun shone brilliantly in our eyes, reflecting off the shimmering sea beneath us, as we inched our way along beaches and clifftops. Opposite us sat an Englishwoman, a long-term resident, and her friend who had come to visit for a week or so. No English reserve here, I noticed: far from murmuring quietly so as not to disturb the other passengers and keep her conversation private, she raised her voice unself-consciously above the din of the engine and the dozen other voices echoing around the carriage. Spain, it seemed, could have a radical effect on foreigners.

The train shuddered up the coast, pulling beyond the built-up areas of Alicante, past Pedro's house, San Juan and out onto the cliffs perched over the clear water of the Mediterranean. Looking out the window, I felt I had never properly understood the term 'sea-blue' until that moment. It was an infinitely rich, passionate experience of colour, deeply satisfying, the shifting tones of turquoise and purple contrasting sharply against the yellow, white and green of the rocks and trees around us.

Just before we reached our destination, the mustachioed inspector, complete with peaked cap and missing shirt button, arrived to sell us our tickets. Eduardo and I paid up reluctantly, irritated at having come so close to a free ride. A Scotsman grunted, handing over the largest note he thought would cover it. The Englishwoman opposite struggled to get the tickets she wanted using sign-language, pidgin Spanish, and clearly and loudly spoken English. The inspector couldn't understand what she was saying, or at least he was giving nothing away. Eduardo and I intervened and translated. As the beleaguered inspector moved on the woman leaned over: 'You know I've lived here for twenty years and I can still barely say a word.'

No wonder the ex-pats needed their own newspaper.

The offices of the *Costa Gazette* were on a narrow street no more than a hundred yards from the sea-front, in a low building set among soaring white towers with orange and green sun-blinds flapping in the breeze. We climbed the dim stairs, entering what seemed to be a collection of holiday flats, cheaply constructed and producing a permanent sense of unease from the thought that they might collapse at any minute. It felt like entering a house of cards.

The newspaper offices were shabby. A teenage girl sat in reception behind a beaten-up old desk, wrapping papers with a sulky look on her face. She said nothing, but gestured with her thumb for us to enter the main room. Walking through, I almost fell as my foot caught in the gaping holes in the dirty brown carpet. Inside the main office piles of papers, clippings and negatives littered every surface. It was small and cramped and dingy. Everything was a dull, non-descript colour. A few curious eyes peeked up to ascertain the source of the break in the monotony, then looked down again, satisfied that we posed no threat.

After a moment or two, a cheerful woman with thick glasses and a northern English accent approached us and asked if she could help. Eduardo explained we wanted to see the editor. Half-expecting to be told to return later – editors were, after all, busy people – I was surprised when we were immediately taken into what looked like a kind of glass and wooden shack in the corner of the main room. Glamour photos of busty women adorned the walls. Some of them looked familiar from copies of the newspaper I had read before coming. A middle-aged man with a bright yellow silk shirt and lazy, bored eyes stood up.

'Eduardo, my boy. Always a pleasure.'

I shook his hand.

'Barry,' he grunted.

We sat down, sinking into a corner on a low sofa.

'What can I do for you two gents?'

Eduardo took the initiative, speaking quickly in an authoritative, colloquial Spanish, which somehow seemed to shift the balance of power. He explained he was here to introduce me, a journalist friend of long standing who was looking for work in Spain. I sat quietly, trying to look engaged, as my attention wandered from buttock to breast to buttock again along the row of pin-ups.

'What's your background, then?'

I tried to say something, but Eduardo butted in, racing on with his big sell. A string of untruths was elaborated, detailing my professional record – editor of the university newspaper, contacts in Fleet Street – and I nearly choked when I heard that I was married to one of his journalist colleagues.

'Oh, lovely!' Barry's dull eyes lit up at this point.

'Well, Jason. I'd be happy for you to come in a couple of days a week for a trial period,' he drawled. 'But I can only pay the usual rate: five pesetas a line.'

I nearly choked again. Was he joking? Two pence a line? But a dig in the ribs from Eduardo held me back. I nodded my approval politely, and the interview came to an end. We shook hands and left.

I was glad to get out of there. Barry's odd eyes bothered me as my attention oscillated between the conversation and the incredibly large breasts of a woman in a lime-green G-string pinned to the back wall. Eduardo tried to reassure me about the job.

'Don't worry, son. They'll be asking you for more and more in no time. And the pay will get better.

You'll probably be running the place in a few months.'

A week later, I returned for my first day. I was introduced to Jonathan, the only full-time journalist working there. A slight, narrow-shouldered man with a mild manner and an undisguised look of fear in his eyes, Jonathan made up for the lack of other hacks in the office by swilling a steady flow of San Miguel beer and smoking eighty cigarettes a day. So strong was his addiction to nicotine, that his whole family once had to fly to their holiday in Florida via Iceland so that he could have a mid-Atlantic puff.

Jonathan was a good journalist, though. He'd previously worked at a selection of national papers in England, and had once famously exposed police complicity in a smuggling racket in Gibraltar. The photos he'd taken almost cost him his life, and, in his rush to get away from the mobsters, he had lost his contacts book. Over time, this notebook had taken on mythical qualities, and everyone from King Juan Carlos to the Mayor of Marbella could have been called directly 'if only Jonathan hadn't lost that bloody contacts book'. Family responsibilities had led him to seek something more settled, and he'd ended up as the news editor at the *Costa Gazette*. Over the following months he showed me the ropes.

'Here, boy. Let me look at your nails.'

We were not having a good lesson. I had cancelled one class as a result of commitments at the paper, and Juan had not been impressed when I told him the reason.

'Oh, I see. So you're off all over the place like a stupid *guiri*, while I'm trying to teach you something serious here. Eh? You don't think I came out of retirement just to be messed about?'

In my own mind, although Juan was teaching me how to play the guitar, Eduardo was closest to being my real flamenco teacher, bringing me up to speed on such things as history, regional variations, and something of the philosophy of simply being a *flamenco*. Juan could take me through the motions, but Eduardo, I felt, could show me what it all meant. I needed them both and wanted to avoid conflict at all costs. But Juan had begun to push me even harder in our lessons now. No more simple *Rumbas* – *Bulerías* had been passed over for something more 'fun' – now I was expected to do things with my fingers I had never thought possible. Every class, he came up with a handful of incredibly complicated chords for me to learn. These required twisting my hand into ever more excruciating positions, and I was convinced he was enjoying the pain I was suffering.

'Enough Gypsy Kings,' he said. 'Serious flamenco from now on. Now you're mixing with all those *guiris* up in Benidorm, you'll be wanting to do *Verdiales*, or *Sevillanas* – all the touristy stuff.'

I looked up. Despite the months of practice, I still felt like I couldn't really play anything anyone else would want to listen to – without either being paid or heavily sedated first. But *Verdiales* and *Sevillanas* were great party pieces, the sort of thing your Aunty Marjorie would be able to clap along to.

'Well forget it,' he said. I groaned. 'It's time for a *Soleá*, the Mother Chant.'

The *Soleá* is supposedly named after a female singer in flamenco folklore called Soledad (the d's, already softened by Spanish pronunciation, almost disappear when uttered by Andalusians or Gypsies). A slow and emotive style that often seems to evoke the 'loneliness' of its title, it forms, along with other *palos* – *Seguiriyas*, *Polos* and *Cañas* – the backbone of the 'deep song' of flamenco, the *cante jondo*. Singing is the first principle of flamenco, and deep song, as any aficionado will tell you, is what authentic flamenco is all about; it is the heart, root and soul of the whole art-form, the least accessible to outsiders and the sound most likely to produce *duende*. It is what takes the listener closest to that charged, primitive experience that seems like an echo from an older, lost age.

'Deep song is imbued with the mysterious colour of primordial times,' Lorca once famously said in a lecture he gave before the 1922 Granada festival. 'Its notes carry the naked, spine-tingling emotion of the first Oriental races.'

Palos that fall outside the deep song category are often referred to in lighter terms as *cante medio*, middle song, or *cante chico*, baby song, or even sometimes as *cante flamenco*, as though deep song were something distinct from flamenco altogether. All these can produce *duende* in their own right, but there is a kudos attached to deep song amongst flamenco circles, where the *jondura* – the depth – particularly in the *Seguiriya*, makes it revered as the aristocrat of all the song forms.

There are singers who specialise in deep song, as there are those who are known principally for their *Tarantas* or *Tangos*. But a guitarist is expected to move in and out of each *palo* with ease; one minute slow and emotive, the next fast and rhythmic, like a fiesta.

Juan began to play mournfully, a look of pain on his

face, counting the twelve-beat rhythm out loud as the music lurched forward.

I listened intently, my eyes fixed on the guitar as I concentrated on his technique. But another part of me was secretly cursing him. His moodiness was beginning to annoy me. I didn't want to learn *Soleá* at that moment. It just didn't feel right and I secretly wished we were doing something else. And now, as it was my turn to copy him and play what I had just heard, my fingers kept catching on the treble strings in the complicated double arpeggio movement.

'Here. Show me your hand.'

I stopped and reluctantly held my right hand out towards him.

'OK. I thought that was the problem. Right, put your guitar away.'

Confused, I did as he said. We were only halfway through the lesson. This was unusual, even for him. What was going on? Was there something wrong with my hands? Perhaps he was about to tell me I had a fundamental problem with my fingers which meant I would never be able to play the guitar at all. Hesitantly, I placed the instrument in its case and turned towards him.

'Right, boy. The rest of this lesson will be dedicated to nails: how to look after them, file them, strengthen them, everything.'

I laughed with relief.

'Hey! What are you laughing at? You think I'm joking?'

I shook my head obediently.

'Some guitarists have been known to turn violent if their nails broke. Someone cut off my teacher's nails when he was sleeping and he almost burnt the guy's house down. The police stopped him in the street carrying a fire-bomb.'

I laughed again.

'I'm deadly serious. Here, look at mine.' He thrust his hand forward. It was fine and sinewy, delicately manicured so that not a single nail was out of shape, each one shining with varnish, the thumb nail filed at an angle to give better purchase on the strings. The skin was soft and white, as though never used: no cuts, no roughness, not even at the knuckles.

'Now look at yours.' By contrast mine looked like a road-sweeper's. 'Right. Let me show you what to do.'

Over the next hour we filed, glued, varnished, refiled, sprayed, blew and generally pampered ourselves like a couple of tarts on pay day. If ever Juan needed a job on the side, I was sure there were plenty of people who would spend a fortune for such treatment. He had turned the simple care of the human nail into a craft on a par with art restoration. At one point I thought I was even going to get a silk job – when thin pieces of silk are glued onto the nail to give it strength. But after much twisting and poking, he decided mine were healthy enough.

'Just be careful when opening tin-cans and that sort of thing,' he said. 'Start using your left hand for ordinary tasks. Your right hand is sacred.'

I nodded in bewildered agreement. I was beginning to have doubts about this. All I wanted to do was play the guitar, for heaven's sake. But he hadn't finished. There were the finer points of filing to master. It all depended on the shape of your own nail and how it related to the rest of your finger. Each one might be different, as was the case with my unfortunate hand. He filed, I put my hand in position on the guitar, he tutted, he filed again, I assumed the position, more filing – sometimes just one stroke at a time – then back to the guitar. It was endless.

'Always file in the same direction. Otherwise, disaster!' There was no irony in his voice. 'And never, ever cut them. That's fatal.'

We finally came to an end, and, to my surprise, the arpeggios were now much easier. I was converted on the spot.

'Thanks, Juan. I just had no idea . . .' I said.

'That's fine. But you must look after them now. OK? You must learn to love your hand, your right hand. And your left. They are your tools. Without them you won't be able to play our beautiful music.'

A call came in. A fire at a hotel in Benidorm. I was told to go and investigate – my first real story. Rushing out with a notebook and camera, I got to the hotel and dodged past security to find everyone lying by the pool as though nothing had happened. There were certainly no signs of a fire. A few people told me some-one's dustbin had caught alight and they had all been evacuated for a few minutes, but that was all. My heart sank. Some story.

'Which paper are you from, love?' asked an old Liverpudlian woman. It was a great chance to advertise my employer, I thought. I might win a new reader.

'The *Costa Gazette*. It's . . .'

'Never heard of it. You should work for a proper paper like the *Sun*.'

I went back to the office. I had been gone for two hours. Barry was not impressed.

'You took your time. Went for a stroll by the beach,

82

did you? Still, wouldn't blame you. Heh, heh.' And he rubbed his hands together lasciviously.

I explained I'd had difficulties but had some great quotes.

'You shouldn't have bothered,' said Jonathan. 'We usually just make them up.'

As the weeks passed I was gradually initiated into the murky world of local journalism and the even murkier one of the ex-pat community. Whole sub-cultures had been created, where each nationality had its own schools, bookshops, newspapers, travel agents, doctors, lawyers – anything where you might want to avoid having to deal with any of the natives. For the readers the paper, as Barry had said, was a bible: absolutely required reading to survive in what was certainly perceived as a hostile environment. Underlying it all was a form of racism, a deeply rooted idea that at heart all 'dagoes' were corrupt and dodgy bastards, only too ready to pull a fast one on innocent foreigners. The ex-pats didn't come here for the people or the culture, they came for the weather – the warm, sunny winters – and they did their best to recreate life in the *Youkay* here on the Costa. The British class system was alive and kicking too. Torrevieja, to the south of Alicante, and to some extent Benidorm itself, were working-class ghettos where folk with little more than a state pension would settle in search of a better life. North of Benidorm – Altea, Jávea and Moraira – was the reserve of the golf-playing, middle-class and professional elites. Not that even they could compete with the gaudy wealth of the Costa del Sol . . .

Spain did rub off on the English in one respect, how-ever: the development of their own argot, formed from seemingly random, mispronounced Spanish words. I first encountered this when I called an English bar-owner in Benidorm to get some details about a break-in the night before.

'Not much damage,' he said. 'But of course they had to break the rackers to get in.'

'Rackers?'

'Yeah, mate. Made a right mess of them, they did. It'll cost me a tidy sum to get those fixed.'

I could hear stifled sniggers from Jonathan opposite. I had no idea what the bar-owner was talking about.

'Just where were these rackers, then?' I asked.

'Where they always bloody are! Where else are they gonna be?' He slammed the phone down. I turned to Jonathan, who by now was quite beside himself.

'What the hell are rackers?' I demanded.

'*Rejas*,' he said, wiping the tears from his eyes. 'He means *rejas* – window bars.'

In a flash I understood. The Spanish word – pronounced 'rekhas' – had been anglicised into 'rackers'. I could see that a knowledge of English and Spanish was not going to be enough. There was a third lingo to learn: ex-patese. Over the months I picked up as much as I could. Houses, it turned out, were always referred to as 'cazers' (*casas*), especially when in the countryside, when they became 'cazers del campo'. You never lived on an estate, but an 'urbanisation' (*urbanización*), where the rubbish men collected the 'bazura' (*basura*), and every once in a while you were visited by an 'alcaldy' (*alcalde* – mayor), who came from the 'ayuntamientow' (*ayuntamiento* – town hall). If you wanted a drink, the largest concentration of English bars in Benidorm was on the 'cally londreez' (*Calle Londres*). This last one cost me many minutes scanning a map, trying to find something that might resemble the sound uttered by the woman on the other end of the phone, until Jonathan once again took pity on me and pointed me in the right direction.

I went down to Ginés's bar alone. Juan couldn't make it that night, and when I saw there was no-one else there from our little group, I resigned myself to a quiet evening. I sat at the bar and ordered a brandy. If nobody arrived by the time I had finished my drink, I would simply head home.

The old men were playing their usual game of dominoes, feet scuffing the sawdust-covered floor as they twitched on their seats. Their voices rose and fell in waves like an unpredictable flock of birds.

I drained the glass and turned to go but was stopped by a tug on my elbow. It was Lola.

'Well,' she said. 'How about a drink?'

I smiled yes and ordered two more brandies. I was glad to see her here away from the school.

'Would you like to sit at the table?' I asked.

'No. Let's stay here.' She pulled up a bar stool and sat next to me. 'I get so bored always doing the same thing.'

We sat close to one another, drinking. There was a hesitant smile on her lips.

'Teacher couldn't make it?' she asked after a pause.

'No, Juan had to—'

'Are you learning fast?' she interrupted.

'I don't really know. It's not easy to say. I think Juan pushes me quite hard.'

'I thought perhaps . . .' Her voice tailed off and she seemed to forget what she was going to say. She brushed a thick strand of dark red hair away from her eyes.

'It looks like the others aren't coming today,' I said.

'Yes. It happens like this sometimes. Although I'm usually the one who doesn't make it. Pilar doesn't like that. She thinks I should make more of an effort. But she doesn't know what it's like.'

I studied her as she spoke: hair swept back over slightly rounded shoulders, revealing thick gold earrings; her fingers playing with the end of her long, fleshy nose; deep mischievous eyes that flicked around the room, never still. She seemed bored, or melancholy, but at the same time she radiated energy, like a hot coal waiting to burst into flame.

'Doesn't know what what's like?' I asked.

She sighed, paused, and looked me hard in the eye. 'She doesn't know what it's like being married to an *antiflamenquista*.' There was a sense of inevitability in her voice, and I had an impression of crossing a threshold.

'What's that?' I asked.

'Vicente,' she said. 'Your boss, my husband.' I waited. 'He hates flamenco. Can't stand it. Always has.' She paused. 'And he hates me having anything to do with it. Says I shouldn't dance, tries to stop me from coming here to the bar, or going to our little get-togethers in the country. He hates it.'

She buried her face in the glass and her hair fell over her eyes. I wasn't sure if she was crying.

'I don't understand.'

She sniffed and lifted her head. 'Vicente . . . Vicente likes to see himself as an intellectual. Rejects traditional Spain, folklore, that sort of thing, as barbarous. It's horrendous. But they all look to France and Britain – especially Britain – as the heart of all that is good. Spain bad, Britain good.'

'What?'

'Oh, don't worry, *guiri*. He thinks you're wonderful. Admittedly he is a little confused by your interest in flamenco, but he's convinced it's just the passing infatuation of a northern European with his primitive southern cousins. You will see the error of your ways, probably under his guidance. He already has plans for you.'

I only half-registered what she said. Her sudden opening up to me had caught me unawares.

'But I don't understand. Why are you and he . . . ?' I hesitated to ask. It seemed so familiar to be discussing such matters.

'Yes. Good question. I ask myself the same. Of course, I know the answer. But . . .' She knocked back her brandy and ordered two more.

'You did want another, didn't you?'

I nodded. The two glasses were placed down next to us on the metal bar with a clink. Lola lent across me reaching for a tissue, brushing her arm lightly over my chest. She wiped her mouth, then screwed the paper into a tight ball before tossing it to the floor.

'I've been dancing since before I could walk,' she continued, lighting a cigarette and drawing on it with her full, wide lips. 'It was all there, from the beginning: my father with his old records, my mother teaching me steps in the kitchen. I was going to be a dancer, a good dancer. Everyone said it was in my blood.'

'You *are* a good dancer.'

'They had it planned for me: go to Madrid, study, dance, turn professional.' She shrugged.

'What happened?'

'I met Vicente.' She took another mouthful from her

87

glass. 'Got pregnant when I was seventeen. That's kind of terminal for a dancing career.' She laughed weakly. 'But I could still have done it. I could still have been a dancer, maybe not professional, but, you know, here and there. But he held me back. Said I needed to stay at home. Then the school, and . . . well, that's it.' Her head bowed once more. 'I've asked him for a divorce,' she said quietly, looking down.

I was both embarrassed and thrilled that she should be telling me such intimate details about herself. But this was quickly absorbed by the surprise of seeing the image I had built up of her dissolving in front of me: this strong, fiery woman, who instilled fear in those around her, was helpless and trapped.

'I have to go.' She threw her head back and stared at me. 'I'm a mother, remember?'

We paid and left, out into the pools of light cast by the streetlamps, walking together for the distance that our two paths coincided, silent, our shoulders almost touching. As we reached the corner she turned to face me, stepping away as though to be any closer meant danger.

'I'm going this way,' she said. I nodded. Normally when we parted from social encounters, we kissed one another on the cheeks, but this time there was hesitation. She wavered, stepping backwards and forwards, as though undecided.

'Do you think . . .' I began.

'I'll see you at school tomorrow,' she said, turning away and heading down the hill. I stood, watching her walk, the gentle rhythm of her hips.

It was late, and very quiet. A Tuesday. One of only two nights off for the town's revellers. Guidebooks on

Spain always cite figures showing there to be more bars per square inch than people, or more cafés in Madrid than in the whole of the rest of the world put together. I forget what the real numbers are, but the impression they give is generally true. You can barely find a street that doesn't have some sort of watering hole, usually several, and this is reflected in the night life. The party normally starts on a Thursday, because having a hangover on a Friday doesn't really count. Then of course there are Friday and Saturday nights. This usually drags on until Sunday, because once on a roll, why bother stopping? And Monday hangovers don't really count for much either. For the really hardcore, even Monday night can swing. Not that the Spanish ever get really drunk in an Anglo-Saxon way, though. Alcohol is merely a means to an end – having fun. And for such a devout and social race, having fun begins to take on almost religious dimensions, where sleep is an act of apostasy and only the hardened allnighters are guaranteed a place in the Kingdom of Heaven. Tuesday and Wednesday are the real days of the weekend in Spain – the only days when rest for all is a certainty and religious duties are excused.

Walking back home under the palm trees along the empty road, I could hear my footsteps echoing against the buildings on the other side. At my front door, I paused. A woman struggling to carry a mattress had turned the corner and was coming up behind me. I asked her where she was going.

'My house is just around the corner,' she said in a strong French accent. 'Can you 'elp me?'

I picked up one end of the mattress and we set off. Five minutes around the block, I thought, and I'll be back before midnight.

We headed towards the market, walking in silence, trying to keep a grip on the old mattress as it kept slipping between our fingers. I could feel the dust from it rising up in clouds and tickling my nose. We went past the market, past the bank and down onto the Rambla, the wide road leading to the beach. Hardly around the corner, I thought, but we must be getting close by now.

'I live just here, in the *barrio*,' she said. We walked on into the old quarter. My hands were tiring and the sweat made the surface of my palms even more slippery. It felt like carrying an enormous fish. And who was this strange, slight Frenchwoman? She certainly wasn't talkative. I felt cheated. Surely my compensation for all this effort was a little conversation.

'It's a heavy old mattress you've got here,' I said. She didn't reply.

We kept walking, through the narrow alleyways, past all the bars, the little cinema, the decrepit square. Where were we going? She said it was close by. I was beginning to regret my act of charity. On we went, up the steep hill into the cluster of white houses at the foot of the castle, deep into areas I had no idea existed. In the moonlight I could see blurred graffiti on crumbling walls, written in a language I didn't under-stand. I was sweating from the exertion now, cursing this woman for taking advantage of my willingness to help. Where the bloody hell did she live? Perhaps she didn't have a house at all and was looking for some-where to bed down for the night.

Finally we arrived at a line of small houses on the very edge of the old town, to the rear of the castle.

'It's 'ere,' she said. Her house was the final one in

the row. We got to her door, put the mattress down and she went inside to turn on the lights.

'Thank you. I can manage now.' I stood there. It seemed strange just to turn on my heel and head straight home. I felt I had been through something with this woman, even if I was cursing her most of the way. She noticed my hesitation.

'Did you want to come in?' she asked.

'No. I think . . .'

'Here, then. Take my card. Come back whenever you like.' She reached into her pocket and handed me a torn piece of paper. 'Christine' it said. 'Psychic'.

I returned one afternoon the following week, justifying my visit with the thought that she owed me something. Perhaps she could tell my fortune.

She welcomed me matter-of-factly and beckoned me in.

The house was small, white, and decorated with Moroccan rugs, Indian shawls, and sweet-smelling candles. There were symbols hanging from the walls: ankhs, pentacles, peace signs.

After a few moments she emerged with some camomile tea. 'Here,' she said. 'It's all I 'ave.'

We sat in silence on brightly coloured cushions strewn on the floor. Now that I'd come I wasn't quite sure what to say.

'Mattress all right?' I tried.

'Hm? Oh, yes. The mattress is fine.'

She was looking at me, or rather staring at me quite intensely. I tried to concentrate on the decorations on the walls, the books on the shelf. Works on healing, magic, mysticism.

'I can read the cards for you,' she said suddenly, 'if you like.'

'OK. Sure.' I was relieved something was going to happen. I had been drinking my tea so quickly it had burnt my throat.

She handed me a pack of large cards and I was asked to shuffle.

'I take it you are heterosexual?' The word sounded odd in her thick accent.

'Er, yeah,' I said, taken slightly aback.

'You know, it is better to ask these days. You cannot know, you know?'

'Of course.'

'I might see your partner and not know whether to say "he" or "she".'

'No, "she" is fine. Just fine.'

She laid the cards out on the floor between us and began to concentrate. I looked down. No death card: that was a relief. What did the others mean, though? It looked like a mess.

'It hits me straight away,' she said. 'You have many good attributes, but here,' she rapped her fist hard against her chest, 'you have not grown up here. In your emotions.' She paused, then said, 'You are emotionally immature.'

Her words rang inside me like a bell and I sat back on the cushions, confused. How could one be *emotionally* immature? It seemed such a strange idea. Surely one just grew, and developed. It took care of itself, didn't it? Maybe not. Somewhere, part of me understood just what she meant. Wasn't that one of the reasons I was here in Spain, after all, this most emotional of countries? Hadn't it been the warmth, the emotional ease of the Spaniards that had kept me here, had attracted me to flamenco and the country in the first place?

The Frenchwoman continued.

'You feel as though the universe is pushing you towards having a relationship with a woman, a woman you know. But it is for you to say, for you to decide. It is of no concern to the universe if you do or you do not.' She now had my undivided attention.

'You may suffer, it depends on you. But there will be grieving soon. In the next year. But also change. You will not recognise your future self.'

She picked up the cards and put them away. 'That is all for now. I must ask you to leave.'

I stood up and brushed myself down, still dazed by what she had said. Heading out into the sun from her cave-like home, I was temporarily blinded by the light. I turned to say goodbye, but the door had already closed.

chapter FOUR

Por Alegrías

Ay Dolores,
como huele
tu cuerpo a flores!

Oh, Dolores,
your body
scented like flowers!

'You can't order passion. It has to come in its own time.'

I sat in Juan's living-room on his red sofa tuning up my guitar. The place smelt of stale cigarettes. We hadn't begun yet and he was still in a good mood.

I was beginning to discover something about my playing, about how I would be drawn to particular *palos* depending on my mood or emotions: a *Taranta* for melancholy, *Alegría* for a certain type of joy, *Tango* for sexual energy. Eduardo had already talked about it, but I wanted to hear what Juan had to say.

'How can we perform a *palo* on cue? Flamenco is a way of life, not something to be produced on demand. Anyone who thinks otherwise is a fool. Flamenco is love. Passion. Not something we can control with a click of the fingers.'

After months of him telling me this, I felt I was close to understanding what he meant.

'It will all become clearer as you get better.'

Enough theory, back to the playing. I looked down at the guitar. Progress was not achieved step by step, as I had expected it to be. It seemed cyclical, if anything.

'Eventually the guitar will become your *novia* – your fiancée,' Juan had said. 'You will love her more than any woman. A guitar is more responsive and as long as you treat her well, she will never betray you.'

For the first months it had felt like a foreign object: a strange, cold, varnished being never comfortable in my grasp, always rejecting me and pulling away. But I persisted, forcing it into place, my arms and fingers constantly inching around it in an intuitive search for the correct position. It began to take on symbolic importance: only when I had successfully reinvented myself as a *flamenco* would the guitar accept me, went the thought. Often I would sit for hours with it on my lap, not playing, just holding it there against me, warming it with my body, resting my arms on its curves as I gazed out the window or read through notes for the English class I had to give later in the evening. With time it would come, I told myself. Real skills needed sacrifice and hard work. And so I continued, spending hour after hour in repetitive practice, training my hands to perform new and complicated tasks until slowly the instrument began to feel like it belonged.

Right-hand techniques are the most difficult, and modern flamenco guitar players pride themselves on them. The left hand creates the melody as it forms the chords and notes, but the right hand is the more important, creating rhythm as it strikes both strings and wood in complex, dextrous movements. Flamenco guitars usually come with a plastic plate stuck to the soundboard to protect the wood as the player taps the rhythm hard with his ring finger. In earlier times the instrument served mostly as a musical and percussive complement to the singer, and many performers accompanied themselves as they sang. With time, as both singing and playing developed, they were separated, and now it is very rare to find people who do both.

I always practised on a white plastic fold-up chair in my living-room, palm fronds brushing against the bay windows in the breeze and creating whirling patterns in the dirt on the panes. Bent almost double over the guitar, I'd strike down on the strings one by one in a roll – a *rasgueo*. It was a strain at first; my fingers were not used to working independently of one another, but little by little they began to loosen and strengthen and the pain would lessen. And I had a sense of satisfaction when, for the first time in my life, seeing myself reflected in the glass door to my bedroom, I could see the individual muscles flexing on my forearm. I tried to alternate techniques for each day, two hours or more spent simply trying to improve my *triple* – a sideways roll of the wrist involving the thumb and middle finger – or striking the strings quickly with my first and middle fingers, the *picado*. Nights came and I often ended up entering a kind of trance, with a loss of all sense of time, until I fell into bed around three or four in the morning.

Over the previous week I'd been practising a *Rondeña*. The *palo* was named after Ronda, a pretty town perched on the edge of a precipitous gorge in the Andalusian mountains. It involved retuning the guitar, dropping the sixth string to a D and the third string to an F sharp, to create a deep, rich, evocative and immediately recognisable sound. Juan had composed this one, he told me, when he was living in Seville near the Giralda tower.

'A wonderful time in my life,' he said. 'Such beautiful people.'

I had been playing it almost non-stop, my mind absorbed by the meeting with Lola at the bar. I couldn't tell if I was just imagining a spark between us that night, and while we were both at the school there was no chance of talking to her. Her hard, professional mask meant that even when we looked at one another, which was seldom, there was nothing, no recognition, no lowering of the barriers that had previously, if momentarily, seemed to come down. I was in a foreign country; they did things differently here. Perhaps in Spain a man and a woman could experience that kind of intimacy without it carrying another – *the* other – meaning. I was young, inexperienced, and struggling hard to understand things I had barely mastered even in England. In the confusion, and partly to escape the anxious workings of my own mind, I had thrown myself into the music and Juan's piece. Sitting at home playing the guitar for hours on end, trying to lose myself in the emotion of the composition, my mind still focused absolutely on her.

We started the lesson and I began tentatively with the first chord. My fingers were often shaky at the start of the class; Juan was never hesitant to break in almost immediately with his first rebuke of the day, as though in protest at having to teach. But today there was a difference. As I continued playing for another minute or so there was complete silence where normally there would have been some degree of groaning, tutting, or simply an order to stop and start again. I couldn't look up – I still needed to concentrate on the strings – but I knew, somehow, that for the first time I was playing the music from the inside, not the outside as had previously been the case, and that Juan was being carried along with me.

I hummed the tune quietly under my breath as I played on, eyes focused on the strings. My playing had improved as a result of continual practising, I felt, and I wanted some recognition from Juan of my efforts. But despite my concentration, I was dimly aware of some other music starting from somewhere. At first I thought it might be a neighbour or a local bar turning on a sound system. Then slowly it became clear: it was another guitar, very gentle, almost inaudible. I glanced up quickly – Juan had begun to accompany me. It was unusual as I only knew *Rondeñas* as solos. He played harmonies; haunting, fascinating chords I had never heard before. Yet they fitted perfectly. His fingers moved effortlessly over the fretboard, sliding and stretching in incomprehensible combinations of notes, feeling his way around my playing, with no rhythm to guide him. In an ordinary moment it would have been impossible to follow me, to gauge my timing, to feel the piece with me. But this was a form of communion, an intuitive link between us, allowing us to perform in unison, producing something greater than our individual parts.

We both looked at each other when the piece finished.

'*Ole*,' he said slowly and quietly. The hairs lifted on the back of my neck. Juan got up and went to the kitchen to make some coffee. I put the guitar down and stood at his window, looking down into the street. *Ole*. He had never said it to me before. It was the nearest I would ever get to praise.

'You like it black, don't you.'

He lit the hob to heat milk for his own drink. The

fire caught the remains of his dinner and the smell of fried garlic flooded the flat.

There is an art to saying *ole* in flamenco, usually pronounced with the stress on the first syllable; only in bullfighting do you hear *olé*, with the accent at the end. You need both a technical knowledge of the music and an intuitive feel for the performance. Exclaim it – or its equivalents: *arsa*, *eso es* – at the wrong time, and at best you will be laughed out of the room. There are even *flamencos* whose speciality is the precise use of these terms – the *jaleo*. They stand or sit at the side of the stage trying to help the singer or dancer to perform their best. *Vamos ya*, 'let's go', is for encouragement. *Ole* is reserved for that special emotional climax: the *duende* moment.

'I think you've fallen in love,' Juan said handing me the coffee. I blushed and pretended not to have heard. He didn't press me and we sat down to continue the lesson.

After some ten minutes spent polishing a few points and discussing what we might look at for the next class, the doorbell rang. Juan stood up and went to answer, disappearing from view into the hall.

'*Hombre!*' He gave out a stifled cry of surprise as the door opened.

'Hello, Juan.' It was Lola. 'Sorry for not calling. I was in the area and I wanted to borrow your video of Belén Maya.' Her voice was hard, like the one she used at school.

'Yes, yes. Of course,' said Juan. 'Wait just a minute.' He darted off into the other room, as wrong-footed as I was by her sudden appearance. I sat with the guitar in my hands, frozen, not sure what to do. It seemed odd that Juan hadn't invited her in. Why had she come? The line about the video didn't quite strike true. Should I let her know I was there? I wondered how she would react. This could be a great opportunity.

But there was no need to decide. Before Juan reappeared she popped her head round the door, her smile framed by red tresses, and mouthed a silent greeting to me. I returned it with a grin of surprise, scrutinising her face for a clue. She winked, and returned to the door. She had known I was there all along.

Juan walked past with the tape.

'Here,' I could hear him saying. 'I didn't know you were still studying.'

'We never stop learning, Juan. *Adiós.*'

And with that she was gone.

I stood up and packed away my guitar as quickly as I could. I might be able to catch her if I hurried, I thought, but I had to be careful not to make it too obvious to Juan. Especially after his earlier comment. He came back into the room with a confused look still on his face. It wasn't normal, this visit of hers, and he seemed to be struggling to work out what it meant. As he dithered, I took the opportunity to pay him for the class and begin my exit. We exchanged a few words – thanks for the class, same time next week, I'll call you – and I headed for the door, all the while trying to resist breaking into a sprint. We said our final goodbye, shook hands and when the door closed, I threw myself down the stairs, guitar case crashing against the narrow walls. I had to find her. Which way would she have gone?

I reached the main entrance hall, and walked out of the darkness into the bright street, a smell of hot tar and steam drifting from where workmen were re-laying the road. Standing on the opposite side, a cigarette in her hand, was Lola. *She* was waiting for *me*.

'Come on,' she said, flicking her head to one side. 'I've got the car just around the corner.'

I followed as she turned and walked away. Even here, on the street, there was an ever-present sense of dance in the way she moved her body. Half-dazed, yet still trying to hide my surprise, I placed the guitar in the boot and climbed silently into the passenger seat. All the things I had wanted to say, all the questions, began to fade.

Lola said nothing as we set off with a jolt and headed away from San Blas and its brick-block apart-ment buildings towards the wide palm-strewn avenues nearer the sea. Powering through the traffic, she swerved from lane to lane, passing through red lights, honking her horn to clear the road ahead of us. The slight haze of the morning had given way to the clear, shining air of midday that gave Alicante its name – Lucentum, the city of light – and the smell of the last batches of bread being made for the lunchtime rush flooded through the open windows in hot waves.

We jerked our way through the crowded streets, her thin brown arms twisting over the steering wheel as she carved a path down to the harbour. For a long time I kept my gaze fixed out of the window, watching the blurred colours and shapes of people and cars flash by. I was almost laughing with excitement, even though my hands were shaking very slightly as I gripped the seat. She'd planned her visit to Juan's. She knew I was there and had come for me. After so many days of uncertainty, the situation had changed. Now, it seemed, I was the prey.

I sank deep into the seat as slowly a hesitant realisation dawned on me. This woman, who had so obsessed me over the previous weeks, her full brown eyes flashing in my mind like mirror-reflections of the sun, was seducing *me*. Surely I must have misread the signs. I started to convince myself that this couldn't be happening; that it was pure vanity on my part.

Down Alfonso El Sabio avenue, then on to the side-streets, past the elegant sandstone theatre and towards the Rambla. Her fierce, silent concentration seemed to forbid any conversation. I looked over at her: slender, long-fingered hands, thin gold bracelets wrapped around her wrists drawing out the tan of her skin. She refused to look at me, and as the silence persisted, the thrill began to turn into anxiety and doubt. Perhaps she was changing her mind.

We parked by the harbour. The rigging of the yachts vibrated in the breeze, striking the masts in a chorus of thin, high-pitched chimes. She reached into her bag, pulled out a cigarette and placed it in her mouth, turning to face me for the first time as she switched off the engine.

'Will you light it for me?'

She caressed my hand as I lifted the lighter towards her. Unthinkingly I moved my face closer to hers.

'Wait,' she said, laughing. 'We're going to have lunch first. On Tabarca.'

The ferry gurgled away from the coastline, leaving

behind clusters of Algerians on the quay, laden with suitcases full of carpets and breakfast cereals to take home on the boat to Oran. We stood on the open top-deck, empty but for a German couple and a fisherman nursing his rods and a wooden box of live bait. Behind us Alicante grew smaller and smaller, towers and hotels dwarfed by the great medieval castle perched on the bare rocky hill overlooking the city.

'I've never been to Tabarca,' I said, turning and looking towards the low island on the horizon.

'It's a small place, with a lighthouse and a one-street town. Not very interesting, but they do good food.'

I was beginning to recognise this in her: keeping face. To take me somewhere special would have been a sign of weakness.

'A friend of mine told me about the island,' I said. She looked away, hiding her face from me. It was still unclear why we were on this boat, shading our eyes from the hot spring sun, moving ever further from the city. At least, I thought, I could engage her in conversation.

'He said the first inhabitants were Italians who settled there hundreds of years ago after being kid-napped by a Moorish emir and ransomed by the king of Spain. They called the island Tabarca as a blessing for their release.'

'Blessing?'

'*Tabaraka*. From the Arabic. It means God bless.'

She looked out over the sea, hands grasping the rail as she leaned over into the warm breeze, dark red hair curling around her eyes. Spray was blowing up from the hull of the boat as it pushed through the waves, coating our clothes and skin with a light, salty film. I looked over at her, trying to gauge her expression, but she moved away, hiding herself from me, her face turned back towards the city.

'What do you want?' she said.

I leaned on the rail and looked down at the white foam churning below. Great bubbles of air rose out from below the surface like sighs. What could I say? I wanted her.

'Do you know how old . . .' She stood up and looked at me. I didn't move. 'No, I won't tell you.'

The island was growing as we moved closer. Two long, flat stretches joined at the middle by a low beach. The harbour, with its break wall and low buildings, was just becoming visible.

I turned back towards her. Without warning she stood away from the rail and lifted her hands in the air, clicking her fingers above her head and putting on the intense expression she wore when dancing.

'*Ole*,' she shouted as she stamped her feet on the deck, arching her back and twisting, her face never moving from mine. '*Ole!*'

I clapped, laughing along with her until she stopped, smiled and curtseyed like a ballerina.

'A woman like me?'

'Yes. A woman like you.'

The island was yellow and dusty, with a light so intense it felt it might sear itself onto our eyes. We walked the hundred yards to the other side of the island and found a one-storey house with tables outside and naked children wearing only pink and green plastic sandals running in and out of the door.

'Mari-Reme!' A large woman with a blue apron tied around her full waist stormed out and shouted to one of them. But the little girl had already disappeared around the corner, and was busy running with her friends to the water.

'She'll be gone all afternoon now,' the woman said, turning towards us. 'Come in, come in.'

The restaurant was crammed with fishermen drinking cold *fino* sherry and eating pieces of octopus stuck on the ends of toothpicks. Used paper tissues littered the floor and a delicious smell of fried fish floated through from the kitchens. We sat at a small table by the window overlooking the beach and the wide, open sea stretching out to the east. Lola drew on her cigarette and smiled.

'There are hundreds of different rice dishes in our region,' she said. 'Go to any village on the mainland and they'll have their own speciality. Black rice made with cuttlefish ink, straight paella with chicken and rabbit, crusty rice that you put in the oven. You always know the real thing because they bring it to you wrapped in newspaper. But the best thing they do here is *caldero tabarquí* made with fish caught off the island. I eat it straight out of the pan.'

The woman with the apron came to take our order as a young waitress filled our glasses with water.

'I caught them all myself this morning,' she said. 'Have to. My husband's useless at it.'

'You should see her,' the waitress butted in. 'They all come to her, like a magnet. She's famous for it. Everyone else comes back empty-handed, but she can catch them just by whistling. Isn't that right?'

Lola ordered some wine.

'Rioja. Don't drink Valencian wine, whatever you do,' she whispered to me over the table. I smiled conspiratorially.

'It's horrendous. They make it for tourists and *guiris*

like you. Everyone here drinks this.' She pointed to the bottle arriving at the table. 'But don't tell anyone back home.'

'Are you just visiting?' The magic fisherwoman handed us our food.

'Yes, we're here for the afternoon,' said Lola.

'You must walk into the village, then. There's a church at the far end of the island and then, if you come back and go over to the other side, there are some lovely walks along the cliffs and an old fort.'

'Thank you. We'll do that.'

The rice was served with the broth it had been cooked in; heavy, saffron-flavoured chunks of fish floating in enormous white bowls. It tasted wonderful.

'Saffron's another Arabic word,' I said.

She looked up from her soup.

'*Za'faran.*'

'Yes, they teach us things like that at school,' she said, uninterested. 'How come you know so much about it?'

'I studied it at university.'

'Is that all?' She laughed to herself.

'What do you mean?'

She hesitated for a moment. 'I mean, *guiri*, that there's still much for you to learn.' She continued eating. I said nothing. It was all part of the verbal fencing.

'The word *ole* comes from Arabic too,' I said.

'What?' Her spoon clanged against the bowl as she laughed in surprise. 'What are you talking about?'

'*Ole.* It comes from Allah.'

I could see her mouthing the two words to herself, unconvinced.

'They sound nothing like each other. What makes you so sure?'

'Even the Real Academia Española says so. *Wallah* –

by God. *Ole*. You even hear "Allah!" called out at some recitals of the Koran. It's just like a flamenco concert when people shout *ole*.'

'Flamenco's not about books, Jason.'

I remembered the endless hours I'd spent studying medieval Arabic poetry in Oxford libraries, all beauty in the descriptions of dancing girls and women with gazelle-like eyes lost in the stress over essay deadlines and exams. Now I was on a hot Mediterranean island being seduced by a flamenco dancer.

'Yes, I know. That's why I'm here.'

'Hope we see you two love-birds back here soon!' the landlady cried as we left. I smiled; Lola didn't react.

A fisherman was sitting outside in the sun on a tall wooden stool, repairing his nets with a knife and pieces of rope tied around his wrists. He nodded as we walked past.

'The village is over there,' Lola said, pointing. 'But I want to go up here. We can look at all that later if you like.'

She headed away from the half-empty beach to the scrubland that marked the other half of the island, holding her hand out behind her as encouragement. I followed, waiting till we had moved away from the restaurant and up the slope before gently allowing my own hand to fall into hers. She clung on to it tightly.

We followed the narrow pathway through the thick brown grass, bright blue sea surrounding us on three sides. Ahead of us, the old stone watchtower of San José squatted on the hill, rising up like a fist to the cloudless sky. Lola led the way, silent now as our feet fell into line, shoulders almost touching, our palms pushing against one another. I caught the smell of her skin on the breeze, hints of jasmine and rose. She looked forward, never stopping or turning towards me, as though the contact we already had was enough. Perhaps too much.

The rest of the island slowly receded into the distance as we headed to the far tip of the deserted grassy plain. Stepping over the last of the gorse bushes, we reached the end and started climbing down a stony slope to the water below, hands still pressed together, hanging on for fear of falling as we skidded on the loose pebbles. The beach was empty save for some gulls resting on rocks visible above the waves. The sun, still high in the sky, seemed to bleach everything: no shade anywhere. We walked down to the shore. Lola kicked off her shoes and skipped away as our hands finally parted.

'It's time for a swim,' she said.

I watched as she began taking off her blouse and then her trousers, throwing them on the sand by my feet until she stood naked in front of me. I looked around. There was nobody.

'Come on,' she called, running into the sea. 'Time to live!'

The light had changed to a thicker, richer yellow as we walked back over the grassland, arms curled into one another. From time to time she rested her head on my shoulder, pressing her mouth against my drying salt-caked skin. Long grey shadows streamed from our feet over the shrubs and out beyond the island. The last ferry would be leaving soon and we had to head back.

I felt warmth fluctuating between us as our bodies

moved closer then pulled apart. A sense of her returning reluctance to be involved with me came in waves, while I was caught between willingness and disbelief. She was married, after all, yet she'd suggested her relationship with Vicente was near, or at, an end. But a middle-aged woman with a young man – that was uncommon; there was a sense of taboo about it that thrilled me.

The first powerful surge of a passionate affair and the sense it gave me of being alive rose up inside me as we paced slowly back to the harbour. The redness of her hair, the arch of her small, open ears, the slight flair in her straight-sharp nose all imprinted themselves on me with a sense of harmony. I cared little if it continued or simply ended once we returned to the mainland. I wanted nothing more than to be with her at that moment, and the sex we'd had felt more real than anything I had ever done before in my life.

Our lips met for the last time before we returned to the main beach, as though in recognition that some line was about to be crossed beyond which our intimacy would have to lessen. Letting go of me, she ran down the slope and back onto the sand. Groups of old men were sitting around tables drinking wine. The large woman with the apron was leaning over them and telling a joke. They all laughed as she thumped the table with her fist at the punchline. She waved to us as we walked towards her.

'Hey! Your bag!'

'What?'

Lola's hand moved automatically to her side where her handbag would normally have hung from her shoulder.

'*Ostias!* I forgot all this time. Jesus!'

The bag had been there all afternoon. She glanced at me reproachfully as though I bore the blame, then ran over to the restaurant. The woman was walking inside to fetch it. I stood and looked back over the sea as Lola disappeared behind her. As long as she had it now and hadn't missed it, I couldn't see the problem, but the tone between us had quickly changed. The evening breeze was beginning to blow and the temperature dipped as the sun started its descent. I crossed my arms and rubbed myself for warmth, still sensing the cold of the waves pulling against my body from our earlier swim. Our return was inevitable, but while we were still here on the island, I wanted the moment to last.

I looked round but there was no sign of Lola. She must be talking to the restaurant-owner, I thought. We had to be aboard the ferry soon. I walked up the beach to the doorway. The little naked girl with the plastic sandals had returned and was sitting on the step wearing a light cotton dress, reading.

Before I could step inside Lola came rushing out, handbag gripped tight and a white look of anger on her face.

'What's going on?'

'Let's go.'

The fat woman came bustling behind and stood over her daughter.

'Goodbye, young man.'

I smiled.

'Goodbye, *madam.*'

Lola was already on the quay when I caught up with her, pulling hard on the ring on her left hand.

'Bitch!'

We had almost reached the city before she spoke again.

'I'm sorry.'

We disembarked and I walked her to the car. She drove away, speeding down the boulevard. I watched her disappear, then headed home.

It was the last thing I expected her to say.

The phone rang in my flat. A call from England. I hadn't been in touch for months.

'How are you? What are you up to?'

I struggled to respond. Since the afternoon on the island, I had barely stopped playing the guitar, the skin peeling and hardening on my fingertips as I sat on my plastic chair every moment I could spare, the metronome on the table ticking relentlessly as I forced myself to practise all the things Juan had ever taught me. Everything had clicked and for the first time in my life, I told myself, I was experiencing something real: real passion, real life; learning a real skill. *Duende*, Juan said, was about being in love. And now I knew.

'I'm fine. How're things there?'

Stories from the village, new tiles on the roof, my niece's first day at school. I half-listened as I was brought up to date on a world to which I still belonged, but which I was trying hard to move away from. For a moment, as familiar voices and phrases buzzed down the line, I could feel myself slipping back into old thoughts and expectations like a kind of mental skin: memories of home, university and the girl with whom I had been planning on spending the rest of my life. But I was on my own now, trying to develop my new, nascent *flamenco* personality. I thought of

113

Lola's hand on my skin and our afternoon on the island. The passion and affection I had always wanted, and never found, was here.

The voices on the other end continued. A letter had arrived from my tutor at Oxford. He wanted me to take part in a symposium, to give a paper based on my research on iconographical art in twelfth-century Sicily.

'Isn't that good news? We're so pleased for you.'

I felt nothing, no joy, no excitement. Nothing. And in that moment, I realised I was free. Once it would have meant so much: the beginning of academic recognition, the chance to get funding. It had been a great ambition; now it seemed almost laughable. I was a thousand miles away, involved with a woman who had two children only a few years younger than I was; a woman married to my boss, a flamenco dancer, a recognisable face in a city where she had given a number of performances. It was a situation I would previously have had nothing to do with, tucked against the cold in English libraries and living-rooms, with only daydreams enlivening my stunted existence. Had that really been me? Surely the person I was now was me, the real me. Not that repressed embryonic don.

I slipped her a note at the school as I waited for a class of ten-year-olds to arrive: a hastily scribbled message asking her to meet me at the bar after class. We could head off together from there. She said nothing, her face deadpan. I had learned to recognise this professional guise. It was functional, the harsh, unfriendly mien she wore; the only way she could survive. But I knew she had conceded and would show up.

I headed to our usual bar. It was 10.30. Ginés, the sweaty owner, was sitting on his stool at the far end of the bar chewing on a toothpick and reading *Las Provincias*, the local right-wing newspaper. Behind him postcards from Ibiza and Menorca decorated a corkboard with images of breasts and naked men on the beach. I asked for a brandy. He didn't stir. Despite being a barman, Ginés was always too proud to take any orders. In his mind, we were unwelcome guests.

Pilar, Rafael and a few of the other members of our flamenco circle were all there at our usual table by the window. But so, I saw to my alarm, was Juan. He was the one person I feared: he knew me better than any of them and seemed to be able to read my emotions. Once Lola arrived, he was almost certain to pick something up. I sat down and lit a cigarette, deliberately avoiding the two spare places on the wooden bench next to Rafael. Instead I squeezed in next to Pilar, away from Juan's direct gaze.

Lola turned up a few moments later. The discussion had turned to Vicente Amigo, the young new Córdoban guitarist. He was a rising star, 'the new Paco de Lucía', and everyone wanted to record with him. Pilar loved his music and enthused energetically.

'He's wonderful. He'll be one of the greats, I tell you. Watch him. So good looking! Have you seen it when he lifts his head like that when he's playing? *Ay!*'

'Are you sure it's just his music you like, Pilar?'

'Shut up, Rafa. No really — yes of course, he's gorgeous, but his playing, really . . .'

I contributed nothing, wanting to attract as little attention as possible. But Lola thought differently.

'You're talking shit!' she cried. There was a start.

They knew her for being forthright, but this was a shock. Pilar's bulging eyes bulged even more.

'Vicente Amigo is a complete prick! He's a sell-out. Have you listened to his stuff? It's pure jazz.'

'B-But Vicente is a great guitarist,' Pilar countered nervously. 'What are you talking about? Even Paco likes him.'

'Fuck! Paco, Paco. He's the past. He hasn't produced anything decent for years.' This was close to blasphemy. There was a murmur of indignation around the table. Rafa took in a long, cold breath. I could see him mentally preparing the case for the defence.

'But what about his playing with Sanlúcar on *Tauromagia*. That's one of the most amazing recordings ever made.' Pilar kept up the fight.

'Amazing recording, yes. Ever wondered why they never play it live? Can't. Too complicated. I tell you, this Vicente has had it too easy. Great *flamencos* don't come from getting fat cheques in the post every week. He's soft. There's no edge there.'

Rafa decided to weigh in at this point, the peace-maker, in his logical, bank-employee type of way.

'Well, I'm not so sure about him receiving fat cheques, as you say. Now, yes, perhaps. But not always, I don't think. I met a man in Barcelona once who knew Vicente and . . .'

He rattled off a list of facts, record deals, sales figures . . . and the argument was deflated. Pilar was still upset, though. She took the attack personally. Lola sat opposite, defiantly drawing on her cigarette. Rafa droned on. I looked round at Juan, who had been quiet throughout, and his bright blue eyes looked into mine. There was an expression there as if to say: 'I know something is up here. I'm not quite sure what it is, but something is happening with Lola, and I've half an idea that you might be involved in some way.' I smiled and he raised his eyebrows quizzically.

The conversation continued, empty and lifeless now. Ginés finally brought our drinks after everyone had calmed down. I was anxious and impatient, though. How were we going to move from here? I had got as far as the meeting in the bar, but what happened next?

In the end, it was simple. A glass of something cold and wet knocked itself over her blouse. Surprise, concern, tissues produced to dry it up. But no good. She stood up.

'I'll have to go home. It will stain.' She looked up. I read the cue. My legs straightened, the chair was pushed back behind me and I stood up. The timing was almost right, maybe slightly too fast.

'I'm off as well. I have to get up early tomorrow.' Nods of understanding. We said our goodbyes and passed together out the door. No-one seemed to pay much attention. Except maybe Juan. I pushed the thought out of my mind.

We headed down the avenue, away from the station.

'Come on.' I grabbed her hand impulsively, all need for caution erased in the urgent desire to feel her skin against mine. In all of this, the passion and the excitement of the affair, it was the new experience of simply being touched in her uniquely intense and affectionate way that mattered to me most. 'Let's go to my place,' I said.

'Are you mad?' She pulled away. I blinked in surprise. 'Someone will see us. I can't be seen walking into a man's house at this time of night.'

A couple of teenagers, their arms draped around each other as if they had been welded there, came round the corner and walked between us. I watched them disappear into a doorway.

'But this is a city. It's dark. Nobody will see us.'

She lowered her voice. 'I'm telling you this is a small town and, yes, someone will see me.' She paused. 'And they'll see you, too.'

I shrugged the comment off. I felt indestructible.

'Besides,' she went on, 'I always bump into people. Always. It's just the way with me.'

I laughed incredulously.

'Listen, it's true. I was once walking in Italy, on a tiny mountain path, and I came across the couple who run the supermarket round the corner from me. It happens every time.'

I shrugged. She was adamant. I could see the night slipping away.

'OK, so what do we do?'

'Go to your place, pick up your guitar and wait for me in the sidestreet. The one with the cinema.'

Ten minutes later we were back in her little car, cigarette smoke pouring out of the open windows as we headed once again out of the city, streetlamps and car lights glaring at us as we passed. We drove north, into the shelter of the coastal hills. It was dark and I quickly lost my bearings; the moonless sky gave no clues. After twenty minutes we reached a dirt drive-way and turned off the road. Three or four crude white country houses were partially visible, half-hidden behind pine trees. We carried on for another half a mile, then stopped. There was no sound. Even the crickets seemed to have gone to sleep.

'Come on!' She dragged me along in the dark. 'I

don't want to wake anyone up.'

I picked up my guitar and we felt our way to the door. She pulled out an old, rusty key and fitted it into the lock.

It was pitch-black inside, with a gritty smell that caught in the back of my throat. I walked into what felt like a chair. Lola struck a match and lit an oil lamp, then another, and a candle. I looked around. We were in a single-roomed building with an earth floor. A wooden table with a blue formica top stood in the middle, a sink to one side, some chairs, a rusty fridge and a bunk-bed against one of the walls. Everything was thickly layered with ancient dust, the kind you feel could smother and kill you if overly disturbed. On the back wall was a grubby, colourless picture of the Virgin and Child. A jar of almonds had fallen onto the floor.

'I bought this a few years ago when my mother died and left me some money. I thought it might come in useful one day. Everyone needs a bolthole.' She smiled. I dusted off a chair and sat down while she produced a bottle of wine.

'Here, open this.'

I put down the guitar as she rinsed a couple of scratched tumblers standing by the sink. It was Valencian wine, the stuff she'd warned me against. I said nothing and we sat and drank in silence, an emotional lull after the tension and excitement of getting here.

After half a bottle she stood up with a start.

'Get your guitar out, *guiri*!' I leaned over and did as I was told, lifting the instrument out of its case and resting it on my thigh. It felt good, pushed up against my hip, my hands stretched over it, ready. It was beginning to feel like an extension of myself.

Lola crossed her arms and lifted off her top, exposing a thin white cotton vest tucked into her lilac corduroy trousers. I tuned up as she stretched her legs.

'I only ever dance in skirts or dresses. But this time, I suppose . . .'

She spun sharply with her back to me and began to dance, clicking her fingers above her head. Tak tak tak. Taka tak tak. Her heels pressed rhythmically into the dirt floor, slowly at first, then faster, kicking up more dust in the thick half-light. Her head bowed, one arm stretched out, hands twisting like flames in the air. There was an intense, almost pained look on her face, eyes half-closed, brow tightened, mouth open slightly as she took short, shallow breaths. Something about her, I realised, was only given full expression in dance. At school she was cold and formal. Outside, at the bar or if you saw her in the street, you might notice something about her from her walk. But it was subtle, hidden. Only now, when she danced, did her all-embracing sensuality show itself. I was enchanted and absorbed.

She signalled to me to accompany her. I had to work out which *palo* she was performing. I struggled, watching her feet closely, frightened of failing her. What was she doing? *Fandango*? *Sevillana*? I listened to the rhythm harder than I had ever done before. Then it clicked. It could hardly be anything else. *Tango.*

I started playing, hesitantly at first, missing the beat for a couple of seconds until finally coming into line, like a telescope focusing sharply on a once distant scene. Tok, takadan, takadan, dan dan. Tok, takadan dan-dan-dan. She swayed, pounded, arched, while my fingers hammered the strings. Watching her footwork intensely, I worked hard to keep the tempo. And for a moment, just a moment, it was as if her dancing and my playing became one. The divisions between us faded and a surge of energy passed around my arms and neck. But almost as quickly as I became aware of it, I lost it, wobbling out of beat. I tried to get myself into line once again, to force the guitar to obey, but failed. She brought the dance to an end and stood in front of me, breathing heavily. I didn't look up. I was exhausted and invigorated. She leaned over, kissing my head.

'Not bad for the first time, *guiri*. Not bad.'

We stepped out into the still darkness, the sweat drying on our skin in the warm midnight air. The silhouette of the surrounding hills was faintly visible against the starred sky. I walked to the car, stones and dead wood grinding under my feet, and waited as Lola locked the door. Still no noise. Lola approached and stood facing me. A change had come over her. Despite the blackness, I could see she was anxious.

'You can't be seen in my car with me. Not at this time of night.' The intimacy of a few moments ago had gone.

'What?'

'You can't get in the car.'

'What?'

'Look, you can't be seen in the car. That's it.'

I could barely believe what she was saying.

'It's late, everyone will be in bed. No-one's going to see us. And if they do, you're just giving me a lift, that's all.'

'No, it's impossible.'

'For God's sake, Lola. It's miles.'

She was adamant. 'You're not getting in that car!'

Our voices had risen from high whispers to low, hoarse shouts. I was worried we might wake people up. But we had both taken a position and were refusing to yield.

She made a move to the car and I lunged forward to stop her. I was damned if she was going to leave me here. Pushing against me as I tried to remove her from the door of the car, she turned round and fought back. Her nails tore into my shirt and sank into the flesh of my chest. Hair flew into my eyes as she tossed her head from side to side. I tried to close her in with my arms, aware that if I let her go, her nails would scrape through my skin, but she pushed me back and away. Together we slipped on the loose stones, stumbling to the side and as we did so, her nails gouged deep scratches across my body. I stood apart, bent with the stinging pain, warm blood soaking into my shirt. She knew I was hurt but didn't move. Concerned, guilty even, but she would not back down.

There was a solution to all this, one she must surely have been aware of but had refused to acknowledge in her anger. I stepped towards her, snatching the keys from her hand. She didn't resist. Picking up my guitar, I opened the boot of the car and climbed in, huddled in the tiny, dirty space next to tins of oil and mangled jump leads. She waited a moment, then walked round, took the keys back from my outstretched hand, slammed the black lid down over me, and drove off.

She opened the boot to the orange streetlights of the city, its hot, damp air like a suffocating blanket. We were in a sidestreet near the esplanade. She didn't want to drop me anywhere near my house. That would mean giving in. I climbed out, wiping oil stains off my face, trying to disguise my stiffness and the stinging pain in my chest, but willing to forget our fight. She refused to look at me. I pulled out the guitar and turned to say goodbye, but she ignored me and drove off without a word. Shaking my head, I set off home, unsure if we would see each other again.

chapter FIVE

Por Tangos

El vecino del tercero
a mí me mira con seriedá,
porque dice que yo tengo
con la vecina amistá.

My neighbour on the third floor
looks at me darkly
because he says
I'm too friendly with her next door.

'You're mad.'

It was the first time I had seen Eduardo worried.

'And you tell me she's married?'

I looked down. He laughed and raised his hands to the sky.

'I told you, she's trying to get a divorce, but it's not so easy with the kids and the business.'

'The business?'

I sighed. 'Vicente. He's my boss. At the language school.'

Eduardo grimaced, took a drag on his cigarette, then slowly and deliberately leaned towards me.

'You may think you're becoming a *flamenco*. But be careful, son. Be very careful.'

It was getting hotter, and my clothes began to stick to my skin in the salty, humid air.

'You'll know when it gets over thirty-seven degrees.' The *pied noir* running the photographic shop beneath my flat was fanning himself by the door with an old copy of *National Geographic*. 'When you blow on the tip of your nose it feels cool. That's when your body temperature is less than it is outside.'

I felt suffocated, both by the weather and the situation with Lola. It was impossible to be lovers when she feared all the eyes of the coast were trained on us. Our argument at her country bolthole had been forgotten, but we would never be able to go back there again. It felt jinxed. And so I spent most of my time thinking of opportunities and excuses, or places where we could be together and alone, with no fear of discovery. The school and the bar, the places we would normally see each other, were dangerous, but we improvised by passing notes to each other whenever we could – in between lessons, or if I nipped out to the office in the middle of a class, when she was most likely to be on her own. Once she came to my flat, but it didn't work – too many fears about being seen – and we ended up in another shouting match. 'Never again!' she cried up the stairwell as she raced away. The tension was part of what fuelled our passion, but at times it seemed to strangle us.

I left the newspaper one exceptionally humid day after the air conditioning had failed. Heading through the orange and white tower blocks of Benidorm for the main road back down to Alicante, I could see the coastal mountains half-hidden above the haze. They looked so far away. I had grown accustomed to driving up and down the coast road and it was easy to forget this green and luscious world was, in fact, close at hand. You only had to lift your eyes.

I turned off and sped up the hill. It would be cooler up there, I thought. And less humid, with any luck. After only a few minutes, the change was dramatic. The light became sharper, and as the road wound round, I looked down with a sense of relief at the sea-front and the cloud of dense humid air hanging over it. Pushing on, I drove along olive-lined roads, through La Nucia, where the English had introduced car-boot sales to the Spanish, and through Polop, famous for its spring water. Then narrower roads as I went higher and higher. Guadalest, an ancient Arab castle, appeared ahead, a white turret sitting above a bright blue lake, set like a lapis lazuli in the hillside. There were some tourist buses that made it this far – the castle was a popular day-trip destination for anyone tired of beach life – but I was interested in what lay beyond Guadalest, the unchartered territory further up the valley. That was where I wanted to be: beyond the reach of the coastline.

I started to plan. I would find a village somewhere off the road, walk into the bar, have a brandy, ask the barman if there was anywhere to rent in the area, he would say yes, I would then see it and take it on the spot. A silent country retreat, far away from the city and the coast. Inland, where nobody would recognise us.

I skirted round the elephantine coaches lined up in rows on the outskirts of Guadalest and passed higher up into the valley. Pro-Catalán graffiti was daubed on the low walls at the side of the road: 'Long live Cataluña', 'Death to Spanish imperialism'. The air blowing through the window was cool, lighter and cleaner. My spirits lifted. It was just a question of where to stop, which village to go to. I drove on, and the further and higher I went, the freer I felt.

A sign at the side of the road, near the top of the valley, caught my eye: 'Vistacastell 2 km'. Inwardly, I knew this was it. The road turned off, down the slope, passing meadows and tall arching trees, over a narrow bridge across a ravine, and through more olive groves and lemon orchards, down into the village. Rows of tightly packed white houses, some half-built; a mangy dog. It looked deserted.

The main square was a small space with coloured flagstones, an old cast-iron water pump, and more dogs lying panting in the shade. Beyond lay small farmhouses, streams and copses, and in the distance the white Arab castle, framed by the deep, verdant valley. A bar stood on one side of the square. I parked, crossed over, and went in. It was large and empty, with a billiard table, plastic tablecloths and tacky maritime souvenirs hanging on the walls. I ordered a brandy from a blond, middle-aged barman. As he handed it over, I leaned across and asked were there any places to rent in the village? He looked doubtful.

'*Espera*,' he said. 'I think . . . María!' he shouted to the kitchen. 'Doesn't my mother have some rooms she wants to let?'

She did. I was taken down the road to meet Amparo, an elderly woman with a grey moustache, a grumpy war-wounded husband, and a large house – the top floor of which was now empty. She showed me around.

'It's much too big for the two of us.' She had a thick Valencian accent. 'Don't open that cupboard. That's where my husband keeps his fishing rods. Of course, he hasn't gone fishing for years.'

The flat was dusty, and the walls were papered with dull grey and orange stripes like the brothels in cowboy films. But it was light and cheap and, most importantly of all, from the sitting-room there was a magnificent vista of the valley, the castle and the shining blue lake.

'I'll take it,' I said.

Vicente's second passion in life, after the English, was hunting.

'Fox-hunting. Now there's a noble sport.'

I was watching a group of twelve-year-olds file out of my class after another evening spent trying to make them concentrate on the lesson rather than playing on pocket computer games. It was time to go home. 'You must have done that sort of thing all the time at Oxford?'

I looked at him in amazement. It was a difficult one, this: whether to burst a romantic notion or let it stand. Like being asked by your seven-year-old niece if Father Christmas really does exist. The shatterer of dreams is not an easy role to play.

'Mine was a very academic college,' I told him. 'No opportunities for much outside books.'

'Have you read Sassoon? Splendid, splendid book. Those were gentlemen, real gentlemen. Not like today. So few left.'

The reference to Sassoon was bizarre, but it felt like a cue. 'What do you mean?' I asked.

'In Spain we are somewhat under-represented in certain, er, areas. Gentlemen, for example.'

'What about the Spanish *caballero*?'

Vicente suppressed a sneer. 'It is true, there are similarities between the English gentleman and the Spanish *caballero*, but there is a fundamental difference.' He paused, as though to give weight to what he was about to say.

'Remember that for eight hundred years there were Moors here.' He drew out the word 'Moors' in disgust. 'Africa, you will recall the saying, begins at the

130

Pyrenees. A *caballero* can be a great man, but he can never, never, be pure.' He looked around the corridor to see if anyone was listening, then lowered his voice.

'We are tainted.'

Pedro had once told me that the concept of the 'gentleman' originated with the Arabs. It seemed unwise to bring this up now, though. There was a worrying, fanatical glare in Vicente's eyes. His feelings on the subject were obviously strong.

The lights went out around us as the other teachers shut up for the night. 'Listen,' he said. 'Come for a drink some time. I would like you to meet some of my hunting colleagues. They're a fine bunch of fellows.'

The man was a snob and a bigot and I was having an affair with his wife, but I nodded reluctantly. To have refused Vicente's invitation would have been unwise, I thought. It was the best way to dissimulate.

For all his Anglophilia, however, Vicente was very Spanish. The ritual of meeting in the evening and chatting easily with friends over glasses of *fino* and morsels of ham and olives, standing at the bar in fine, bright clothes – this was all typical of a man of his class and age. Yet 'Englishness' was a label with which he had decided to clothe himself, and the accoutrements went everywhere with him like well-worn props: a pipe, a tweed jacket if it was chilly, and, as ever, the polished brogues.

If the effect was to make him stand out amongst his friends, it worked. They were, on the whole, an unremarkable lot: three overweight, middle-aged men, all character lost in their comfortable, sunny lives, where the most intense experience came from hangovers after a heavy night.

We stood around for what seemed like hours,

drinking, eating and chatting – mostly about hunting. We were out of the main season now, so there was plenty of reminiscing to do, and talk of next autumn. Then a question about weaponry set Vicente off on what appeared to be one of his favourite subjects.

'The best guns are English, of course: Holland & Holland for example, or a Purdey – bespoke. Some prefer American models, like Remingtons, but personally I don't rate them,' he said.

'Are you brainwashing him already, Vicente?' A short, tubby man with handlebar whiskers interrupted with a smile. He turned to me. 'Don't listen to him. He doesn't know anything about guns. Only one thing interests him. Eh?!' He turned to Vicente. '*El Killer?*' The last word was uttered in a strong Spanish accent: 'keelerr'.

'*El Killer?*' I asked. More laughter.

'Only one thing interests *El Killer*. Killing. Doesn't care what he's using. Just blow the fucker away. Blam! Blam!' The fat man mimicked the action of shooting a stationary target. 'He's got a lust for blood, this one.'

Vicente looked uncomfortable.

'But surely that's what you all do when you go hunting. It's all about killing,' I said in an attempt to defuse the tension.

The fat man grunted. 'For me, it's a sport. But this one – you put a gun in his hand and he turns into a madman.' He tapped his forefinger against his temple. 'Blood. That's all he wants: blood.' He leaned over to Vicente and lightly slapped his cheek, grinning. 'Eh! *El Killer!* Wake up! You're pissed.' The hardened look fell and Vicente broke into a smile. Everyone laughed, but I realised I had seen a side of the man I would rather not have known. My hands were sweating, my pulse racing.

'You must come out with us again,' Vicente said, fully clad in pseudo-English sophistication and still drunk. I shuddered. The last thing I wanted was a repeat of this evening.

'Next Friday?' I said.

'See you then, dear chap.'

I took Lola to Vistacastell for the first time. She walked around on a tour of inspection in her proud, haughty way – nostrils flared, head poised – as I prepared some lunch.

'What do you think?' I asked.

'The decoration is horrendous. But it will do – for a *guiri.*'

She walked over to a chair by the window looking down onto the valley, and sat quietly with her back to me. It was a form of approval.

When I returned a few moments later with some food, I found her sitting in the same spot, gazing out, her clothes in a pile on the floor beside her. I kissed her freshly exposed shoulder as I put the plates on the table.

'This view leaves me naked,' she said dramatically. 'It touches me here.' She clasped a fist to her breast and stared beyond me at the valley. 'How can I cover myself in the face of such beauty?'

I shrugged.

'Besides,' she said, turning to me, humour now lighting up her face, 'it's more fun eating like this.'

We laughed our way through the afternoon as the colours outside slowly shifted from the sharp, white definition of midday to the gentler, calmer yellow of afternoon, and then the final rich orange of sunset.

It was time to leave. We crept down the stairs, but I already knew Amparo, the landlady, would be there. Another woman in her house! She had to find out what was going on.

She was at the door, pretending to sweep. This time Lola had taken off her ring.

'Was that flamenco I heard you playing?'

'Yes.' Doubtless she had heard a lot more besides. Lola turned away.

'Do you play?'

'Yes,' I said. 'And she dances,' pointing behind me.

'Good. Then you will perform at our fiesta in a fortnight's time. We need some more music, different music.'

Her little Chinese dog was sniffing inquisitively at my ankles, as if looking for a new territory marker. I shuffled nervously.

'Every year the same folksong from Pere.' She waved her broom at me menacingly. 'No! This year I want flamenco,' she said harshly. Then softening, 'It will be nice to have some foreign stuff.'

'Yes of course we will play.' I could hardly refuse. The broom was now across the doorway and we were trapped.

'Good,' she said, letting us pass. We stepped out into the light and said goodbye. 'A fortnight, eh!' she called to us as we headed up the square. I squeezed Lola's stiff, reluctant hand. I expected a head-on assault as soon as we got in the car, but instead there was silence and resignation.

'We'll be seen. I know we'll be seen,' was all she said.

'Don't worry. We're miles from anywhere. The only people here are peasants and donkeys.'

'You don't understand.'

Juan was delighted when I told him about the fiesta.

'*Hombre*, your first concert. Wonderful!'

He didn't ask for any details, assumed I would be accompanying a dancer, and began teaching me the essentials.

'This is not like playing on your own, boy. Completely different. *Compás* is everything. Forget the fancy *falsetas* and just stick to the rhythm.'

We went over an *Alegría* and a *Tango*. 'These are always popular. Everyone always asks for them.' He seemed to know exactly what I was up to. 'But don't do *Soleá*. People around here don't like it, can't understand it. Besides, it's not a party kind of thing.'

I nodded. He was more worked up about it than I was. I watched him now as he explained it all to me, sweat soaking through the armpits of his red shirt. One day, I thought, he'll wear red trousers and shoes as well, and then I'll know he's really lost it.

'Accompanying is all about following the dancer: giving her the rhythm, but also covering up for her mistakes,' he said. 'Remember, if she messes up, it's your fault. Now listen, there's a whole other world you've got to learn about here. We'll start with the *llamada* and go on from there.'

I was nervous. Maybe this wasn't such a good idea. How on earth had I persuaded myself that I was good enough to play on stage? The whole thing was ludicrous. *Jasón 'El Inglés'* – the greatest flamenco disaster in history. I felt like a man with a note ordering his own execution.

'You have to love the dancer, to feel her, intuit her. One *flamenco* on their own can rarely produce

135

duende. But when there are others, if it clicks . . . *Jo!*'

But I was too busy worrying.

'Hey, concentrate!' Juan snapped me out of my daydream. 'Listen, you'll have to practise a lot between now and then. But don't worry, you'll be fine. Just stick to the simple things.'

My hands were shaking when I left.

I was with Vicente and the hunters, back in the *barrio*; the throbbing waves of dance music spilling out onto the narrow paved alleyways, the stale smells, and the little posters stuck up on crumbling walls pleading for the noise to be kept down.

The local government was trying to clean up the area – grants were being offered to restore the old buildings and paint them in bright, sensual colours, but it wouldn't take long for all the life to be beaten out of them if Alicantinos merely treated the area as their weekend playground.

We went to another new bar. More of the same: ultra-violet lights, very loud music, mirrors on the walls. Only this one was narrower and smaller. Most of the people around us were teenagers or people in their twenties, but there were plenty of small groups of middle-aged men and women – like Vicente's – intent on getting their weekend fix of fun. For the post-Franco generation, the need to party knew no age limits.

Some sort of conversation was taking place, but I couldn't hear what anyone was saying. The fat one with the moustache was lifting his hands into the air and waving, pretending to shoot a flying bird. When people sharing a common obsession get together, you can hardly expect them to talk about anything else, I thought.

I took the chance to watch Vicente closely, trying to work out what it was that Lola had seen in him. There was something heavy and brutish about him behind the elegant English façade he tried to cultivate. And what if he knew about us? I pushed the thought aside, as the adrenaline kicked in.

The heavy thud of the loud, incessant music was beginning to have an effect. I stood drinking, rocking rhythmically with the beat. There was nothing else to do.

Many large gin and tonics later, we tripped our way into the square outside, now filled with people of all ages enjoying the regular street party that was the weekend here. Joking, laughing, back-slapping, we edged through the throng to an outdoor bar where the air was clearer. In the semi-drunken haze, Vicente's pipe had seemed to fill the room.

We settled down in our newly claimed piece of territory and began drinking again under a ceiling of matted reeds. The other three were engrossed in another hunting tale, while Vicente and I stood to one side.

'You're friendly with my wife,' he said.

I had never felt so cold, as if with those simple words he had drained my blood away.

'Yes,' I said, just managing to force the word out without stammering. 'We both like flamenco.' There, that was it. Just a friendship based on a common interest. Like this lot and hunting.

Vicente had an incredulous look on his face, thick eyebrows meeting above his deep-set eyes. I began looking for a way to change the subject. He leaned forward. I tried to step back, but there was no room. His face was now almost touching mine.

'But you're English,' he blurted out. 'How can you like flamenco? Flamenco is for Gypsies and criminals. It's shit.'

He was angry, spittle forming at the side of his mouth, but all at once I realised that he still knew nothing.

'Flamenco is about passion,' I said, parroting my guitar teacher.

'Passion?' he said. 'Drugs, you mean. They're injecting themselves all the time. Drug addicts. Look at that Camarón fellow. Why do you think he died so young?'

I looked away.

'For heaven's sake, Jason. You're from Oxford, why on earth do you like that . . . rubbish?'

I said nothing. It was clear his anger was not directed at me. And it seemed there was more to come.

'I don't know why Lola insists on seeing these people. I don't like her going. I've told her a hundred times. It's affecting her work.'

I screwed up my eyes. I knew this to be untrue. Lola was just as hard, humourless and efficient as ever.

'We have nothing in common,' Vicente continued. 'She has no interest in hunting. Or the English. I only gave her that job because she wanted the money.' He choked for a moment, then recovered. 'Her mother was half-Moor.'

He surprised me. There was little contact between ordinary Spaniards and the Arab world even now, let alone at the time her mother was born. The absurdity of Lola and Vicente's marriage was even clearer now: Vicente, the racist Anglophile, married to a truly 'tainted' *flamenca*.

'I tell you, if it weren't for the kids . . .' he snorted. 'I only married her because she got pregnant.' Then quietly under his breath, 'The whore.'

He looked up. 'Still, it saved her from becoming a complete Gypsy, I suppose.' He took another mouthful of his whisky and Coke – there were some things he just didn't get right.

'She begged me, absolutely begged me to marry her. And of course once the babies came, the dancing stopped. For good, I thought.' He leaned forward and placed his mouth close to my ear. 'You know, I think it's only the physical side that keeps us together.'

The other hunters called us over. Vicente turned away sharply as though suddenly aware of what he had just told me.

Pushing through the crowds, we headed up the hill to the back of the *barrio*, where the ordinary party-goers still wouldn't go. The streets narrowed even more here; the graffiti thicker on the walls. I lagged behind a little. The man revolted me and I wanted nothing more than to slip away and head home. But I was trapped by a desire not to draw attention to myself.

Vicente took me by the elbow. 'Come along,' he said. 'We're going to see some friends.' The others laughed.

'Friends?' I was doubtful.

'Yes. Some very dear ... and close friends.' The others laughed again.

'No, come on, seriously.'

'I am serious. Very serious. We're going to introduce you to some of the loveliest ladies in the province. You'll see.'

I stopped. '*Putas*?'

'We prefer not to use that word. Come on!' He grabbed my arm again, but I pulled it free.

'Listen, Vicente. I can't.'

'What? Why not? Relax, my dear fellow. They're really quite lovely.'

I had to do something. It wasn't the idea of going with the prostitutes so much as who I was with.

'No, Vicente.' He looked at me with complete incomprehension.

'It's just not English, you know,' I said. His face fell. 'An Englishman thinks he should never have to *pay* for it.'

For a moment, I almost felt sorry for him as he stood there deflated. But it had worked.

'I see,' he said. The others were calling for us to catch up. 'I have to go. Perhaps . . . lunch next week-end? I have some things at home I would like to show you.'

Reluctantly I agreed, and he turned and walked away into the blackness.

I met Eduardo at a café for breakfast. We sat outside under striped umbrellas, sipping glasses of peach juice dripping with humidity, the harsh taste of black tobacco still on my tongue.

'Well, how's it going with the fire-woman?'

'I spent last night in the *barrio* with her husband and his hunting mates.'

'For Christ's sake!' He glared at me through his sunglasses.

'And I learned a couple of things too. She's a quarter Moor, he goes with prostitutes, and despite the problems they're having, they still enjoy the "physical side", as her husband put it.' I was surprised at my own jealousy.

'Sounds like a pretty ordinary marriage to me – apart

from the Moorish bit,' he said. 'But watch it, son. You're playing with fire. He might not know anything now, but one slip and you won't have any fingers left to play the guitar with. Once he knows where they've been. You understand me?'

'Lola and I are playing at a fiesta in Vistacastell next weekend.'

'I don't know why I bother.'

'Look, it'll be fine. It's miles away from anywhere. Nobody will see us.'

'I hope not, son. I hope for your sake it fucking snows and no-one shows up.'

'I'm going to accompany her.'

'Ah, well! If it's accompanying you're interested in, you must listen to Tomatito – the Little Tomato.'

I knew the only way to get him off my back was to start talking shop.

'He's the man to listen to. The king of the Gypsy guitarists. Now, the way he played with Camarón was the last word in accompanying. I know it's not dancing, but the principle is the same: drawing out the best performance from the other person with the minimum effort. The guitar is a vital component, but must never distract attention from . . .'

On and on he went. But I'd stopped listening. I was thinking about Lola – and Vicente.

Back at the *Costa Gazette*, Barry was in a good mood. He'd recently become fascinated with a young girl whose father wrote a column in the *Sunday Telegraph* – which reached us on Mondays.

'She's gorgeous. Look at the tits on that!'

He showed me a picture of a pouting Londoner with luxuriant dark hair. He'd written to her asking her to do a regular piece for the paper. Curious, she had written back, asking him to send some details of the paper's rates.

'Well, we can offer her the top amount – twenty pesetas a line. What do you reckon?'

'I think she'll laugh in your face.'

'What the hell do you know anyway. Look,' he said, turning to the impassive, grinning Jonathan, 'tell you what. We'll put all the money in an account for her here, so when she comes on holiday, she'll have a tidy lump sum waiting for her. Spending money, like.'

He vanished into his grotto, triumphant.

'Dickhead,' Jonathan mouthed to me as the door slammed.

'Oh, listen, Jason.' Barry's face was back again. 'There's some fiesta going on somewhere in the mountains this weekend. Some English geezer's going to be playing flamenco, apparently. I want you to cover it. Jonathan will tell you where.'

Jonathan gave me the details. I kept a stunned silence.

I found Lola and Vicente's flat in the suburbs of the city – a large soulless area full of tower blocks and condominiums with swimming pools and tennis courts for the residents; the fruits of the new, prosperous, post-Fascist Spain. I parked and passed through the metal gate at the entrance into what seemed like a fortified camp. The concrete communal area was deserted in the all-embracing midday heat. Even the pool was empty.

I reached the door, found the right bell and placed my finger over it. For a moment my hand refused to obey. As the days passed, I had grown reluctant to keep this particular appointment. Lola had frozen on me when she found out about the invitation and had threatened to disappear for the weekend and abandon the concert. I had pleaded and she agreed to stay. Besides, Vicente would be leaving that evening for a conference in Valencia. We would be able to meet for the fiesta, and perhaps another day beyond that. But a nagging feeling remained.

I rang the bell and a voice came over the intercom. It was Vicente.

'Come on up, dear fellow. You'll find us on the fifth floor.'

He was at the door to greet me, all smiles and a firm handshake. I went inside.

The flat was dark – heavy furniture, browns, greens, mahogany chairs like thrones. The walls were lined with smart, untouched, leather-bound books bought from a book club, or by the yard from a decorator.

'Can I offer you a beer, old chap?'

I watched Lola coming and going from the kitchen, head erect, hair tied back with a clip, tight on her scalp. Yet as she passed backwards and forwards, never looking me in the eye, I realised there was something different about her. I was used to two personalities – the school administrator and the *flamenca* – yet here was a third, one I had no idea existed before this moment. I saw that here, in this house, with Vicente, she was a wife, playing an essential role in the fantasy life they had created. The hauteur was gone, the fire extinguished. The sulking pride I had expected her to display failed to show. Everything about the way she ate, sat listening to Vicente, removed the dishes, brought out more food, bore witness to her acquiescence and self-negation. A ghost. There was no love here. Wife, yes – even physically, as my jealousy reminded me – but not lover.

'I've made some paella. Would you like some?' I had never known her to be so polite.

'Mmm. Payela,' Vicente said, mimicking the English pronunciation. She tittered.

I scanned the room for signs of her presence, of the woman I thought I knew. Only books and old maps of English counties. This was Vicente's world. Then something caught my attention. At the bottom of the bookcase stood a plastic doll in a bright red and black dress with turquoise sequins, black hair held tightly back on the head with a clip. It was a flamenco dancer – the tacky kind sold in souvenir shops. I turned away.

'My daughter is just like me,' Vicente said. 'Loves English. She's reading English Lit. at Barcelona University. Top of her class.'

I congratulated him, his pride quite filling the room.

'While my son, ah, he's more like his mother. Wants to join the army next year.' He leaned towards me. 'All that aggression,' he said softly. Lola was in the kitchen.

'I have a contact – an *enchufe* – in the Ministry of Defence in Madrid. We'll make sure he gets a good posting.'

In the only country where, it was said, power was more important than sex, having *enchufes* was the only way to get things done in this so-called democratic age. The system of favours and local strongmen was the real face of Spanish political life.

Vicente continued to extol his children's virtues, but he spoke of them like ornaments. Again I noticed their absence from our surroundings, not merely physically – the daughter, at least, was away from home, and

144

doubtless the son had better things to do on a Saturday afternoon – but also as visible members of the household.

Lola returned with more plates, a fixed smile on her mouth, an apron tied comfortably around her waist. I barely recognised her. This was not the lithe, leopard-like woman I had fallen in love with. I thought of stretching my foot out under the table to touch her, but didn't dare risk it. Besides, Vicente made great demands on his audience, and I was forced to listen to him like an unwilling passenger on a long-distance train journey.

The meal came to an end and Lola began clearing away. I wanted to get up and help her, maybe enjoy a second or two in the kitchen alone, to see if she was really there. But Vicente kept me nailed to the chair with his barrage of words. As a compromise, I started stacking the plates on the table, but was gestured to leave well alone. I obeyed and Lola carried on.

'Come with me,' he said. 'I want to show you something.' I lifted my leaden body – swollen with heat and rice – out of the chair and followed him down the dark, unlit corridor. At the far end he opened a door and beckoned me inside.

It was dark and smelt of cologne and mothballs: the scent of elderly Spanish people. He turned on a small lamp on a chest of drawers by the door. A dull, grimy light was cast about the room, barely enough to show what was inside. My eyes blurred in the gloom and I had to strain to bring everything into focus. More dark, old furniture, an old Persian rug on the floor, a brown armchair – the covering almost worn off. But more impressively, hanging from every wall, in glass cupboards, on stands, in corners, filling the entire room, were stuffed, dead animals, staring back at me through black, lifeless eyes. Rabbits, falcons, stoats, a boar's head, sparrows, a deer, all arranged around this morgue-like temple, silently paying homage to the violence of the man who had killed them. Their stillness was strangely disconcerting. I half-expected them to reanimate themselves at any moment, draw breath and launch themselves onto their slayer.

'I have a man in Valencia who does them for me. Of course, you can't stuff them all. Some of them are just in too bad a condition after they've been shot.'

In my mind's eye, I could see him in a camouflage jacket, blasting these creatures out of the sky, from the trees, his rifle spitting death wherever he pointed it.

'I'm running out of space. There's only room for special ones now. Like this one.' He pointed at a falcon with its talons outstretched, beak open wide as in the final seconds of homing in for a kill. How had it been when Vicente shot it, I wondered. Sitting quietly in a tree carrying out its morning ablutions, perhaps? Soaring peacefully on the coastal winds? The taxidermist was obviously good at flattering his clients.

'Of course, you can't lose much time once you've brought them down. Sometimes I drive straight up to Valencia with my animals in the back of the car. Don't even stop to go home and change. He likes to get them as fresh as possible. It's the heat, you see.'

We stood in the cool, dark room, his animals staring back at us. The icy layer of fear that had lined my stomach since the first night with the hunters in the *barrio* began to rise into my throat.

'I have worked hard all my life to build what I have, Jason,' he said. 'It means everything to me. I would kill anyone who tried to take it away from me.'

* * *

I stopped at the flat to pick up my guitar before heading back to Vistacastell. Outside the front door, I bumped into Pedro hopping from shady patch to shady patch along Alfonso El Sabio. The road was deserted. No-one came outside in heat like this.

Seeing him brought back a sudden memory of my arrival in Alicante: the deep serenity of his jasmine-perfumed garden, the joy of the new, the hope, and calm. He seemed to carry it around with him.

I went over to say hello. He smiled – his wide, childlike grin – and embraced me. We hadn't seen each other since Christmas, as if I'd almost forgotten he was there.

'My dear Watson, you must take care in this heat. You'll burn up.'

And he walked on, smiling, waving and blowing kisses into the air.

'And . . . Don't worry. Be *kh*appy.'

My hands were trembling when I reached Vistacastell. The square had been decorated with lights, and a pavilion had been set up in a corner full of long, empty tables covered with white paper cloths. There was a bar further inside, and then the stage with a chair and a microphone. I looked at it with dread. Two men were setting up the PA system, tinny popular music echoing around the village to an absent audience. So great was the Spanish lust for noise that even this late siesta hour wasn't sacrosanct. I walked down to Amparo's house wondering if I could do some last-minute practice.

The Chinese dog was sitting by the door like a fluffball. He knew me now, and would be on his feet, wagging his tail unassumingly, as soon as he recognised my steps coming down the narrow street. He sniffed my ankles, I patted his head, and together we went inside.

I crept upstairs, anxious not to wake the sleepers below. I opened the case and picked up the guitar, gazing at the fading valley, and waited.

Lola was late. She said Vicente had caught a different train to the one she had expected. The fiesta was already under way.

'Here, I brought you a present. Take it.' Then to the side, 'Not that you deserve it.'

I smiled. She was back to normal.

I opened the box and inside was a bright red fountain-pen. 'One day you'll write about all this. And when you do, I want you to use this pen.' She kissed my eyes.

I had so many questions. Why had she been so different? How did she manage to do that? And what about her Moorish grandmother? The mystery of it excited me. I wanted her to tell me about it. Surely she knew about Vicente's racism? But there was no time, we were due to perform. No time, even, for a last-minute run-through.

It was gone midnight when we arrived. Mosquitos and moths flew chaotically around the harsh lights hooked up at the sides of the pavilion. It was very hot, despite the mountain breeze, and there was a strong smell of sweat, tobacco and cheap red wine. Mounting the stage, I kept telling myself it was only a small audience of half-drunk farmers who probably knew as much about flamenco as my grandmother did. No need to worry, none at all. But my legs still shook, and

I was relieved when I was able to sit down in the chair placed out for me.

Lola, meanwhile, rubbed her hands together and took centre-stage, her eyes fixed just above the audience. For her, it was about defiance.

'*Mierda*. Shit,' she said without turning round. It was the Spanish equivalent of 'break a leg'.

A fat man with a shiny face introduced us as '*Los Novios Flamencos*' – the Flamenco Fiancés. I cursed Amparo under my breath. Doubtless everyone knew about us. Lola rolled her eyes, and dipped her head.

'For the love of God!'

I saw her mouth the words and her shoulders seized with tension. Not a good way to begin. She was quite capable of storming off and leaving me there to play on my own.

'*Ole*,' came a cry from the audience. They were waiting for us to start. But I could read Lola's mind and could feel the anger and pride rising inside her. This was too much. Why should she, a real flamenco dancer, perform in front of this lot? *Ole*? They had no understanding of the word. How could they shout *Ole*?

The crowd was still waiting, and becoming edgy. Why hadn't we started? Was something wrong?

'Lola!' I hissed. But she stood still, head down, jaw clenched. '*Venga! Mora!* Come on, you Moor!'

She whipped round and looked me straight in the eye, shocked for a second, then turned back to the audience and crashed her feet on the floor. The dance had begun.

The villagers went wild, thought it was all part of the show, and loved us for it. We began with *Verdiales de Málaga*. Good, popular, passionate stuff. Loud and rhythmic and a favourite amongst non-aficionados. Everyone was clapping, mostly out of time, but the pavilion was filled with noise and dance, men shouting, children chasing each other round the tables, glasses being filled, conversations continuing between mothers despite all that was going on around them. I breathed a silent sigh of relief. What better way to cover up my mistakes? No-one could even hear me with all this going on.

My eye briefly caught sight of Amparo at the front of the stage, clapping furiously with her neighbours. She saw me looking at her and waved. I smiled. I could hardly blame her for our billing as '*Los Novios Flamencos*'. It was just how things worked.

The piece came to an end and there was a roar of applause. But we hardly stopped before moving straight into another popular style: *Alegrías*. Lola pulled out some castanets from her bag. 'I need them for the *compás*,' she shouted above the din. 'I can't hear you.'

More shouts from the crowd. '*Vivan Los Novios Flamencos!*' I groaned, but there was no reaction from Lola this time. Perhaps she hadn't heard. The cold was rising in my throat once more, and my fingers began to catch on the strings. Vile, twanging, discordant sounds. 'That's it,' I thought, 'I've lost it.' But the dance and the crowd demanded I continue, and I was forced to press on regardless, hands sweating with nerves. Once back in the rhythm, I realised no-one had noticed. And if they had, it really didn't matter. This was a Spanish fiesta crowd. Nobody was going to pass judgement. Especially not on a foreigner. But just in case, I decided to hold the *compás* and do nothing else.

The *Alegría* came to an end. More cheers. 'One

more, and that's it,' Lola called. The sweat was beginning to stream down her forehead.

We started on a *Tango*, the first *palo* we had done
together. Lola went at a fast pace; I could see her
brought alive by the crowd again, the flowing rhythm
rising through her body.

'*Venga, Morita!*' I cried again. This time she smiled
and danced even harder, sweat flying from her face as
she twisted and pounded the earth, her hair sticking in
wet strands to her cheeks. I remembered Juan's words
about *duende*. *Duende*, he said, was love. My fingers
flicked smoothly over the strings with perfect timing,
in perfect unison.

She kissed me when she finished. The villagers
cheered. '*Vivan Los Novios!*' We didn't care any more.

'This feels like a wedding,' I said.

We climbed down through the smoke and sweat,
through congratulatory crowds of people. The next act
was already beginning, but no-one seemed to have
noticed: they all wanted to meet us. They had probably heard the man now on stage about a hundred
times before. It seemed to take an age to get through.
'Wonderful, wonderful!' Amparo came over screaming
her thanks, and kissed us both. 'I'm sure you'll be so
happy together.'

Finally we got outside the pavilion. Plenty of people
here too, but at least there was room to breathe.

'Well, *guiri*?' She draped her arms around my neck
and stared up at my face, eyes dancing above her
broad smile. 'What do you think of your first concert?'

I breathed, more relieved that it was over than anything else, and let my head fall back to look at the
starry sky.

'Not bad for a first try. Quite beautiful towards the

end. But he should have listened more to what I told him about playing with dancers.'

I turned round, shading my eyes against the lights. With a surge, the bile that had been lining my stomach pitched up into my throat. It was Juan.

'You play so well together.' Lola's arms dropped to her side. 'Why didn't you let us all know, then we could have enjoyed it too.' He stepped closer, a thin smile forming on his mouth. Lola began to back away. I stood still, hovering between attack and flight.

'Such a beautiful performance, my friends. Such *encanto*, so enchanting, such *duende*. I was quite moved. It was almost like old times, eh, Lola? Have you brought Vicente along? Or perhaps you've managed to spirit him away like you used to.' Lola was half-hiding behind me.

'*Los Novios Flamencos*. Ha! Nobody ever gave us such a pretty name, did they? Only ever Juan and Lola. Never did sound right. Maybe that's why we . . .'

'What the hell do you want, you son of a whore!' Lola screamed.

'Ah, yes, the famous temper. It's the red hair, you know. But I suppose you've already worked that one out, haven't you, Jason.'

'Look, Juan . . .'

'Shut up, cunt.' His mouth was beginning to tremble. 'You know absolutely nothing. Have no idea . . . That whore . . .' He lifted his finger and pointed it at Lola. A great torrent of words and abuse sat in his throat waiting to explode. I braced myself against the coming attack, sheltering Lola behind me in case he turned violent, staring straight into those light blue eyes.

But it never came. Whatever it was in him – the fear, shame, belief in himself as a peaceful man, or simply

152

too many years of nurturing the pain so that now it could find no expression – whatever it was suddenly gripped him, took back control, and smothered the anger, dampening it down to the steady smoulder of his normal self. The finger dropped, the trembling left his lips, and the calm, quiet face of Juan returned.

We stood facing one another, and for a second we were teacher and pupil once again. I could almost have imagined it was all engineered as part of my training, part of the process of learning to see the essence of flamenco, the beauty that Juan always talked about, but that I never felt I could quite grasp. But it was a short-lived moment. The reality was that we had been moments away from coming to blows. And now the secret was out.

All of a sudden he smiled, like a father.

'Don't worry,' he said. 'It's safe with me.' And he turned and walked away through the crowds, disappearing into the village.

Lola let out a stifled cry and pulled me away, twisting my arm as she ran from the square and down into the dark, deserted street. Sickness and violence churned in my stomach. I wanted to go back, but she pushed me to the door. I fumbled with the keys, we got inside, and upstairs.

I heard her collecting her belongings chaotically as I went and stood silently at the window, looking out at the now-invisible valley. The gap between us was immediate, inescapable, and filled the entire house. She was leaving, and we had become strangers.

My mind wandered to calm, gentle images of deserts, oases, long journeys over distant plains: a fantasy cocoon against the emotions that were battering my brain.

She came into the main room and stood behind me. I could feel her breath on my neck, but it was cold and hard. I didn't move, but kept looking away through the window, searching for something, anything of my valley that might have escaped the veil of the night air.

'I'm going.'

'Yes, I know.'

We stood motionless, frozen like two of Vicente's animals.

'You never told me about your Moorish grandmother,' I said.

I didn't hear her leave.

'You can't stay here now, son. Believe me, you really can't.'

'Why the hell should I run away?'

Eduardo looked at me incredulously.

'OK, fine, I know he's got a shotgun. Several. But . . . I'm in love with her.'

'Which is why you have to leave. Now.'

'I'm not a coward. Anyway, Juan might never mention it. He said he wouldn't.'

'Look, son, from what you've told me this Juan bloke doesn't sound like the most stable person in the world. We're dealing with jealousy here.'

'But why would Vicente believe *him*?'

'You just don't seem to understand, do you.' I looked at him quizzically. 'It's not just your neck on the line here. What do you think he's going to do to Lola if he finds out?'

I sank down into the chair. Of course, he was right.

'Listen, it's a question of damage limitation. If you leave now, there's a much better chance nothing's going to happen to her. Juan's only going to be interested in breaking you two up. If he's in love with Lola as well, chances are as soon as he's heard you've packed off, he'll leave well alone. At least that's the best you can hope for. You understand me?'

I nodded silently.

'And don't go calling her up every five minutes. This has got to be a clean break. For her sake.'

'But where can I go. I don't want to go back . . .'

'Go to Madrid. Look, you came here to learn about flamenco. You've got to go to the capital, that's where it's all happening. You were never going to find much here.'

I thought I had.

He wrote down some information on a piece of paper: a cheap hostel, flamenco bars I should visit.

'You must leave tonight, you realise that. The bus is at nine.'

'But what about . . .'

'Don't worry. I'll make sure Juan finds out. And don't worry about those jerks at the *Costa Gazette*, either. I'll tell them you've just got a job on the *Sun*.'

Pedro seemed pleased when I told him I was leaving.

'So, my dear Watson. Another adventure?'

He was annoyingly calm, ignoring the panic that was now controlling me, and wanting to tell me everything about a new posting he had in Morocco. I listened with heaving chest. There was all the business of rent and returning keys to think about.

'These things have a way of sorting themselves out,' was all he said.

'Look, Pedro, I think I'm going mad.'

'No, it's all right, Jason,' he said seriously. 'You're not going mad. Everything will be all right.'

I left some money and the keys in a brown envelope with the *pied noir* downstairs, then went to the bus station. It was almost a year to the day since I had arrived in Alicante. Eduardo came to see me off and handed me a tape by the guitarist Pepe Habichuela.

'One of the great masters,' he said. 'If angels could play flamenco, they'd all sound like Pepe Habichuela. He's a Gypsy, one of the best.'

I started to climb aboard.

'They're the people you're going to have to start hanging out with, son. Gypsies. No more *payos* like this lot here. You want the real stuff.'

The doors closed and the bus set off. It was one of the loneliest moments of my life.

chapter SIX

Por Soleà

Si algún día yo te llamara
y tú no vinieras,
la muerte amarga a mí me viniera
y no la sintiera.

If one day I called you
and you didn't come,
bitter death would come in your place
and I wouldn't even feel it.

'You like the *cante*, then?'

The man on the chair in front of me is the hairiest I have ever seen. Sitting here, his brightly coloured silk shirt clinging to his torso, a smell of sweat mixed with sweet, sickly aftershave, he conforms with all my previous ideas of how a Gypsy should be. Gold chains glint faintly through the thick, black mass sprouting at the top of his chest. A half-chewed cigar is twisted in the corner of his mouth as he rolls it with his tongue.

I had found him backstage at the Restaurante Alegrías, one of the more touristy flamenco venues in Madrid. The place was full of Japanese businessmen brought to this gaudy location to be entertained by Spanish hosts who knew almost as little about flamenco as their guests. 'Typical espanish', they called it in Spain, mimicking the Disneyfied image of the country Franco had liked to project in his struggle to attract foreign dollars. For twenty pounds a head you were given a bowl of gazpacho soup, some Serrano ham and bread, and a show. It was the kind of place you would find B- or more likely C-list performers. Which was why I was there.

'*Te gusta el cante?*' he asked again. 'You like flamenco singing?'

'*Sí.*'

The Gypsy had just come off stage with his band and I, a foreigner – a *guiri* – was pushing into a world where I didn't belong.

'*Sí, sí,*' I shouted above the din next-door. '*Me encanta!* I love it!'

It was unintentional, but fortuitous. The man stared at me, puzzled that a foreigner could pun in Spanish. Then a smile crept into the corners of his mouth, opening his lips until he bellowed, his head rocking back with laughter.

'Did you hear that?' He turned to the other members of the band, cramped in this small, heavy room as they packed up and changed after the show. 'I asked him if he liked the *cante*. Yes, he said, *Me encanta!* Ha ha. *Me encanta!* Did you hear?'

They were, to a man, unimpressed, but he laughed on.

'*Bueno*. Tell me about the *cante*. Here, have some brandy. What do you like?' He blew out a long, thick stream of smoke like a fluttering blue ribbon, and passed me the bottle he was drinking out of. From the corner of my eye I could see the other members of the band muttering, anxious to pack up, get paid and leave.

'I like rough voices,' I said. '*La voz afillá*. Like yours.'

In a shop on the Gran Vía the previous day I had read on the back of a record sleeve about the different types of male singing voice. The *afillá* style was named after the great nineteenth-century singer El Fillo. A wandering blacksmith, he was one of the first to have developed the coarse, typically Gypsy style of singing, later continued by Silverio Franconetti, and today favoured by performers such as El Indio Gitano, the Gypsy Indian. They said El Fillo had died in poverty, his voice ruined by so much hard drinking, still mourning the murder of his brother, the singer Juan Encueros, Naked John. An innovator with a vast knowledge of different *palos*, even now there were those who referred to him as the Johann Sebastian Bach of flamenco.

'Yes. *Afillá*. But there are voices much better than mine. Listen to Terremoto – the Earthquake – or Manolo Caracol. Now those . . . oof!' His lips pursed in a sign of respect.

'But you're just as good as they are,' I enthused. 'There's real power in your voice. You're fantastic!'

He sat back sharply and went silent, the smile gone, staring at me intensely. It seemed I'd gone too far. I had learned a little about Gypsy etiquette, and I had the feeling I'd just broken an important rule. This new, sneering expression he wore seemed to demand what on earth I, a *guiri*, was doing telling him what was good or bad.

'So why did you come here? Why do you want to talk to me?' His voice, still deep, had become hard. I saw that the other members of the band were trying to catch his eye. I had to move fast if I was to keep his attention. Time to dive straight in.

'I play the guitar,' I said. 'I've been learning. I want to play with a group. I thought . . .'

His eyes grew darker, like a bull staring down its prey with a dull, earthy, disrespect. I was sure I'd blown it. He'll laugh me out of here and that'll be the end of it. Stupid even to try. Any minute now he will simply stand up and walk away.

Somewhere inside me, though, I knew I had to take up the challenge. If I backed down now, this opportunity would be lost for good. Tales my grandfather had told me about his life as a professional bare-knuckle fighter came to mind. Taking on five policemen at a time; putting his fist through solid wooden doors as training. It was time to use some inherited northern grit.

I straightened my back, drew my chin in, and looked back at the Gypsy as fiercely as I could.

'How long have you been playing?' he asked.

'Two years.'

'Here,' he said, pulling out the guitar that was leaning against his chair, 'play me a *Fandango*.' I hesitated, then took the instrument from his hand. Some of the other band members were already walking out with their cases and bags. The door to the stage opened and the jarring echo of a hundred hysterical voices poured in.

'. . . unspeakable, my friend. Unspeakable!' A well-fed German was delivering his punch-line above the screaming laughter of his companions.

'It doesn't matter,' something inside me was saying. 'Just play. It doesn't matter.' I lifted myself, breathed deeply and played the first chords.

There was an interruption. A younger man with long, curly black hair tied back in a pony-tail – the other singer in the group – came over and spoke in a low tone, his back turned against me. I couldn't hear what was being said – there was too much background noise and chat from the others standing at the side – but it was clear they wanted to leave.

161

The younger man left abruptly and the Gypsy got up.

'I'm off,' he said, taking the guitar back out of my hand. I stood up. He made to leave, then turned.

'Come back tomorrow. We'll talk about it then – if you're as good as you say.'

The sharp, unforgiving stench of cat-piss filled my nostrils and woke me once again. I opened my eyes to the grey half-light filtering through the tall, grimy window. We were at the end of an alleyway, all direct sunlight blocked out by the buildings around us. The smell and the thick, ancient dust made breathing difficult and my chest tightened in revolt at the foul air. I looked up at the ceiling. A cockroach was negotiating the bubbles of yellow-brown mould that were forming under the plaster. As he fell, a piece of the ceiling fell away with him and he landed on my stomach, legs kicking frantically in the air.

I flicked him off and dragged myself out from under the sheet. Now it was summer again, this dark flat was pleasantly cool despite the piercing heat outside. Although God only knew how I had got through the winter. The snow had only just melted from the tips of the distant Guadarrama mountains and memories of sub-zero temperatures with little or no heating had left their imprint in my bones. Madrid air cannot blow out a candle, they said, but it can kill a man.

My flipflops dragged along the dusty floor of the corridor outside my room – sticky in places where urine had not been cleaned up – past towers of mouldering paperbacks lining both walls from floor to ceiling. A shadow moved quickly, low down ahead of me. A pause, flashing green eyes, then it vanished with a low groan of fear and frustration.

I trudged on. The bathroom was empty but the loo was blocked again and close to overflowing. The cheap, red plastic seat was already stained. Retching, I grabbed the plunger, and went to work. I was becoming an expert at this, my arms performing the necessary twisting, heaving motion mechanically. Two minutes and it was cleared.

The hot water of the shower blanketed me as I turned on the jet. A year on, and I still found Madrid to be a dry, heartless city. The change from Alicante couldn't have been greater: people everywhere, squeezing, bumping and jarring their way up over-crowded streets full of beggars and pimps; an ever-present sense of aggression, anxiety and franticness. The area I lived in was particularly bad: a dark, labyrinthine quarter near the Calle Pez, with several whores for each street corner and hunched junkies scratching for pieces of bread in the gutter. One used to catch my eye as he'd prostrate himself half-naked on the pavement, forehead on the floor, knees pulled up, arse sticking in the air, a grubby Coke cup held in his hands above his head, pleading as loudly as he could to the passers-by for change. I had to fight a persistent desire to escape and flee back to Alicante, or even give up everything and leave for good. Even the weather was less friendly than on the coast, shifting from extreme heat to extreme cold, with no shades of autumn or spring. The people were proud and provincial, lacking the warmth I had grown used to. Looking at the angry, lost, concentrated faces, it seemed over 70 per cent of them were mad, un-balanced or teetering on the edge. I hated it, but saw it as city energy, something to plug in to if I could, and ride along with. After all, this was where the real flamenco scene was, as Eduardo had said. That thought alone kept me on track and held me down in the city – a reason for being there and staying in Spain when it felt as if I had lost everything.

One thing in Madrid's favour, though, was the water – wonderfully soft rain piped straight from the mountains. I let the jet flow over my rapidly thinning body. My ribs and hip bones were quite visible now.

My landlady was sitting in the kitchen, a cigarette hanging precipitously from her mouth, a cup of weak tea in one hand, and a skinny, incontinent cat on her lap.

'What the hell do you do in there?' she screamed. 'I've been waiting here for hours!' She scuttled past, ash flying in all directions, burning holes in her nylon dressing-gown.

I went back to my room, dressed quickly, grabbed my guitar and walked out into the black, meaningless streets.

Carlos lived in the sprawling Madrid suburb of Vallecas: a grubby, concrete area south-east of the city centre that sat like a giant slug-like parasite on the belly of the capital. Ordinary Madrileños referred to it with awe or loathing. 'Vallecas?' they'd say. 'That shit-hole?' It was an area of cheap, redbrick tower blocks that absorbed waves of immigrants seeking work: Basques from the Sixties; North Africans wearing thin leather shoes; short Latin-Americans who spent most of their time calling home from wooden booths in grocers' shops offering cheap international calls. And Gypsies, moved by the authorities from their shanty towns into modern flats.

'They're not like us. Water in buckets – *when* they wash – and they cook over fires on the kitchen floor,' a balding bar-owner had told me. 'I tell you, I haven't got anything against them. A Gypsy comes in here and I serve him as I would anyone else. But he's got to have respect.'

It was an echo of the past, only today the Egyptians, or New Castillians as the Gypsies were often called in the nineteenth century, were kept on the outside not by city walls, but by a ring-road dividing them from the main city.

Non-Gypsies, *payos*, said you were taking a risk just by walking into Vallecas. The change from the city centre was clear: another drab, modern suburb with lifeless architecture. But there were subtle differences, something more edgy and run-down about it. The kiosk where I bought cigarettes from a ghost-like woman and her daughter had sawdust on the floor and a red neon strip flickering around the door like a nervous twitch. Thin-trunked, blackened trees stood by the side of the road like starving refugees, unable to stand straight under their own weight. Graffiti was everywhere: '*Pásate al la Resistencia*', or the Basque spelling of 'Vallekas' painted in bright colours like a standard proclaiming the 'otherness' of the place and its people. Most of the roadsweepers were women. You'd see them drinking in a bar and then see them again in the street a couple of hours later, transformed into dawn workers with tight green overalls and workmen's gloves, throwing cigarette butts into the gutter they'd just brushed clean. Here there was a wearing away of strict divisions. Where normal people saw a world of lines, Vallecas was more of a blur.

Carlos's flat was on the fifth floor. I didn't trust the

lift, and so took the stairs, past children with dirty faces and bright, animal-like eyes. They had been there the first time, when Carlos brought me back with the other group members, playing on the steps at four in the morning. They had looked at me strangely. *I* was the one out of place, as far as they were concerned.

Carlos's threat to test my guitar-playing was never carried out: I returned the next night to Restaurante Alegrías but he wasn't there. We met up again by pure chance after I got to know some aficionados who took me to a flamenco bar, or *tablao*, where Carlos was performing. It was a lucky break after almost a year of trying unsuccessfully to fall in with *flamencos*, particularly Gypsies. Until then my search had produced nothing, thwarted mostly by the complete unwillingness of Gypsies to have anything to do with me. At best they might offer to give me lessons for exorbitant amounts of money. That night, though, things began to turn.

'Eh, *churumbel*!' Carlos said when he saw me, as though he had expected me to find him in this other venue. From then on, he always used the Gypsy word for 'kid' when addressing me.

We spent the night at his grubby flat, playing, singing and drinking heavily. I was drawn to a joyous spontaneity about him. When he sang, the veins on his neck stood out, his face reddened, spittle flew from his mouth and I feared he might collapse. But once it had been captured – the raw essence he was seeking – his expression reverted to calm self-assuredness and a deep relaxation, as though he had rid himself of something cathartically through the song.

> *Me asomé a la muralla*
> *me respondió el viento:*
> *'Para qué dar esos suspiritos*
> *si ya no hay remedio?'*

> I climbed up to the town walls
> And the wind said:
> 'Why so many sighs
> if you can't change anything?'

You could tell when the moment had come as the *jaleo*, the flamenco cries of encouragement, increased in a sharp crescendo of '*Ole*', '*Eso es*', and a surge would pass around the group, as though something had happened. And all the while, the incessant clapping rhythm of the *palmas* pulsated in the background. Then the other singer – the younger, darker man with the pony-tail – would take up the song.

Was this *duende*? There was enormous energy carrying us all along but it was different to my first experience in Alicante, when I heard the woman sing in the Plaza Mayor. There I had been captured, as though by an invisible, sentient being. Here there was an intense group emotion that vivified me. It was impossible to say. I simply sat on the sidelines, grateful that I had been allowed even this far into a closed and very hierarchical world.

Halfway through the night, Carlos told me to join in and accompany one of the dancers on the guitar. I had drunk heavily, but still had enough sense to know that turning this down was not an option. As they passed me the instrument, I realised to my relief that two other guitarists would be playing as well, and so I kept the rhythm as best I could, following the chord

changes and trying to make as little sound as possible.
With the racket surrounding us, it was all I could do.
It even boosted my confidence and they had to prise
the guitar away from me later as I tried to accompany
a piece Carlos always sang on his own.

The faux pas was ignored, though. More brandy was
poured into my glass and a line of cocaine placed in
front of me. I hesitated. Since arriving in Madrid, I had
heard constant condemnation of Gypsies for their
drug-taking. I lifted my head. Although no-one was
obviously watching me, I could tell my reaction
was under scrutiny. It was a test. Not to take it would
mean remaining on the outside.

I snorted.

'I think the *guiri*'s shit-faced.' The old Gypsy sitting
next to me started prodding me.

'I'm fine, I'm fine,' I said, shaking myself.

'Hey blondy, where d'you learn to speak Christian
so well?' I was amazed that someone who appeared to
have no teeth could articulate so clearly. His expression was a throw-back to the past when anything
Spanish, or 'Christian', was acceptable, and anything
foreign – typically deemed 'Chinese' – was dismissed.

'Alicante,' I said.

'Alicante?'

'Yeah. You know it?'

The old Gypsy snorted and turned his face to the
side with a jerk. Grey hairs circled his ears in an otherwise black mass of curls. I took another drink.

'Alicantinos taught you to play?'

'Yeah.'

'Gypsies?'

I thought for a moment. Eduardo had told me that to

be accepted by one group of Gypsies meant to be at least taken seriously by others. It gave you a sort of badge, a letter of introduction into a closed society. But I didn't know any Gypsies in Alicante, and there was a risk in pretending I did. What if I was found out?

'Yeah,' I said as confidently as I could, waiting for the next, inevitable question: Who?

But instead, he smiled and raised a rough, thick hand on the end of what looked like a partially withered arm.

'Juanito,' he said. 'Your mother gave you a *guiri* name?'

'Jason,' I said.

'What?'

'Jason.' Still no sign of comprehension. '*Khassón.*' I pronounced it the Spanish way.

'Sounds Chinese,' he said.

I reached the fifth floor, walked down to Carlos's door and let myself in, stepping carefully over the ducks in the hallway, past the donkey standing mournfully in the corner. At first I had been surprised that it never seemed to move around, but it had claimed its own little stable and now refused to move, perhaps out of fear of losing this safe enclave.

The place was a mess. Animal droppings were everywhere, the walls were smeared in grime, and black scorch-marks dotted the lino floor where people had previously lit fires. The smell was overpowering.

Carlos was with Jesús, the other singer, on the tiny balcony that looked directly onto the blank, brick wall of the next-door block of flats. Thin blue and white metal chains hung over the door to prevent flies from entering, and were coated in a thick layer of city dust that rubbed off onto your clothes as you passed through.

'*Eh, churumbel! Qué tal?*' Carlos's teeth flashed with a smile as he quickly ended the conversation. Jesús flicked his chin up casually in greeting, then turned away without a word. I watched him walk back into the flat, tall and proud, his long, curly hair shiny with brilliantine. I was still unwelcome. The others at least pretended I had my foot in the door – Juanito was even treating me like a friend after my line about the Alicantino Gypsies – but Jesús held out, never talking to me directly, hardly even looking at me or recognising I was there.

'We were waiting for you.' Carlos was dressed, as usual, in his brightly coloured shirt, open all the way down to his hirsute navel. Today the shirt was red, with blue and yellow anchors, the kind you could buy at the market in packs of five for 2,000 pesetas. He was a short, stout man, with thick, rock-like features. Greying black hair was swept off his forehead with grease. The powerful stench of his aftershave mingled with the animal smells to create a sickly pot pourri of perfumed shit.

'Come on inside! Today I want to hear you play properly. You've managed to avoid it till now.'

Approaching him the first time at Alegrías and then finding him again the following night had gone down well. Assertiveness was appreciated among Gypsies. But it had only got me so far. Now came the real test. I'd only ever joined in when everyone else was there – the dancers and the two other guitarists – and my own playing was easily hidden in the great noise they all produced. Often I couldn't even hear my own mistakes. But I had stayed and had returned now three or four times for more dance, music, cocaine; arriving with bottles of booze as the price of admittance.

'How do you expect me to play without my backing group?'

He gestured for me to sit down on the black fake-leather sofa, unimpressed by my weak attempt at humour. Jesús had disappeared, I was glad to see. His cold, critical gaze would make it worse.

I sat for a moment with the guitar in my lap, trying to think of a piece that might impress without demanding too much technically. Nothing seemed right. *Tangos* had too many associations with Lola and a time I had painfully blocked out, if not actually recovered from. A *Bulería* was exciting, but complicated; I was more likely to make a mistake. Besides, I sensed that Gypsies viewed it as belonging to them. I was foreign; I still had to tread carefully. An *Alegría*? I didn't know enough *falsetas* well enough, and, besides, the mood wasn't right. There was something too light about them. *Seguiriyas* were my favourites, a slow *cante jondo*. They were seen as one of the 'strong' *palos*, understood only by serious *flamencos*. But again . . . I wasn't sure if I could pull it off. My fingers began to sweat. From the corner of my eye I could see Carlos fidgeting.

'Come on, blondy. Play!'

The ducks in the corridor began quacking at each other and the direct sunlight on my exposed neck was burning my inappropriately white skin. A cough, and finally I began, my fingers falling into a *Taranta*, a sorrowful mining chant from the Murcia region. I felt relieved that somehow the decision had been taken. No rhythm to worry about, and ideal for self-expression. This'll show him, I thought. It was a piece

I prided myself on being able to play well.

I moved my fingers over the strings trying to extract every ounce of feeling I could. Perhaps, I thought, as the question unceasingly played itself out in some part of my mind, perhaps this is *duende*: the emotions, the sensation the player puts into his performance. If I tried hard enough, he should be able to feel it too. I crouched even tighter over the guitar.

'Yes, yes. OK. Fine,' Carlos interrupted. I looked up, startled. 'Come on, give me something with more life. Rhythm, rhythm!'

I started a spluttering, haltering *Bulería* in my confusion, fingers slippy with sweat now and almost sliding off the strings. Something the other guitarists had played a few nights previously came to mind and I tried to copy it, but usually the singer dictated what piece he wanted, not the guitarist. I had no idea what was expected of me. The situation was absurd. Carlos clapped in time to urge me on. The chorus of ducks started again.

'*Venga*. That's it.' Then he started singing:

> *Me lo encontré en el camino*
> *y nos hicimos hermanos.*

It was a song Camarón used to sing.

I had to count the rhythm to myself – *un dos TRES cuatro cinco seis SIETE OCHO nueve DIEZ un DOS un dos TRES* . . . After tapping it out in my head for a couple of years, I thought I owned it. But he was singing, I was nervous, and it was essential that I get it right.

My lips moved as the digits raced through my mind. Straight rhythm, just straight rhythm. Keep it

172

mechanical, like a clock. Listen to his singing. I fought to keep in time.

Samara fue elegida por los moros reina de la morería . . .

He stopped singing and nodded to me to play a *falseta*. I started on the first one I could think of, one I had learned in Alicante – an old-fashioned, very traditional tune that was inappropriate here. Its melodiousness jarred with his more anarchic, modern style.

He took up the singing once more and we crashed into a finale.

I stared down at my feet. Not my best performance, and I hadn't been able to play with anyone else since the fiesta with Lola almost a year before. In the meantime, I'd got by playing along with the cheap cassettes you could pick up at petrol stations for 500 pesetas. But playing with a singer, like playing for a dancer, was completely different. The singer often accentuated off-beats while the guitar was expected to hold the *compás*, yet at the same time following his pace and changing as required. When a singer and guitar-player were in harmony it created a complex syncopation. But I had little idea of where the song was going.

Someone was trying to hand me something. I looked up and saw a glass of beer thrust towards me by Jesús's outstretched arm. I took it and tried to look at him, but I saw his disapproving face and close-set eyes and lost my nerve.

'Rhythm,' Carlos said. 'If you want to play with us you need perfect rhythm. It's the most important thing.' The gas spitting up from the cold beer wet my face as I brought the glass to my lips. I thought my rhythm was pretty good.

'So what's my rhythm like?'

I realised as soon as I had spoken that it was the wrong thing to say. Carlos laughed. Jesús turned away again and stepped silently out onto the balcony, tying his hair into a bunch at the back of his head with an elastic band. Carlos went out to join him, while I strummed a quiet *Soleá* – the *palo* of solitude – to console myself. I could hear their voices but could make out little of what was being said. Jesús, I could sense, was reluctant to bring me on board. A *payo*, a *guiri*: it just made him suspicious. But I also knew, from my little experience with them, that Carlos was the boss, and what he said went. Age seemed to count for a lot in the rigid pecking order.

The tone of disagreement filtered back through into the main room. I shifted my hot, uncomfortable body away from the intense light pouring through the open window. It felt odd, knowing my future was being decided out there. I had flattered myself that I had made it in through the back door without anyone noticing, but this was feeling more and more like an audition. The donkey caught my eye. His sad, tearful face betrayed a broken, self-pitying spirit. The rope around his neck was superfluous: this animal wouldn't make a break for it if you left him a trail of carrots and whipped him down the stairs. He seemed to be suffering from some sort of donkey institution-alisation. I could only feel pity for the pathetic creature. As I watched, he defecated on the floor where he stood, and a fresh wave of manure-smell passed through the flat like a cloud of mustard gas.

Carlos beckoned me to join him on the balcony. Jesús had walked off.

'Well, *churumbel*.' I could tell it wasn't going to be straightforward. 'Listen, we haven't got anything lined up, so you can't play with us for now. But you keep playing, and we'll see. We might take you along with us. In the meantime, you listen, you watch and you learn. *Vale?*' He passed a thick finger from his ear to his eye and then mimed the action of playing the guitar. It was his way of reassuring me.

I turned back to the window, disappointed, yet relieved I was still 'in'. There was nothing I could say anyway. Not to Carlos. He didn't discuss things.

Music started from somewhere inside the flat. I looked in, and passed back into the main room. My eyes adjusted. Jesús was standing with one leg on a chair, my guitar resting on his thigh, playing a *Soleá por Bulerías*. Pure, hard notes like crystal.

He finished with a long, smooth *rasgueo*, fingers striking the strings one after another like a machine-gun, then looked at me with defiance and pride. I didn't care that he was using my guitar, but somehow it was important.

'I haven't played for five years,' he said. Then he placed the guitar on the floor and left, with every air of a man with something important to do.

Carlota, my landlady, was in a foul mood again. The electricity bill had just arrived and was far higher than expected. We had useless old Franco-era wiring that only provided 125 volts, so the flat was littered with rusty transformers boosting the power to 220.

'I shall have to put your rent up,' she said. 'It's all that time you sit in your room with the light on. And

175

you play cassettes all night. You think that doesn't use it up?'

This was true, but I doubted it was the explanation for the big bill. There was only one transformer in my dusty room and I had to listen to music in the dark.

I snarled.

'Don't look at me like that.'

She couldn't see how I was looking at her; thirty years as a virtual troglodyte had left her yellow-skinned and half-blind, eyes pale and dull from reading in the gloom. The ash fell from her cigarette onto the cat sitting in her lap. It leapt up, scratching her as it darted into the dark, dirty safety of the corridor.

'Damn you! *Me cago en la leche!*' she cried, and tottered off to get some antiseptic: a necessary house-hold item in this place. I had only taken the room because it was probably the cheapest place in central Madrid. She could hardly charge any more for such a dump. All her income came from lodgers. There was absolutely nothing in the bank, no reserves, no relatives, nothing. Which was why the place had slowly deteriorated over the years to reach its present shoddy state. There was only ever enough money to eat badly and pay the odd bill. Nothing for repairs or redecorating. The house was slowly crumbling around her and the cats like a tomb.

There had been the odd lucky break. One room had been unrentable as it had no window and only a small wooden bed. But then a man arrived who wanted to use it occasionally for illicit rendezvous with his mistress. The rest of us were under strict orders not to talk to him and to disappear when he came round. There was the rumour that he was someone important and well known . . . I only ever came across him once, but the corridors were so dark I couldn't get a good look at him.

Now there was the threat of higher rent. I had barely earned anything since arriving in Madrid. For months I had languished in depression, eating little, sleeping late, yearning for my easy Mediterranean life and the woman I saw then as the greatest passion of my life. Lost love. It had felt like a kind of death. I dreamed of her searching embraces, her breath on my skin. Just to see her once more. She wouldn't even have to know I was there . . . But a sensible inner voice, the spoiler of so many ideas, would always hold me back, haunting me with visions of Vicente pressing a 12-bore up against his shoulder. I couldn't take the risk. A complete break, Eduardo had said. Much as I hated it, I knew he was right.

Occasionally I did some stand-in teaching for a nearby English school if the money situation got too bad, but I stayed in the flat because it was Madrid – the promised centre of flamenco, still driving me on – and it was the only place I could afford. And in some ways, too, because the dark awfulness of it reflected my mood. Now, after so much time and so many wasted chances, there was an opportunity to fall in with a real flamenco group. I couldn't afford to pay any more, so I had to think fast.

'I can sort out the electricity for you,' I said, 'as long as you promise not to put the rent up.'

She looked suspicious. 'What the hell are you talking about?'

'If I sort out the electricity meter for you, will you promise not to put my rent up?'

She sneered. 'I never promise anything.'

'Well, it's up to you. I can guarantee a lifetime of low electricity bills,' I said, trying to mimic the sound of an advert.

Her dull, grey eyes brightened. 'Really! How?'

'Promise?'

'Well . . .' It was the most I was going to get out of her.

'Have you got some old 35mm camera film?'

She hurried off, slippers scraping in the grime, then returned with a film in her hand. 'Will this do?'

I grabbed a chair and climbed up to the meter above the kitchen sink. As long as it was the right make . . . I was in luck. Slipping the film into the tiny slit on the side of the box I was able to catch the wheel and stop it dead. It was a trick I had learned from Carlos.

'There you go,' I said, looking down. 'An earthquake won't make that thing turn now.'

She looked hard. 'What have you done?'

'The meter won't turn any more. I've blocked it. All you have to do is not answer the door to the electricity man, fill in a low number on the form when it comes round, and they'll never suspect a thing. The cheapest electricity in all Spain.'

'Oh, you are an angel,' she said. 'This is wonderful. We can switch on the fans, turn on the lights. And of course, you can play as many tapes as you want, my dear.' And she tugged on my arm affectionately.

'And the rent?'

'Oh, don't you worry about that. You can stay as long as you want.'

It was the only time I saw her genuinely happy.

Back at Carlos's place. Despite not being officially taken on board, I continued visiting the flat almost every night. There was always someone there, and apart from Jesús's reaction, I never felt totally unwelcome. If I was around for long enough, I reasoned, I would be regarded as part of the furniture.

I usually arrived with a litre bottle of wine or some brandy if I could afford it. And a few packets of cigarettes. Ducados black-tobacco cigarettes were essential for anyone who saw themselves as part of the counter-culture. They came in blue and white packets, had a tar content as high as a cigar, and tasted like floor-sweepings dipped in diesel. But, most importantly, they were cheap and enjoyed a symbolic status not unlike Gauloises for the French. To smoke Ducados was to make a statement rejecting the system, and as such, they were as good as the official cigarette of the flamenco world.

Most members of the band were as happy smoking them as they were breathing. There were exceptions: hard men, like Carlos, for whom even the venomous fumes of Ducados were not strong enough. He usually smoked cigars or, sometimes, Habanos filterless cigarettes. He said he needed them to keep his voice in shape. I tried one once and could barely speak for a whole day afterwards. But it left me with a greater fondness for a country respectful of its citizens' right to poison themselves to death.

Spaniards didn't care much about smoking in public places. No bar waiter, belly straining behind the obligatory vest and white shirt tucked into tight, black trousers, was complete without a cigarette – usually a Fortuna or Nobel – hanging out of the side of his mouth, as he took out the rubbish at the end of another sweaty shift. Middle-aged women preparing the food in workers' bars nonchalantly lit up as they whisked the eggs for another *tortilla de patatas*. There were even – and this pleased me the most – men in their sixties shuffling in their slippers and puffing happily away on thick Montecristo No.3s in the Vallecas supermarkets. It took the edge off so much bright, white packaging somehow.

The other members of the group had gathered at the flat. Javier, a young *payo* dancer from Valencia, was standing on the balcony stretching his legs and seeing how high he could kick.

'Look, I'm out of shape,' he'd say as his toe touched the top of the door-frame. 'And I'm getting fat.' A tiny roll of skin round his waist would be pinched. 'Look!'

He had a slight build, narrow shoulders, a turquoise bandana in his hair, and an unnerving way of looking at everyone as though he were in love with them: head tilted to one side, eyes wide open, and a demanding smile.

The other dancer was Carmen, a buxom woman in her late thirties with high blood pressure and dyed blond hair that came out a sort of thick, streaky orange. She was known as 'La Andonda', the knife-woman, for having attacked her husband with a kitchen-knife after she found him with another woman. The nickname came from a previous 'Andonda' from the nineteenth century – the explosive younger wife of the singer El Fillo – who was equally known for her knife-wielding exploits. Carmen's situation had ended disastrously, Carlos later told me, and the husband had kicked her out – a catastrophe for a Gypsy woman. The community might well have ostracised her completely, but Carlos had taken her into his group because she was a distant cousin. 'She doesn't dance too badly, either, the fat old thing,' he said.

The other two in the group were guitarists. Antonio, the first guitarist, was a thin, young *payo* with dark blond hair and long sideburns who performed finger-breaking feats on the fretboard. Always clean-shaven, he wore fresh white shirts every day that quickly wilted and lost their sheen in the smoke-filled air of Carlos's flat. Someone – it must have been his mother – even ironed his jeans. The other members of the band needled him in an attempt to bring him down a notch or two, but he fought back, always failing to receive the respect from the others he felt he deserved.

Juanito, I was surprised to discover, was the second guitarist. At forty-seven years old, he was younger than I had thought, and his shortened right arm was the perfect length for playing. He told me it had been partially severed in a car accident and the surgeons had been forced to cut some of it away before sewing it back on. The result was that his hand fell exactly into the right playing position, and he was spared all the torturous straining and pins and needles that bedevilled the more 'able-bodied' guitarists. He could never play the complicated *falsetas* that Antonio liked to show off with, but he had the most perfect *compás* I'd ever heard.

'*Hombre*,' he said as I eased myself down next to him. We had gone beyond first-name terms, although, in contrast to *payos*, he never shook my hand or touched me in the way most Spaniards did. Gypsies seemed to have different ideas about physical space. He lit a cigarette, took a drag and then squeezed it into the gap between the strings and wood in the head of the guitar.

'So it doesn't get in the way when I'm playing,' he said.

As with every group, I later discovered, the hierarchy was everything. Antonio had been one of the founders of the band, and had even sought Carlos out as a singer, but from the day he arrived, Carlos had been the leader, the *jefe*. As a singer and a member of the same extended family, Jesús was second-in-command. There was something distracted about him, as though his mind were elsewhere, on other, more important things, giving the impression that the band was not everything in his life.

The others filled various middle-ranking roles, with Antonio jockeying for a higher position and always failing. He used his guitar-playing as a weapon in a political game, not realising that no matter how well he played – faster than Paco de Lucía, with more feeling than Tomatito – he would always be near the bottom. In the end I decided it was partly a *gitano–payo* thing, but I couldn't help thinking things would be easier if he just stopped trying so hard.

The flat was crammed with people. Apart from the group members, Carlos's two teenage daughters and their friends were there, a handful of neighbours, and more friends from across the road. Every few minutes other faces would appear at the door, some staying, some just having a look and then moving on. At one stage an old man with a green hat and a purple face showed up and everyone stood up respectfully. How wonderful to see him.

'*Ostias*, is that guy still alive? Look, he can still walk, how old is he? Did he make it all this way on his own? Oh, no, look, there's his daughter, how terrible for her, having to look after him after all these years, she's never been married, you know . . .' She was nearly eighteen. Almost an old maid.

We all went quiet. The old man lifted his hand, muttered something totally incomprehensible through toothless gums, turned and left. Cries of joy; some people clapped. What a great old bloke. Then we sat down again. I never did find out who he was.

The noise was unbelievable. While other Spaniards would talk loudly and on top of one another at large family meals, here everyone was shouting, singing and screaming, usually with the TV on full volume in the background. One of Carlos's daughters was even dancing to make her point to her neighbour. The result was a ceaseless cacophony which you either stepped inside or were overwhelmed by. As morning approached, I would often begin to doze off and find myself listening to the full crescendo of it all, like a wall of noise, rather than a particular voice or conversation. And I would throw myself back into the fray to avoid going mad.

Jesús's black, narrow eyes were staring at me from across the room. I felt his gaze like a tingling sensation in my shoulders, then turned to see him quickly look away. Nobody seemed to have noticed his return. He came and left with no questions asked. There was sweat on his brow and I knew he had been running.

The women began clearing the table after another heavy broth – *potaje*. Carlos's quiet, Indian-looking wife, María-José, made it by the bucketful, throwing whatever was to hand in a pot along with oil and water. Tomatoes and garlic were the only consistent ingredients I could detect, accompanied by anything from eggs, spinach and onions to broad beans, fish and *chorizo* sausage. On a good day you might even find some black pudding – *morcilla* – floating in it. Soaked up with bread, at least it filled you up.

I got up to help, but was pulled down forcefully by Carlos.

'Woman's work,' he said, drawing on the cigar stuck fast in his thick, full lips. Traditional gender roles were strictly adhered to. Juanito told me it was common in some houses for women to wait for the men to eat first before taking what was left over for themselves.

'*Pero aquí somo medio apayao* – but here we're half-*payo*,' he'd say, almost shamefully.

More cries and shouts as the table was cleared: 'María, pass me the big dish, no the one by Juanito, fuck it's hot, did you pick up the glasses, hey *moza*! I haven't finished, you pig, you eat too much, and you need to fatten up, there's no meat on you, what do you know, hurry up there . . .'

Antonio had already pulled out his guitar and was playing the elaborate opening of a *Fandango*, showing off with modern, jazzy chords that stretched your fingers to breaking point. I felt Juanito squirm. Pedro had told me the *Fandango* was one of the *palos* with the strongest Arab influence. It was haunting, rhythmic, very distinctive, interweaving itself amongst the clatter of plates, screams from the kitchen and snippets of conversations slowly fading away. And then Carlos began to sing.

> *Los arroyos cristalinos*
> *tu nombre van repitiendo*
> *las campanas repicando*
> *en la torre de una iglesia,*
> *el mío están murmurando.*

> The crystal streams
> are repeating your name,
> while the bells ringing
> from a church tower
> whisper mine.

The girls and many of the others had left. The music continued and cocaine was passed around. The drug made playing easier, increasing my self-confidence to the extent that I felt inspired on it. And the nervous energy it gave me meant the sound I produced on the guitar was more akin to the harsher, stronger style of the modern players I wished to emulate. Under the circumstances, I quickly lost any qualms about taking it. It was part of the lifestyle I was buying into, a necessary step, I told myself, in my search for flamenco knowledge.

Juanito had become my main contact in the group. Without being obvious about it, he would always make sure we sat together so that he could guide me through passages I was unsure about, or teach me *palos* I had yet to learn.

'Hey, try this,' he'd say in his high, boyish voice. He played old tunes, standards, the sort of thing everyone was expected to know, yet no-one heard any more, because guitarists were all too busy experimenting, trying to find the latest jazz or funk sound. To out-Paco Paco. They were the sort of pieces you heard at weddings, festivals, on old records from the 1950s and 60s – a bedrock for most of the ideas in flamenco, but in danger of being lost these days.

His thick fingers would move rapidly on the fretboard, producing an earthy sound that was almost non-existent now – most modern guitarists play 'cleanly', without the mistakes and buzz of tradition. He played a proper flamenco guitar too – spruce and cypress, no rosewood – with its harder, shallower sound.

We spent hours like this: informal tutorials on the side that allowed me to get a taste for a more 'Gypsy' style of playing – often appearing to change rhythms and stressing off-beats. It might be five minutes, half an hour, or even the whole night, but whenever we were all together, he would find time to show me something. A chord variation or a little lick to throw into the middle of the *compás* just to vary it, to give it more life and a certain magic. It was invaluable, a crash course in the sort of things I would need if I was ever to have a chance of playing professionally with the group. But I had to be careful about what I said. If I started trying to ask him questions about the piece – 'What was that? A minor?' – he would withdraw, or rebuke me. For him you either played at the top, *por arriba*, or in the middle, *por medio*. Anything else went over his head.

'Don't talk to me in Chinese. We only speak Christian round here,' he'd say.

Carlos's mother-in-law was a seer. Or, rather, she looked at the cards for people and came out with the phrases they expected to hear.

'Blondy!'

It was my turn.

She leaned over me, gold teeth glinting dully in the low light. Her fat wheezing body was wrapped in a white scarf that she held tight at all times over her black and red blouse. One of her eyes was covered in an unnerving milk-like mist. I got up and joined her at the table as indicated.

'Watch out for her,' said Javier, flaring his nostrils as he stretched his leg up to his ear. 'She might tell you things you don't want to know.' He spoke slowly, as if I couldn't understand Spanish properly.

The old woman handed over the cards for me to shuffle, then took them back with thick, grubby fingers solid with fat, gold rings.

'You will marry a fair-haired girl,' she proclaimed. Not a good start: I'd never been attracted to blonde girls and began to laugh. She realised her mistake.

'Although you prefer dark-haired girls,' she said. That was more like it.

She stared at the images on the wooden table in front of her. 'You are waiting for something.' She pointed to the card of the Suspended Man. I thought of Carlos and his promise of gigs some time in the future. Surely she already knew that.

'If you follow my advice and pay heed to the omens, you will fulfil your destiny.'

I sighed.

'Soak a white handkerchief in your own sweat, wrap some jasmine flowers in it and leave it to dry on the windowsill for three days. On the third day, throw the flowers away, burn the cloth, and within the year you will be married and have witnessed the birth of the first of your three sons.'

I flattered myself that the reading was one step further in the group's acceptance of me, even if the woman did manage to extract 1,000 pesetas ou' of me for her wisdom. She grasped the money greedily and stared at the note to make sure it was real. I wondered who was laughing at whom. I justified my folly by thinking of it as an act of charity. But 1,000 pesetas was a lot for me now and I couldn't afford to lose money so easily.

'Make sure you listen to her and do what she says.' It was La Andonda. 'I did, and everything turned out good.'

I looked at her. First, the woman's husband had been unfaithful to her, and then she'd been thrown out of the house for trying to knife him. I decided to ignore the soothsayer's advice.

'You. Come with me.'

Jesús beckoned to me with a casual flick of the fingers. I stood up, confused. He hadn't spoken directly to me for days. As the lowest in the hierarchy, I had to obey. I walked towards him and he turned and headed out the door.

We walked down the stairs and out into the dark street, orange and pink lights flickering over our heads. It was three in the morning, but the streets of Vallecas were full. A singing Gypsy woman was blocking the pavement, unconcerned by the wailing car alarm just thirty yards from where she stood. She had placed her home-made sound system – a 3-foot metal frame on wheels bearing enormous speakers, a keyboard and a microphone – in the middle of the path so that everyone had to cross the road to get past. It seemed an odd way to busk, but what with her flat, tuneless singing, cheap backing track, and the accompaniment of the high-pitched squeal of the Audi up the road, you had to wonder if her intention was to earn any money at all. People couldn't get far enough away from her. I looked at her two sons crouching in the doorway behind her. They were dressed in grubby nylon tracksuits, with that proud, bored, menacing look of so many Gypsy kids.

Jesús walked over and handed them some money,

which they accepted grudgingly, hardly looking him in the eye. We moved on.

A beaten-up old Renault was waiting for us. We stepped inside and drove off. There was no greeting or chat. I never saw the man behind the wheel again.

This was the bohemian, flamenco life I had been looking for – not the imitation I had experienced in Alicante. Even my time with Lola began to pale through the filter of cocaine and the excitement of hanging out with real *flamencos*. Eduardo would be proud of me, I thought, convinced I was finally on the inside. And as I identified myself more and more with this world – regardless of whether *it* had accepted *me* – I could sense myself absorbing a new code of honour which, above all, involved a loathing of those on the 'outside'. Non-*flamencos*. It became a knee-jerk, anti-establishment sentiment that existed purely on the level of 'us' and 'them'.

Twenty minutes later, we were dropped off in an area of the city I didn't know. Residential, by the look of it. Short trees were dotted along the pavement; a school with tall redbrick walls stood opposite. The Renault drove away. Jesús walked ahead and then cut into one of the side-roads. I hurried behind, careful not to lose him. The streets round here were empty. We kept on walking, cutting in and out between the cars: first on the pavement, then in the middle of the road, and back onto the pavement again. Jesús was silent and seemed to be looking for something. I started to wonder what we were doing there. He intimidated me, with his obvious mistrust, and my mind buzzed with possibilities.

We heard voices. I was thrown into a lightless doorway and pushed against the wall, his hand on my throat. For a moment, I thought he was going to kill me. But the people walked past – just a group of kids coming back home from the bars – and he relaxed his grip on my shirt.

Back on the street, he moved swiftly, like a shadow. I stayed behind, frightened now, watching him as he cruised past the cars like a hunter. Then he gave a low whistle. I walked over reluctantly.

'Go to the top of that street and wait for me there,' he said softly. 'If you see anyone before I arrive, hold the cigarette in your left hand. Got it?'

I nodded.

'Go on!'

I ran off, uncertain why I was hurrying, not knowing who or what I was supposed to be looking out for. I ignored my misgivings, driven by the desire to do well, to be accepted.

Standing at the corner, underneath the canopy of a shoe shop, I was faced by rows and rows of empty knee-length boots. There were trees on either side of the road – plenty of shelter from the streetlights. I had to think how to make myself less conspicuous. The most suspicious thing in the world would be just to stand there, at this time in the morning. I lit a cigarette, waiting to transfer it into my other hand for the signal. But if there was anyone to look out for, they would spot me instantly. And I wasn't quite sure who 'they' were. The police?

There was little time to wonder. Jesús appeared from around the corner.

'Get in!'

I jumped inside and we sped off. He was driving a black Mercedes.

* * *

Racing down deserted boulevards. Tower blocks, road signs, bus shelters, trees like semi-conscious flashes in the corner of my eye as we sped effortlessly and gracefully through a night-lit city.

'*Me cago en Dios! Me cago en Dios!* I shit on God!' Jesús screamed out of the open window as he drove at high speed through the pulsating rhythm of the streetlights crossing over us in a steady, constant beat. *Un . . . dos . . . TRES . . .*

'Have you ever seen this city? *La has visto?* Seen it like this? I'm going to show you the city. This is going to be the best fucking tour of the city there has ever been. By the time we've finished – Oy! Almost, almost.' He swerved to avoid a kerb that had loomed up from nowhere. I looked over at him: the quiet, moody Jesús was transformed; screeching in a high voice as though having five conversations at once, and shouting for the whole city to hear.

'*Me cago en Dios!*' For most people it was an expression of annoyance, but here it seemed more like a statement of faith.

'*Qué te parece este coche, eh?* What do you think of this car? You want the car? You can't have it. It's mine. Of course, we could go for a long drive. You need some money? All the way to Córdoba, Seville, Jerez. Wherever you want. *Ah, las tías*, the girls in Andalusia. Not like the tarts here. *Zorras*, they're all tarts. Carlos, he's mad. You take my advice, steer clear of the girls in Madrid. They're all tarts, tarts. Good Andalusian girl, that's what you— Look how fast this fucker can go. I can beat them all, *hijos de puta*. Look at that. See that? That's the old Post Office. See it? There on the left. He's taking it too far. They've been cleaning that fucking place for years. Fucking pigeons shat on it so much the place began to fall down. Ha, ha. What a bunch of fuckers. *Gilipollas. Guiris* like you. They can't even build a building that's pigeon-shit-proof. Fuckers. That's where Juan Antonio used to live – Andonda's husband – before she cut his bollocks off. Poor bastard. No more bollocks for Juan Antonio. What a fucker. Of course, I told her "You should have used a blunt knife, not that razor-sharp thing, then the fucker's prick would have fallen off by now as well". Ha! Fuckers.'

The lights racing past my window were beginning to merge with one another, the speed pinning me back into the leather seat. Down the long, straight avenue of the Paseo de la Castellana, past the Torre Picasso which looked less like a symbol of modern Spain than a toaster placed on its side. Then on down the Paseo de Recoletos, past the classical columns of the National Library and the Torres de Jerez – black and grey twin towers from the Seventies that looked like firemen's practice buildings – and on to the Plaza de Cibeles. I put my feet up on the dashboard and listened to the one-man rant sitting next to me.

'Hey. Get your fucking feet off my dashboard.'

I lifted them off instinctively, but he grabbed them and placed them back.

'Ha! Only joking. Do what you like. Only don't make a mess.'

I stuck my head out of the window, eyes rolling back, watching the tops of the trees and the towers pass by, as though in an alternative, upside-down world that existed in the sky. We swerved sharply and I felt a shadow pass near my head.

'Watch out kid. Don't lose your head. Ha! Don't lose your head. Fucker.'

192

I sat bolt upright and looked back: we had almost smashed into a road sign. Jesús grinned over at me.

'Here. Your turn.' We skidded to a halt in the middle of the Paseo del Prado. 'Come on! Your turn to drive. You don't think I'm going to do all the fucking driving, do you. Come on. Let's see if a *guiri* can drive.'

The car was in the middle of a broad tree-lined avenue opposite one of the most famous museums in the world, but all I could think about was not getting run over and killed. I got out and jumped in the other side. Jesús leapt into the passenger seat.

'OK. Let's see what you're made of. Or just another Juan Antonio. Eh? Come on, kid.'

I pressed on the accelerator and, with a start, we set off, our heads jerked back against the rests with the force of it. 'Christ, this thing is powerful.'

'Powerful? This is a pile of shit. I'll show you something really powerful.'

We sped on. At the traffic lights I stopped.

'What the fuck are you doing? Drive, drive. We haven't got time to sit here for the fucking lights. Keep driving. Go! *Vamos!*'

We took off again. Even if it was dawn, this was Madrid, and there were still plenty of other cars around to make passing through red lights a hazardous hobby.

Down towards Atocha, up, and round the back of the Retiro. It was quieter here. Jesús leaned half of his body out of the window, waving his fist at the trees like a great hammer about to strike each one down.

'Fuckers! Fuckers! Fuckers!'

But then came a flashing light – blue – and another car pulled out sharply behind us and headed our way.

'Put your foot down. And listen to my directions

carefully.' His voice was suddenly calm. I glanced across: the manic, screaming fool was poised and self-possessed, watching the road ahead like a fighter pilot.

The police car was still some distance away. I felt a sharp surge passing through my brain, shortened breath. I had total confidence – not in myself, but in Jesús.

'Kill the lights. There's a turning on the right coming up. Get ready to turn, but don't brake. Slow down, slow down. It's coming up. There, whatever you do, don't brake.'

'What are you talking about? How can I not brake?'

We turned. I braked.

'*Ostias*. I shit on your father. I told you not to brake! I told you—'

'How the fuck! Why?'

'Because they see your brake lights and they know where you've gone.' He was gentle, reassuring. 'Right, just keep going straight. Keep straight.'

'But the streetlights. They'll see us anyway.'

'Keep straight.'

The street was narrower, cars parked on either side. We were doing sixty, with barely a foot between us and disaster. There was no space for panic. It was a question of not thinking about it. Letting go. The individual cars disappeared in my mind and we entered a smooth-sided tunnel, with only one possible path for us to follow, like a ready-laid track. I pressed the pedal even harder. Jesús looked round through the windscreen, just a brief check, and then back, staring out through the rear window.

'Keep it going, kid. Keep it going.'

We were coming to the end of the street. The police had dropped behind.

'Where do we go?'

'Left, left.' We swerved off. I didn't use the brakes. Jesús lifted the handbrake gently. My God, I thought, we're going to spin this thing right off the road. The car tilted to one side, we skidded, but somehow managed to stay on course.

'Straight, straight. Then left at the bottom. Use the gears more.' Smoother this time, but the engine sounded like it was about to explode. 'That's it. Go, go!'

Back onto the boulevard. No need to say which way. I knew the plan by now. But the police car was still there. Faster, we had to go faster, and find a better way to lose them.

We raced down the hill, away from the centre, moving inevitably towards the south, and Vallecas. It might be dangerous to lure them there, but it was probably our only chance. I saw Jesús feeling around for something.

'A phone, a phone. This bastard must have— Watch it, this junction's a tough one.' We flew over the crossroads, narrowly avoiding a moped. The police car slowed up to avoid a collision. A few precious yards gained. But they were fast, probably faster than us. We couldn't lose them on the straights. We had to shake them off some other way. My heart was beating overtime, blood pulsing violently in my hands as they gripped the steering wheel. I felt locked in this position, as though after the crash they would find me still clinging on, a wild, staring look of horror in my eyes.

Jesús was dialling. 'Keep it going kid. Come on, come on, answer the bloody— Roberto!'

Blue lights still flashing in the mirror, like a fly that

refused to die. Jesús was talking rapidly to the man on the other end. Short, fast instructions. I didn't hear what was said, too busy watching the road – behind and in front.

He switched the phone off. 'Just keep going. It's sorted. Head towards Carlos's place.'

There were more cars down here. People setting off early to put up their market stalls. We had to weave madly between three vans that were driving slowly in convoy, turning out onto the main road and taking up half the lanes. They were lucky not to be hit. But I realised I didn't care. We were moving forward and nothing was going to stop us.

We crossed under the ring-road and headed up the hill into Vallecas, careering past early-morning buses and swerving to avoid old women walking out to buy bread. The grey, concrete football stadium sped past almost unnoticed.

'Take the second right, towards Carlos's place, then the first right again. We can do it, they're falling back.'

I drove as instructed, trying not to brake, no lights, relying entirely on the streetlamps.

'Here, on the left. That garage.'

I swerved in, braking for a final time, with a great screech of tyres on tarmac. The car entered a small opening in the wall, the door was closed, and we were in total darkness.

'They might have heard us.'

'Don't worry about it. Come on, this way.' We got out of the car, my knees trembling, and headed out of the garage, and into a shop at the back. Someone was locking the doors. I could barely take in what was happening. We could hear the sirens circling around the area. There seemed to be more than one of them now, but it was difficult to say. We stood, poised, ready to run if we had to, unsure how safe we were here. The police car came down the road and passed by the garage door without stopping. Then a second one. Then nothing.

We breathed a sigh of relief. Jesús put his arm around my shoulder.

'Here,' he said, placing some dope in my hand as I collapsed into a chair. 'Take this. You need it.'

chapter SEVEN

Por Bulerías

En esta vía maldita,
siempre le faltan las cosas
al que más las necesita.

In this damned life,
the people who need the most
are the ones who go without.

*T*wo Gypsy sisters aged six and eight are taking turns to swing their little brother by the arms in a circle. Their clothes are cheap and dirty from rolling around in the dust. They laugh enthusiastically at their game, swinging the child, then changing places and swinging him once again. Their skin is dark – like Indians' – and their ruffled, unwashed hair hangs about their eyes like overgrown ivy. They break from their playing to beg at the nearby bar. An old man with dyed black hair, streaked over a scalp dotted with liver spots, attracts most of their attention thanks to the yellow Labrador lying lazily under his table. The dog and the Gypsy kids get on well, but the man is uncomfortable and tries unsuccessfully to shoo them away. Eventually a barman emerges from inside and moves them on. They stare back at him in a playfully defiant way, denying him moral victory while obeying his order to leave.

They go back to the entrance of the ugly modern church, where a woman in a brightly coloured floral dress stands with a pram, holding out her hand expectantly to the exiting parishioners. She looks old enough to be a grandmother. The sisters start clapping a *Bulería* rhythm as the congregation, in their fine blouses and shirts, anxiously side-steps them. The lesson has ended. No charity today.

'We've got a tour next month. I want you to join us.'

Carlos knocked back his brandy and indicated to the barman to bring another. The cigarette smoke caught in my throat.

'You'll be famous,' he laughed. '*El Niño Rubio* – the Blond Kid. Great for the *guiris*.'

I was in.

'Two, three gigs a night,' Carlos continued. But I wasn't listening. My mind had returned to the night with Jesús. I wondered if he had had a hand in this, if I'd passed the test. I was pleased, a great chance had finally come. But at what price? Even then, half-stupid as I was with my desire to be accepted, a voice of conscience could still be heard. 'Car thief,' it said. And a wave of guilt and fear would flood through me. 'What if you get caught?'

The group wasn't just about flamenco for me, though. It could give me something far more important. I had made virtually no friends in Madrid, insulated as I was against the world by my unhappiness, and I desperately needed the company of other people and a social life. With Carlos I thought I had found that. And so, I reasoned to myself that I hadn't actually stolen the car: it was Jesús. I'd helped him drive, true, but I had no idea how he'd got it, or what he'd done with it afterwards. Didn't that clear me?

Carlos continued speaking as my educated brain

drew on years of intellectual training to justify what I'd done.

'We're hiring a villa near Valencia.'

Valencia. Just up the coast from Benidorm and Alicante. Not around Madrid. Not in Andalusia. I'd half-expected a tour to head down into the flamenco heartlands. No. Back to the coast. Back to the tourists. And worryingly close to a past I now wanted nothing to do with.

'Oh, and there'll be something in it for you.'

Nothing specific, but I was relieved. My money had almost run out, and I was only just managing to survive by starving and doing odd jobs for Carlota in lieu of rent. I'd lost almost a stone since coming to Madrid, and my clothes were beginning to hang loosely on my body.

'There's just one thing,' Carlos added. 'You need a new guitar – a proper one. We can't have you on stage with that plank of wood you carry around.'

I needed at least 100,000 pesetas to buy a decent guitar. I couldn't ask Carlos for an advance; I had no idea how much he was going to pay me. Besides, I was still definitely a *payo*, an outsider, even if I was on the fringes of the group now. It was clear from the body language.

I thought of Jesús. His attitude towards me had changed, but this would be too much. An important part of the code seemed to involve not being indebted to anyone, which meant not making requests of others. If I had asked, he would almost certainly have helped, but it would not have been right: the relationship would have changed.

Just to get something moving, I decided to advertise

English classes. Language schools were out of the question. I was free, a *flamenco*, I told myself proudly. I couldn't work for anyone but myself. A two-line advert appeared in the local rag, *Anuntis*, with the phone number of the flat. Then I waited.

Days passed without a call, not even a simple enquiry. I started to get angry with Carlota, convinced that she hadn't been picking up the phone.

'There've been no calls, I tell you. No calls.'

'You should get an answering machine.'

'Then *you* pay for it!'

Finally the phone rang. Did I teach German? The old man didn't want English lessons. His daughter had gone to live in Hamburg and he thought he might go and see her one day, maybe next year, or the year after, when his hip was better. Anyway, he thought he might start learning now, because you can't start learning a language too soon, and he wasn't as sharp as he was when he was young, so he might take some time, but if I could be patient with him, and he didn't have too much money either, he was saving for the air-fare, you see. But he'd heard that English and German were very similar, so perhaps . . .

Everything depended on me being able to make enough money to buy the guitar. Otherwise no tour, no flamenco. They would all leave and I would be stuck in a hell-hole of a flat with a mad landlady trying to disinfect cat wounds all day.

Another call. I rushed to the phone.

'*Sí?*'

'I was calling about the English classes. I need four hours a day, intensive tuition. Is your flat very private?'

'Yes, I suppose so. Well – how do you mean?'

203

'Will we be disturbed?'

'No. We'll have a room to ourselves.'

'Good. And will anyone be able to hear us?'

'Well . . . there may be some other people in the flat at the time, but they won't mind.'

'No, no. I need absolute privacy.'

'OK.'

'Good. I'm very looking forward to it. Will you provide all the necessary equipment?'

'I have some text books we can work from.'

'No, I mean *other* equipment.' Silence. 'You know, the *other* equipment.'

'I'm sure I've got everything you need.'

'Very good. Now, about payment.'

'It's 1,000 pesetas an—'

'I was hoping I might do some house cleaning for you instead of payment.'

'House cleaning?'

'You see, I don't have that much money. But I'm very well trained, sir.'

'Look. I don't really need—'

'I can do wonders with my tongue.'

They all thought it was very funny when I told the story later on.

'*Ay!* Sounds like you really hit it off with him,' Javier said.

The laughter stopped. For a moment there was an uneasy silence, then Juanito started playing quietly from the corner, Jesús started singing, and we all took up the cue.

Javier's homosexuality was one of many undercurrents in the group. It was rare for him to make such a slip.

* * *

The solution, when it arrived, came in the form of a Japanese car.

'I needed something simple,' Jesús said. He was almost apologetic it wasn't a BMW or another 'luxury' car. I began to wonder how often he did this. He seemed to view cars as other people did apples on trees.

I drove him out to the western suburbs one night, past the illuminated Atlético stadium, over the Manzanares, and out into the character-free area of tower blocks that hugged the capital like a lifebelt. Jesús gave directions in a haphazard, strangely illogical, way. There was no grid of streets in his head, perhaps he searched for landmarks or memories. I couldn't be sure. He was his more usual reticent self – not reeling out the mad, flowing monologue I had expected.

'Stop!' he cried. We had, quite unexpectedly, reached our destination. I saw a bar – dark, half-lit, as though just closing and in the process of cleaning up – and braked hard. We came to a sharp halt, skidded a little, and there was an almighty smash into the back of us: the car behind had been too slow to react. With a lurch, we shot forward several feet across the road and came to rest.

I lifted my hand to my neck – a pain from the jolt rang inside my skull. Jesús was already out of the car, storming down to the driver behind us.

The shouting began as I checked myself for any damage. Jesús, I was sure, would be inches away from murdering the other driver. But, to my surprise, as I got out I saw that the noise was coming, not from the Gypsy, but from the other man: a slight, thin-mouthed character with a moustache trimmed in bank-manager fashion.

'You lot should be taken off the roads!' he screamed. 'You're only fit to drive bloody donkeys!'

Jesús stood impassive.

'*Me cago en tu padre!* You bastards drive worse than women,' the man went on. He turned to look at me and was confused for a moment. What was a blond foreigner doing there? But he'd found his theme and wasn't going to change.

'You're all bloody criminals . . .'

The door of the bar flew open with a tremendous roar. The man stopped. We all looked round. Four very wide, hairy men in vests stepped out and stood on the pavement opposite us. The leader tilted his chin up in Jesús's direction to ask what was happening, flicking the ash from his cigar menacingly to the floor.

'None of us can drive, he says.'

The men from the bar said nothing, but stood with their arms crossed. The leader sucked hard on the stub resting between his fingers.

'Well, er, yes. That's right!' After a moment's hesitation, the man foolishly decided to continue. 'None of you can drive. I mean look at this. What do you call this? You can't just stop in the middle of the road. Something like this is bound to happen. Don't you think? I mean, really. Surely. N-no . . . ?'

He gave up. The man with the cigar had stepped down, walked across and was now eyeballing him, the burning stub no more than an inch from the well-tended whiskers.

'Get your papers,' said the cigar-man.

'Papers?'

'Insurance.'

The man said nothing, but stared, petrified, into the

206

eyes of the fat Gypsy who seemed about to smother him with his bulk.

'Papers!' the Gypsy whined.

'Listen. I haven't really got . . .' The *payo* was struggling. He looked around him for a way out, but was trapped. It was clear he wasn't completely on the right side of the law himself.

'Look, could – could we . . .' His voice was shaking with fear as he trailed off, his sentence unfinished.

'That car's worth four hundred thousand,' the Gypsy said. It wasn't worth even half that, but I managed to check my look of surprise in time. We couldn't give anything away.

'Look . . .'

The others from the bar began to pace towards the car. It was perfectly timed. Jesús placed his hands carefully into his jacket pockets.

The *payo* took one more look around him. Fear seemed to rise in him like a lava flow, slowly at first, and then with a sudden explosion. He panicked, and capitulated.

'Yes, all right. Christ! I'll have to . . . I'm not carrying that much.'

'Give me your wallet!'

The man's hand went down into his jacket automatically and fished out a leather wallet. The cigar-man took out a credit card and called to his two colleagues. 'Take him to a cash machine.'

They moved off, two of them as though unused to walking, the other like an empty bag. Within a couple of minutes they had returned and a wad was passed over. Nothing was said. The man got back into his car, reversed from the pile of broken glass on the road, and drove away, a screeching noise coming from somewhere underneath the bonnet.

'He won't get far in that,' the cigar-man said. 'The radiator's fucked.' And he turned to go back inside. Jesús motioned for me to stay behind outside. I went to look at the back of our car. It was fine: the back bumper was dented, but it could still be driven.

An hour later Jesús returned. He took the keys from me and we headed back to the centre. Slow driving, not worth trying anything in this car, but there was still the usual disregard for traffic lights, one-way streets, pavements. Again, the pulsating, hypnotic effect of the streetlights passing over my eyes like waves.

'One thing,' I asked. 'How did he know the driver of the car didn't have any insurance?'

'He didn't. But then no-one does. Except rich kids and Cataláns.'

He dropped me off and I slid back inside the flat, screwing my eyes against the ammonia-filled air. I threw my jacket on the bed with a sigh, then looked down. Something had fallen out. Bending over to pick it up, I found an envelope with 150,000 pesetas stuffed inside.

I knew exactly where to go. Juanito and Antonio had both mentioned him. Alejandro, *el Mallorquín*. He had a flat somewhere behind the Plaza de España.

I walked up the narrow streets. There were chickens everywhere; strange, deformed creatures with small bodies and oversized feet. I found the house, walked in through wrought-iron gates, and up to the second floor.

A man with narrow shoulders and a tight-fitting nylon shirt opened the door.

'Alejandro?'

He nodded.

I had imagined an old man with bad eyesight working obsessively over minute veneer carvings. But he was young, much younger than I had expected. I went to shake hands. He took mine limply, as though just to be polite, and beckoned me in.

We passed into a bare room. Hard wooden floors, white walls, a naked table, two chairs, and a kind of bench running down one wall. The air was filled with the most wonderful perfume of raw wood.

'Would you like some tea? I have some mint tea, from Morocco.' He passed into the kitchen and returned some minutes later with a teapot and two mugs. I hadn't had tea made for me since living at Pedro's.

'Come about a guitar, I expect.' His smile exposed crooked teeth.

'Yes, I'm a friend of Juanito and Antonio. They both play with Carlos.'

'Ah, Carlos. Is he still singing?'

We drank the tea. It tasted like sand.

'You'd better come with me, then.'

The workshop was light, whitewashed, with guitars hanging neatly from the walls. I passed along the rows of instruments, eyes agog. It was hard to know where to start.

'What sort of thing are you looking for?' He looked at me sympathetically. I would be happy to buy a guitar from this man, I thought.

'I'm looking for a *negra*,' I said. 'Rosewood back and spruce front.'

The traditional combination for a flamenco guitar – a *blanca* – is a back and sides made of cypress and a spruce top, with a shallow body to give a more percussive feel. Classical guitars, on the other hand, are deeper and often made of rosewood and cedar. The *negra* is a hybrid, with rosewood to give richness, but a spruce soundboard to produce the harsh, bright edge needed for flamenco. And you have to pay a lot to get a good cypress back.

'Yes,' said Alejandro, 'I have a few of those.' He pulled out five guitars from the rack and handed them to me one at a time.

'How do you like the action?'

'Low,' I said. This made it easier to play, especially the *picado* technique, but you often paid by losing some of the higher notes: on cheaper guitars, the strings were so close to the board they would catch on the frets at a certain distance and you would not be able to distinguish between two, possibly three notes. But this also gave a buzzing sound, more like the style of players of the past, such as Sabicas or El Niño Ricardo. The last thing I wanted was for it to sound like a classical guitar. It was a sort of inverse snobbery I had picked up since coming to Spain. Classical guitarists were seen as lightweights; *flamencos* were the 'real men'. While classical guitarists played in a relaxed way, hand over the hole to create a resonant sound, we strained into an unnatural, contorted position, fingers as far behind the soundhole as possible, to give a raw, meaty feel. Some even said that classical guitarists actually envied *flamencos* for their right-hand technique, and that we were the secret, unsung masters of the guitar world – a bit like the anonymous blues players in the Deep South living in their wooden shacks, from whom all the rock 'n' roll greats were said to have stolen their ideas.

I tried the guitars, one by one. It was going to have to be a matter of feeling the right one. I remembered how Juan had always referred to the guitar as *la novia* – his fiancée. I now knew what he meant.

In the end, I was restricted to a choice between two – the only ones in my price range. I played each guitar for half an hour. It was important to take my time, and Alejandro, to my relief, understood this. No pressure, no standing over me. He passed to and fro, smiling every so often in encouragement.

There was little between them, but finally I selected one: the richness of its bass notes was magical, and seemed to fill the room, and resonate through my entire body.

'I am happy you chose this one,' Alejandro said. 'I didn't want to say, but your playing was much more meaningful and stronger with it.'

I handed over the money.

'Look after it,' he laughed as I was leaving. 'It's special for me. I finished it the day my mother died. I made it for her, in her name.'

We arrived at the villa late one night. The place had the false, man-made smell of a recently constructed building: a mixture of cement dust and paint. It was dark, and we all scrambled out of the mini-bus with cases, bags, digs in the ribs, and sore heads. It was like a school outing. Antonio, ever the organiser, went in first to scout the place out while the rest of us stretched our legs in a more carefree manner and Carlos opened a fresh bottle of brandy. I knew immediately that I didn't like the place; there was a superficial feel to it, as though a simple puff of wind might lift it from its foundations and blow it clean away. It was a summer house, built quickly as a simple shelter from the sun, with a patio and white, bare, square-walled rooms. Not enough rooms for all of us, though. Someone was going to have to share. Me, of course. The question was, with whom? In the end, despite all his running about, Antonio was ordered to join me in a boxroom round the back. He was incensed. It wasn't big enough for him on his own, let alone with the *guiri*. I didn't know it then, but he had a clear reason in his own mind why he didn't want to share. The tour was about more than just playing gigs. A few words from Carlos, though, and he seemed to calm down. Again, I was surprised to see how complete Carlos's grip over the group was.

In the bedroom, I unpacked my boots. As well as the new guitar, I had bought some *camperas* – Spanish cowboy boots. They were plain, flat, with only a single strip of leather running down the length of each side from the top to the heel as decoration. They were another symbol of becoming, and belonging, as far as I was concerned. I had built up an image of them as authentically Andalusian from photographs, TV, and people I'd seen walking in the street. They were heavy on my feet and I wanted them to give me a greater connection to the earth, to root me somehow. But when I tried them on, they were ridiculously uncomfortable, too narrow for my wide, Anglo-Saxon feet. I would break them in, I told myself. Spanish leather was supposedly the best in the world. A folk-singing uncle of mine had even sung a song about it – about the lady of the manor who was swept off her feet by the Gypsy Davy, and how her husband rode off to look for her and found her by a camp-fire:

Take off, take off your buckskin gloves
made of Spanish leather.
Give to me your lily-white hand
and back right home we'll travel.
Back right home we'll ride.

But she didn't go back. The draw of the Gypsy way
was too strong for her – and her husband returned to
his sedentary life alone.

Jesús arrived later that night in another car. He had
a double room to himself and called me in for a line of
cocaine that was carefully drawn on a plastic table by
the window. Before long, Carlos's wife, María-José,
poked her head round the door.

'*A jalar!*' she said. Jesús got up to go.

I didn't understand and as we headed out to the
patio, I asked Jesús what she'd said.

'Eat. It's *Caló*: Gypsy language. She's telling us to
eat.'

I had gathered that Carlos's term for me – *churumbel*
– was some sort of Gypsy word, but had assumed the
phrases they used that I didn't understand were
simply Spanish words I had yet to learn. As it turned
out, a lot of the colloquialisms I had already picked up
were of *Caló* origin: *sobar* for sleep, *chungo* for bad,
parné for money. But as I listened harder to their conversations, I discovered that all kinds of words and
phrases in the flamenco songs we were listening to –
particularly the more modern stuff from bands like
Ketama – that previously I had been unable to understand began to make sense. Like the word *camelar* – to
love.

Mira si yo te camelo, te camelo de verdad.

Every other song seemed to use it.

Few Gypsies seemed to speak pure *Caló* – it was more a source for their own slang, which they would interject amongst the ordinary Spanish they spoke every day. But it was a badge, a sign of belonging, and, more importantly, of not being a *payo*.

Jalar, jalar. I rolled the word over my tongue as we headed out for food on the patio.

After the meal we rehearsed. But it was more serious this time; the last opportunity before playing in front of an unknown audience.

'*Churumbel!*' Carlos called me over. 'I want you to play the *Alegría* with Javier on your own.' I knew the piece. It was short, a kind of filler, and we had been playing it as a group for weeks. But I was shocked to think I was going to be put in the spotlight like this. I nodded and the rest of them filed out of the room. We were left alone to practise together.

'Just you and me, eh?' Javier said under his breath and winked. He could joke with me, but there was a sharpness to his humour.

'*Venga.* Let's start. I'm sure you can do it.' He stood with his back to me, waving his arm at his side in time.

'*Siete ocho nueve diez un DOS.*'

I plunged in, but got no more than a few seconds into the piece.

'No, no. For God's sake! Keep in time!' he shouted over his shoulder.

We tried again, and got slightly further.

'*Compás! Compás!* Come on, Jason, do me a favour and keep time, will you.' His lips turned down in a sulky frown of indignation.

I tapped my foot on the floor like a metronome to make sure of the rhythm. It wasn't gelling, but I couldn't feel where I was losing it either.

'Jason!' He stopped again. 'Look, I'm sure you can do better than this. I'm quite sure. Carlos wouldn't have asked you to come along otherwise. You must keep the *compás*.'

I snarled as he turned his back on me to start once more.

'Now let's take it from the *solo de pie* again, then come in with the *Bulería* at the end.' I placed my hands ready to play. There was a tap on my shoulder. Turning, I saw Juanito at my side, a big smile on his face. He motioned for me to pass him the guitar. I handed it over quickly and he began to accompany Javier's dancing behind his back. He kept it simple, even throwing in a couple of dud notes for authenticity's sake. But it only lasted a few moments. Once again Javier came to a halt.

'*Me cago en la leche*. I told . . .' He turned, and with a look of horror saw Juanito there with the guitar in his hands.

'B-but . . .' He stood motionless, crestfallen for a moment, with a look of sheer disbelief. Then, with a rush, the blood and anger flooded his face. '*Hijos de puta!*' he cried and stormed off.

Juanito and I just couldn't stop laughing after that. For weeks all we had to say was '*hijos de puta*' in a fake Javier voice and we'd be on the floor.

Javier hardly ever spoke to me after that.

What surprised me most about the tour was the speed at which it all happened. It was like our life in Madrid, but wound up like a spring and set off to run at three times the usual pace. We played two, usually three gigs a night, starting at ten in the evening and not finishing until four or five in the morning. Sound check, playing, packing up, dashing somewhere else, unpacking, playing, packing up . . . Most of the time, I had no idea where the venues were.

The first night was a shock. By the end of it, my hands were shaking from so much exposure in such a short period. I felt wrecked. But it simply carried on. This was work. Most of the time we were at small places: low-key brothels, bars, cafés, with the occasional concert hall, local festival, or wedding. The gigs themselves were fairly mechanical affairs. I had been expecting something else: real tension, of the kind I thought preceded all creative endeavours. But after the first couple of nights, I began to calm down, and understood that this was just a job, what they did for a living. You couldn't worry about how well you were playing, or how much feeling there was. We weren't artists, more like craftsmen, making ends meet. And once you had played and mastered a piece more than a certain number of times, it was difficult not to start switching off while on stage and going into autopilot. Antonio suffered the worst. He played with a look of utter boredom on his face.

At the end of the night we would return to the villa, change out of our black and white costumes – simple shirt and trousers – and stay up till at least ten or eleven in the morning, drinking, playing and singing. This was when the real music was made: a time for new pieces or the *palos* only we liked; the ones the audiences wouldn't appreciate. Then we'd sleep till about four in the afternoon, have a shower, practise some more, eat, and it was time to go once again. It was hectic, pressured, non-stop. And what made it possible, I realised, was the constant supply of cocaine

– always there, keeping me going like some sort of magic fuel. Jesús would provide the supply, and we would take it in his room or on the patio. I had thought that we were all on it, but was surprised when I later discovered that it was only really Jesús, Antonio, Javier and me – the younger ones. Juanito never touched it, and Carlos always stuck to brandy. As for La Andonda, she didn't need it; she was manic enough. I felt foolish, in a way. Perhaps I'd only imagined the group pressure to take it. But I was hooked now, and life on tour dragged me deeper and deeper under the drug's self-aggrandising influence.

Meanwhile, we all ate together, played together, woke up together, slept the same hours, turning ourselves into some sort of collective creature, a unit in which all individuality was lost. The thinking was done for us. We simply obeyed and fell into line. Back into the bus again, another hour's drive to the next gig, unpacking, playing, packing up, and then moving on once again.

Occasionally something would break the routine. The real reason why Antonio was so upset about sharing a room became clearer one night when he managed to impress a girl in the audience with his fancy playing; he forgot all about the rest of us and went off on some musical tour of his own. She later showed him her appreciation in private – it turned out she had a room of her own they could use – but in the process, he provoked La Andonda's fury for making her look a fool on stage. It was something she would never forget.

For the most part, though, there was almost no time to do anything else but play. Carlos would entertain us in the early mornings back at the villa, sitting on the balcony doing impressions of other singers: El Lebrijano, El Indio Gitano, or a high-pitched Pedro Pinto – voices from the past.

Antonio would complain. He wanted us to launch off into a more jazzy sound, in the way that guitarists such as Tomatito were doing.

'Look, guys, like, we really need to be doing more, like, modern material. You know? I mean, look, we could be like Ketama, or Karakatamba.'

'Karakatamba,' Carlos snorted mockingly. It was taken for granted that Antonio was simply looking for a vehicle for his own, more elaborate, playing style.

'Hey, listen. People like that are the future, you know?'

'Play your modern material in your own time. But here, we play flamenco.'

Antonio went quiet at this point, then stormed out. We all carried on talking: this kind of thing happened every day.

'It's a shame they have to get so upset,' Juanito said. 'Carlos is right: Karakatamba – pfff.' He shrugged. 'But Ketama? Now they can play. They're from the Carmona family. Granada Gypsies. Good *flamencos*.'

The sun was already high in the sky when I knocked back the last of my drink and went to find sanctuary in the darkness of my bedroom.

'This is flamenco, *churumbel*.' Carlos grabbed my arm as I passed him. His breath smelt like a distillery. 'This. This life. Not all that shit you were up to in Alicante. You want to experience real flamenco? You want to know what *duende* is really about? It's about this. It's about living on the edge – *a tope*. It's about singing so hard you can't speak any more. Or playing

218

until your fingers bleed. It's about taking yourself as far as you can go, and then going one step further.'

At that point, I believed him.

Jesús continued much as he had in Madrid. The group's travels around the country were further grist to his mill, supplying him with opportunities to pick up 'prizes'. He was still cautious about the others knowing about my involvement, and his behaviour towards me when we were with them hadn't changed from the beginning. Every so often, we would return from the gigs in a different car, and such was the curtain of silence surrounding his activities, there would be no comment. It was out of bounds.

The high-speed driving was exhilarating, and I further buried any doubts by pretending the cars weren't stolen at all, or that Jesús would return them once we had finished. We were just joy-riding, having fun: a necessary distraction from the boredom of touring. Somewhere in the back of my mind, a voice questioning how I had fallen into all of this tried to make itself heard, but it stayed in the background, barely audible above all the noise.

One Sunday night we played a gig at a home for deaf people. We didn't realise what was wrong at first. Then La Andonda noticed their hearing aids and the penny dropped. We cranked the amplifiers up to maximum and deafened ourselves in the process. When we finished, they all sat there stony-faced, not knowing when to clap, or even if the concert had come to an end. Javier took the initiative and stood in the middle of the stage, motioning to everyone to start the applause, and finally it came. But the rest of us were already packing up and getting ready to leave. It was our only show that night, and we wanted to enjoy an evening off.

As we were passing outside, Jesús motioned to me to follow him. I handed my guitar to Antonio and we left, walking away into the hot, dark streets. We usually cruised the quiet residential areas, looking for the best cars, but sometimes we'd find something right where you'd least expect it – a car outside a nightclub, where the owner had just popped inside, leaving the engine running. I was on watch-duty, scanning the streets, peering round corners, pricking up my ears for the sound of a car, a police patrol, anything. At which point I would give the coded whistle and vanish into a doorway until it was safe to reappear once again and continue the hunt. If there was ever any crisis of conscience, it would emerge in these seconds spent alone waiting for Jesús to appear. For a few moments, a moral anxiety would force itself upon me, strengthened by vivid images of getting caught by the police, but then it would vanish again as soon as we were inside the car. After all, we only took cars from rich people. They were insured or could afford the loss. There was no money in it for me. This was the price of my acceptance.

Jesús beckoned me over and I climbed into a BMW.

The streets were narrow here and too choked with other cars to drive fast. We headed away and out into the hilly countryside. Jesús accelerated along the empty, blackened roads, headlights streaming ahead as we reached up to 70, 80 miles an hour, bulleting down what were little more than windy, unmanageable tracks. Even in a car like this, it was a bumpy ride. He pushed the accelerator closer to the floor, throwing my head back. Through the window, I could see the full moon.

'Dad died – a night like this, just like this, cold, the fucker, left us, my mother, me, two sisters, no money, spent it all on drink, fucker, had to go out and work, only thirteen, needed *parné*, always needing money, can't get by in this *puto mundo* – this fucking world – without money, it's what you need, to keep you going, you want some money, I can lend you 50,000 if you want, got it in my pocket, ha, ha, you're not going to get me, you fuckers, I bet the fucker who had this car was a real fucker, bet he cheated on his wife, bet he had his mistress right there on the back seat, giving it to her, one-two, one-two, taking her *por el culo*, up the arse in the back of his BMW, ha, ha, *gilipollas*.'

'Perhaps he was gay.'

'You're absolutely right, you're absolutely right, he might have been gay – gay fucker, ha ha. Ugh! I'm driving a gay car! Ha ha. *Joder!* Fuck, this thing can move, look at the acceleration on that. *Joder.*'

We scraped a tree that was leaning partly over the edge of the road. Jesús looked round to the side it had hit.

'Have to get that fixed up quick. Can't sell the fucker with chipped paintwork.'

We drove on, speeding in the empty, white light of the moon.

Something appeared up ahead: lights, vehicles. It was a roadblock.

'Slow down,' I called.

'It's all right, I've already seen it.' His voice was calm and professional again. We stopped several yards short, the headlights on full beam.

'Quick. Change seats,' he said. We crossed over

clumsily, catching ourselves on the gear-stick. I could see someone approaching the car. It was the *Guardia Civil*; gorillas with machine-guns.

'Talk *guiri* to him,' Jesús ordered.

I felt a thudding in my throat as a heavily armed man in green uniform tapped on the window. My greatest fear was finally coming true.

'Good evening, sir.'

'*Buenas noches*,' I said in my thickest English accent, looking up with a smile. He would want to ask questions, want to know why I was driving at this time of night, why I was in a Spanish registered car, would want to see my documents, had probably heard us scraping the tree up the road, and would probably want to know who my travelling companion was. But I also knew from my time at the *Costa Gazette* that they were probably on the lookout for ETA suspects. Not stupid Englishmen. I had to get in there quickly, it was our only chance.

'We're trying to find the Valencia road,' I said before he could say anything. 'I've been driving around for some time now and I can't find it. Could you possibly point me in the right direction. My wife's just had a baby.'

For a moment, I thought I might have given the game away. It was a stupid thing to say, but fear had made me blurt it out. The guard hesitated for a minute, as though it were the last thing he had expected to hear, then snapped to attention in honour of my new role in life as a father, and barked out the directions. I was going the wrong way, he said, would have to turn back in the opposite direction.

I spun the car around and set off, leaving just the slightest trace of rubber behind on the tarmac. The roadblock receded in the rear-view mirror. I could barely breathe for shock.

'Nice work, Dad,' Jesús said. 'Good job they didn't get me. Fine time they'd have with me. Driving for fifteen years and never had a licence. Ha! Fuckers . . .'

We drove up to an ordinary modern block of flats in a bland neighbourhood on the outskirts of Valencia. The flat was small and dim; there were no lights anywhere. Every room was lit with plain, white candles, with the odd red, blue, or twisted translucent one to break the monotony. The smoke made the air thick and heavy, and the walls looked grey and greasy in the haze.

The dealer was a skinny *payo* with a forked, scraggly beard and trembling hands. His black hair fell from a central parting down to his shoulders, making him look like a sort of walking pyramid. He and Jesús greeted each other in the twilight warmly, and we moved into the kitchen. A candelabra emitted a gloomy glow over a wooden table and chairs.

We sat at the table and snorted a line of cocaine each. I watched as the puddles of wax on the floor slowly grew with each drip from the candles, reflecting a distorted image of the candelabra.

The dealer brought out a plastic bag from another room.

'It's good,' he said.

His trembling hands shook nervously as he passed it over. Jesús took it and laid it on the table, opening it as carefully as he could. He reached for a knife from his pocket, then flicked it open to fish out some of the white crystals. The dealer looked away, stood up suddenly, and walked over to the cupboard, fiddling with the cups and plates.

'Hard to keep everything straight when you live on your own,' he said unnecessarily.

Wax was now falling onto Jesús's black hair, but he didn't seem to notice. His attention was totally fixed on the little pile lying on the end of the blade. He lifted it up, brought it to his nose, then sniffed it lightly.

There was a smash. Three plates had fallen out of the dealer's hands and were lying in pieces around the kitchen floor.

'What the fuck are you playing at?' Jesús screamed.

'Sorry, Jesús, sorry.'

'This is crap! You trying to fob me off with rubbish or something? *Me cago en tus muertos*, I shit on your ancestors . . .' He leapt out of his chair, knife in hand, and began to lunge towards the dealer, who was cowering in the corner.

'Jesús!' I cried. In an instant I saw what was about to happen and had managed to hurdle the chair and grab his wrists from behind as the blade sliced forward.

The dealer collapsed into the corner. Jesús lunged again, his body taut, muscles like cords. I hauled him back, and he struggled to free himself from my grip, thrashing from side to side. I was taller than him, though, and the drugs had given me a nervous strength. I was more worried about the knife, about not getting caught on the end of it myself.

The dealer sat up and began crying.

'Jesús, it's me. For God's sake, Jesús. It's me.' He quivered, white-faced, shaking with fear. 'Jesús. You can't do this to me. You don't know what it's like . . .'

'You son of a whore! *Me cago en tus muertos*.' Jesús bellowed the Gypsy curse, still wriggling to get free.

'Come on Jesús. You can sell that on. Please, I really need the money.'

Jesús began shouting again and the dealer slid back into the corner, making himself small and sobbing violently.

Jesús seemed about to lunge again. With a final effort, I steered him out through the kitchen door and into the corridor, then threw him into the stairwell, shutting the door as he stumbled backwards, dizzy with rage.

I ran back inside. The dealer was still in the corner, crying.

'You OK?'

He said nothing.

I checked around for blood to see if the knife had touched him. He was fine. I made to leave.

'T-tell Jesús, please, tell him. I love him. He's my best friend.'

I left some money on the table as I went out.

Jesús was outside in the street, waiting for me. He seemed calmer now, not the bloodthirsty lunatic of only a few moments ago.

'You shouldn't have done that.'

'I did what I had to do.' I was surprised at myself. I had never answered him like that.

We walked off, neither of us saying a word. Then, as we reached the car, I felt his hand on my shoulder. I turned and unexpectedly he put his arms around me and embraced me. I stood awkwardly for a moment – an Englishman once more, stiff with embarrassment, caught off my guard by a foreigner – until my arms relented and I returned the embrace. This was Jesús, who never seemed to need anyone. An independent Gypsy, weaving his way slyly through a strange, adverse world where he didn't really belong – a world he rejected, and which, in its turn, rejected him. But all he wanted now was this.

We stood together, patting each other gently on the back, until at length, he pulled away.

'You drive,' he said. 'I need to sleep.'

chapter EIGHT

Por Soleá Por Bulería

Compañera de mi alma,
Diós te había dao sabiduría.
Que una palabrita tuya
vale por doscientas mías.

Companion of my soul,
God has given you wisdom.
So just one of your words
is worth two hundred of mine.

*T*he guitar barely left my hands now. I felt its absence when it wasn't there, searching for it in my sleep as I mentally rehearsed, fingers twitching over invisible frets. Playing became my main means of expressing moods and feelings, my hands naturally falling into *palos* or chord sequences that seemed to come from some previously unacknowledged part of myself – a more confident, self-aware yet vulnerable side of me. I'd wander around the villa working out new *falsetas*, or trying to perfect my rhythm, perched on a table or sitting on the edge of my over-sprung bed. The acoustics were particularly good in the loo, as the closed-in walls created a kind of echo chamber that made the music resonate through my entire body. The others laughed but with a tone of reproach – this was just a little too weird.

But playing, driving, or just stoned out of my head, a need was growing inside me. Subtle at first, I felt it only in short flashes or absent-minded moments as I was cleaning my teeth, waking up from a siesta, or feeling sunshine on my face for the first time in days and blinking heavily with eyes accustomed to the dark. Like a drowning man conscious only momentarily that he cannot breathe, passing the rest of his time unaware of his steady progress downwards, breathing water in place of the air he needs.

La Andonda realised there was something wrong, she could see that I was becoming restless. One afternoon she decided to teach me knife-throwing, presenting me with an old, rusty knife she had never used. We spent a couple of hours in the garden flicking it into the ground, she with a deft wrist action I had expected of her, while my own efforts resulted in the knife bouncing around in the dirt on almost every attempt. It was as though she understood that I needed something else, that I was no longer satisfied. And while I appreciated her kindness, there was more to it than the desire for a new distraction.

One afternoon I set off away from the villa, walking on my own into town. The sun was intense but I felt a need to get out.

The old baroque church with its blue-tiled dome was surrounded by soulless blocks of brick, five or six storeys high, punctuated by aluminium windows with cheap pink and green sheets pegged out to dry in the dust and sand. Stepping over an upturned, broken child's buggy lying among a pile of plastic cups, I headed towards a phone box in the middle of the blanched, empty street. It was like an oven inside. I pulled out a handful of change and began dialling.

I hadn't spoken to my family for months. After the initial surprise, they began filling me in on what they were doing, asking about my life in Spain. It was difficult to reply: I had told them little about what I was up to and now, just when I felt a deep need for conversation and to be able to speak to someone about what I was feeling, the distance that had grown up between us seemed insurmountable. It was a strange sensation: a strong desire to connect with my former home and a simultaneous awareness of how far away from it I had grown. I was in Spain now, this was my life, but I was isolated.

The phone went dead. I had no more change. Light-headed from the oppressive heat in the phone box, I stepped out into the street; into the piercing, exposing light.

'Where've you been?' everyone cried when I returned to the villa. 'We couldn't find you.'

'Of course you couldn't find me. I went for a walk.' It was unusual for me to be sharp with them.

'A walk? At this time? *Estás chalao* – crazy. Come in and have some *potaje*. María-José has just put it out on the table. We were going to start without you.'

I fell back into line and ate my soup.

It was our last gig of the night. I was already beginning to feel tired. Strange, as we were only really halfway through our day. The bus stumbled along. Carlos had drunk too much brandy, but it was the only way he could sing. Never sober – it just wouldn't happen, he said.

We came to the edge of a town. Lights, blocks of flats, car-lined cicatrised streets. It looked fairly ordinary. A bump lifted us off our seats momentarily. I looked out of the window and saw we had crossed a little train track. There was a station. The name on it flashed by too quickly for me to see it, but I already knew – we were in Benidorm.

I gazed in horror as the familiar roads appeared

230

on the other side of the glass: bars, English theme pubs, the infamous 'Cally Londreez', the beach-front lined with palm trees, the discos full of pink tourists sweating out all the lotions and creams they had smeared on their skins in the evening to sooth the burning of the afternoon sun. I was caught between wanting to peer at this past world and a strong desire to drop deeper into my seat and vanish. But my curiosity won, and I began scanning for familiar faces. I might catch Jonathan and Barry out having a late drink, or some of the characters from the town hall. I remembered my desperate flight away from here. I couldn't expect a warm welcome if I did bump into anyone.

And then there was Lola.

I hadn't thought about her for at least two weeks, the longest time since I'd left. The mixture of pain and passion surfaced with a jolt. We were not in Alicante, I told myself. Not Alicante. There was no reason for her to be here. She didn't even like Benidorm. But my emotions wouldn't listen, and were busy tightening their grip. We were a flamenco outfit. There was every chance that she would be drawn here to see a concert, would be sitting in the audience, was probably there already. I started to feel sick.

'I saw Camarón sing here once,' Carlos said. Everyone went silent at the mention of the great man.

'He played out at the bullring. Gypsies there from all over. Everyone was going mad. It was incredible. People trying to get in any way they could. One kid tried to get in on a ladder and broke his leg when the security guard kicked it out from under him. It was like rising up to heaven and seeing the face of God.

'Afterwards we all left and went out into the streets,

full of disgusting white *guiris* falling over and being sick. I tell you, it was the worst experience of my life.' Everyone grunted in sympathy.

'*Churumbel!*' he called back to me. 'You must feel at home here, eh? Among all your *compatriotas*? How does it feel? Make you homesick?' They all laughed.

'Sure you don't want us to stop off and pick up some "feesh and cheeps"?' He pronounced the last words slowly and deliberately, his mouth unused to the foreign sound. I was surprised he had even heard of fish and chips.

'Or shall we go to the chemist's for some skin creams?' More laughter. I was beginning to wonder if he was taking out his anger from all those years ago on me.

'You're gonna sit up near the front tonight – next to Jesús. There'll be lots of *guiris* in the audience. They'll love it. I want you to talk to them in *guiri*. Introduce us, that sort of thing.'

If Lola was there, I wouldn't be able to hide.

The venue was on the sea-front, one of the hundreds of bars, cafés and restaurants that lined the esplanade. As expected, a lot, though not all, of the audience were foreigners. Some English, Germans, Scandinavians. I tried to explain to Carlos that it was probably not worth me saying anything. No common language.

'These people are here to get pissed and have a laugh. They're not interested in us,' I protested.

He grunted and looked away.

'Why else do you think you're here?' he said.

I was stung, but put it down to the brandy, and the memories of the night of Camarón.

Backstage, for the first time, I asked Jesús for some cocaine. He gave me some without hesitation, but there was a question in his face.

*　*　*

Carlos led us onto the stage, brandy bottle in hand, followed by Jesús, then me. I felt totally out of place, like a peasant invited to dine at the landowner's table. This was against the pecking order – a pecking order which, tonight especially, I was more than happy to remain the same. The drug was giving me its usual lift; the comforting boost of confidence and rush of self-belief. But not for long. Its effects seemed to last shorter and shorter periods of time.

I stepped forward, scanning the audience for those large brown eyes, the flash of deep red hair, but saw nothing.

'Ladies and gentlemen,' I heard my voice, high-pitched and nervous, casting out like a thin, feeble net. 'We are gathered here to hear one of the finest flamenco performances in Spain today.' There was a titter. I blushed. The lights were hot, burning on my forehead as the warm air flowed in from the open door. More people were arriving, sitting down. A man and a woman. I peered into the dark, trying to see who it was.

'Er, all the way from Madrid, the capital Madrid, for your very delight . . .' The woman was standing up to take her coat off. I couldn't see her properly. Damn it. If only she would turn around, I might be able to see her in profile. I peered again. From the back of her head, it could well be her. But there was a knock behind me – I was being told to hurry up.

'Carlos and his Flamenco Friends!'

The audience clapped enthusiastically, more out of relief that the half-wit making a speech was finally finished. I slumped back into my chair, my mind wandering to that distant corner, and the female

233

late-comer. I couldn't see her at all now, there were too many faces in the way. Had she seen me?

The gig got under way. I had other things to think about, and the drug made it very difficult to concentrate on anything with any clarity. Antonio was playing the opening of the first piece, then Carlos started and we had to follow him, his pace and signals. I heard him filling the room with his low voice, screwing up his face in an attempt to create the necessary intensity; the emotional concentration that was fundamental for any flamenco performance, good or bad. Without it, the music simply became a meaningless cacophony.

Perhaps it was the thought that Lola might be there, or somehow reconnecting with my earlier life by arriving in Benidorm like this, but as I played, something unexpected happened. No longer the intense concentration of before. The mechanicality I had seen in some of the others – especially Antonio – I was beginning to experience myself. The same songs, the same rhythms, the same chords. I had played them all so often now, I could almost, almost, manage them in my sleep. We were all there, dressed in our uniforms, the only break of colour the ever-present turquoise bandana on Javier's head and La Andonda's red and white dress. She was clapping and calling out the words of encouragement – the *jaleo* – to squeeze out a drop of enchantment for this emotionally dead audience. Graceless as she was, she could do it sometimes – usually when she was annoyed with someone, dancing back at the villa. She would lift her skirt menacingly at the knee and thigh and fill us all with some strange, twisted erotic energy. But tonight? I doubted it. She didn't look angry enough.

With a great rolling *triple* Antonio finished his *falseta* and Carlos took up the song once more. For the first time, I listened with a critical ear. I had never wondered what I thought of his singing before. My concern had always been to ingratiate myself with him, win his approval, to be accepted into his circle. But now as he sang, it dawned on me that this was really only a mediocre singer whose band I was in. His voice was flexible – he demonstrated that with his impersonations of other singers on the patio at the villa – but in concert? It was thin, sharp. It never moved me in any way. The facial contortions he performed to express feeling were only skin deep, but they did the job. Our audiences were mostly made up of tourists and ordinary Spaniards – who probably knew as much about flamenco as the tourists – or people at private parties more interested in the person standing next to them. The truth was, we were just so much entertainment, wallpaper – colourful wallpaper, but little more.

La Andonda was on stage. She had changed her clothes for the *Farruca*. Dressed as a man, she danced a male dance, stripped of the fiery hand movements with more footwork and a leaner line. Unfortunately La Andonda herself was not lean, and, squeezed into the tight-fitting black trousers and even tighter black top, she was all buttocks and breasts. She loved it, thought it was the best thing she did, but you could hear the collective groan from the rest of the group every time she stood up to waddle her way through the piece. The people here, at least, seemed to appreciate it, and when she finished the applause was tremendous. One man at the back even wolf-whistled. La Andonda lapped it up. But for the rest of us, it only served to demonstrate the ignorance of the audience.

'We should get her and Javier to swap places,' Jesús whispered to me.

It was important to have a crowd that knew and understood what it was listening to. A good performance was a dialogue, and could only be achieved if the audience understood its role. The band was the prime mover; but without something coming back, it could only play, dance and sing. There was nothing else – no passion, only an outer shell. Looking over at Antonio, his face dull with boredom, waiting anxiously for his next chance to show off, I began to doubt if this lot could ever produce anything special, whatever the circumstances.

'The problem with this bunch is they don't know how to listen,' Carlos said as he sat down after his final song.

Yes, I thought, but do we really know how to play?

When we finished, the lights went on and I stood up quickly to get a glimpse of the woman in the corner. She was sitting with a drink in her hand, her face half-covered. But the hair was wrong. Too dark, not red. She put the glass down and caught me staring at her. I looked away. It wasn't Lola.

We drove up the hill, away from the coast and out of Benidorm. This time I didn't look out of the window, and allowed the streetlights, the bars and tourists to pass by unobserved. It was all dead to me.

The following day, Carlos called me over. He was sitting in his usual place on the patio, next to the jasmine plant that somehow, miraculously, had managed to grow and survive. None of us were looking after it.

'*Churumbel*. I want to talk to you.' His thick features

glistened in the fading light, an oily film covering his skin as he drew on his cigar. I walked over to him. He sat back on his chair.

'Sit down there.'

I sat.

'Cigarette.' It wasn't a question.

'You know what the most important thing is in all this?'

I shook my head.

'*Pasión*. You've got to have passion.'

With a sense of guilt, my mind went back to the previous evening. Had my thoughts not been so silent after all? It wasn't always easy to tell.

'I was fourteen when I decided I wanted to be a *cantaor*. Course, I'd sung before then, but it was more like a game, childish. But one day my mother took my hand and said, "Son, you see that eagle up there. You know why he flies? Because he has no choice, because it's his destiny, because he's an eagle, and that's what eagles do." '

I was wondering where this eagle was supposed to have been. I didn't know Carlos had been brought up in the middle of the Sierra Nevada. He seemed pretty urban to me. Still . . .

'And she said, "You're going to have to decide what you are. If you want to sing, you have to know it in your heart. You have to do it because there's nothing else you can do. You have to do it because it's what you are." '

'And since that day, I've felt it here.' He pummelled the centre of his chest with his fist. 'Right here. And you know what, *churumbel*? Since that day, I can see it in others too. I can see if someone has it in their heart.'

He stood up and started unbuttoning his shirt to reveal an off-white, immensely hairy torso, half-covered by a greying vest. Removing the shirt completely, he handed it to me without a word.

I had heard of this. It was a way of symbolising acceptance, like sharing bread and salt in some parts of the Middle East. But it had always been described as an interesting anthropological detail. I had no idea it was still practised, and it took me a few moments to work out what was happening.

After a moment's hesitation, I stood up and took the sweaty shirt from him.

'Thank you,' I said, looking down.

'What you did last night touched me. It touched me here.' His fist was beating his chest again.

'The way you stood up there and – I don't understand *guiri*, but I know that what you said, you said it with feeling, with passion. And that's what counts, *churumbel*. Last night you had feeling. I could tell from your playing. Don't think I wasn't listening to you. I can hear you, you know, even when you're furthest away from me. But last night was very good. Last night was special.'

I crumpled the hot, damp shirt in my hands and looked up.

'Now go and fetch me some more brandy.'

The shirt was the kind of admittance I had longed for. I took it gratefully, but there was a hint of insincerity about the act – a trait I recognised more and more in Carlos – which niggled at me. My fear was that I *was* only there for the tourists, as he'd said the night before; an adornment, or freak. A blond foreigner playing basic flamenco accompaniment for a two-bit band. But for my novelty value, I might never have got here.

Antonio was angry when he found out. Carlos had never treated *him* like that, and he was the principal guitarist.

'I think, you know, he likes you.' His main grudge was with Carlos, but he was annoyed with me too.

I sometimes wondered if Antonio wasn't the real outsider. He wanted respect as a great guitarist and all he got were complaints that his *compás* was too fast or too slow. He practised a lot, working out ever more complicated *falsetas* to show off his skills. But it was a case of trying too hard, it seemed. Nobody wanted a *manitas de plata* – silver hands – in the group. It was all about singing and dancing and putting on a good show for the audience. The guitarists were just the musical background. There were times when the guitar element was important, but not many. This was not a modern flamenco set-up, where *tocaores* had become as important, or more important, than singers and dancers. It was a fairly traditional, basic flamenco that we played. Nothing too spicy, or innovative, or ornamental. Antonio simply didn't fit in.

The truth was, though, that none of us really fitted in. Javier the homosexual, La Andonda the homicidal maniac, Juanito the cripple, Jesús the cocaine-snorting car-thief. All misfits, in our own way.

I crashed back in through the high, narrow, wooden doors at Carlota's flat and was greeted by the familiar sting in the eyes as the ammonia hit. She had kept the room for me while I had been away, letting it only for a couple of months to a friend from the Basque country who was attending a course over the summer. We had grown used to each other, and although she needed the money, she preferred a familiar face and wanted to avoid the stress of taking on a stranger.

'Oh, you're back! How lovely to see you. Come into the kitchen. You must tell me all about it.'

I dumped my bags and followed her through. The cats leapt out of my way in panic. 'Bloody fools!' she cried. It was a good day. The closer to the cats she was, the more you knew you had to be on your guard.

I walked over to the window and looked out into the murky street. A junkie was sitting opposite, against a wall, inserting a needle into a much-abused vein, blood rushing into the syringe as he found his spot. I turned round. Carlota was sitting by the table, pulling on her cheap cigarette.

'*Bueno*. Well, then. Tell me about the tour. Are you famous yet?' she asked me eagerly. I sat down to begin. There was the sound of water pouring from somewhere. I looked at the tap. Then a reflection from underneath Carlota's chair caught my eye. A stream of urine was flowing unhindered onto the floor from the cat on her lap.

'Excuse me a moment,' and she hurried off to the bathroom. I mopped it up quickly.

'Will you have a drink?' she asked, scuttling back.

'Yes. I will thanks. Back in a moment.' I had my own call of nature to answer.

The cheap, red, plastic loo seat must have finally given way, and had been replaced with a fluorescent green one. But apart from that, everything seemed, as I eased myself down, more or less the same. The same grimy floor, the same broken mirror, the same noise of buses and mopeds coming from the open window.

My hand reached round for the loo paper. It had all gone. Carlota must have forgotten to buy some. I thrust my hand into a pocket to see if I had anything suitable, pulling out what looked like a flyer. It was a glossy advert for the Gypsy Kings I must have picked up from somewhere. I thought for a moment, then gladly applied it to its newly found function.

chapter NINE

Por Taranta

En diciendo ¡gente ar torno!
todos los mineros tiemblan
al vé que tienen su vía
a voluntá de una cuerda.

Calling 'Get in line'
the miners tremble
at the sight of their lives
hanging by a thread.

'Come on. To work.'

Jesús came to pick me up, carless.

'You must ask your friend to come in, Jason. He doesn't always have to wait for you outside, you know,' said Carlota. Expecting Jesús to sit and drink tea while fighting off vicious incontinent cats did not seem like a good idea. I looked at the clock: it was three in the morning.

'Maybe another time,' I said, stepping out the door. The end of the tour and returning to Madrid hadn't slowed things down as I had hoped.

We started walking. It was a week night and the city was still half-deserted as people delayed their return home from holidays on the coast. A couple of Gypsies by the side of the road were furtively syphoning off petrol from a parked car, sucking the liquid into an old water-bottle into which it flowed, bright greeny-pink. For a moment I thought Jesús might greet them, but he passed as though they weren't there. The sense of fraternity amongst Gypsies I had expected to come across was hard to find.

We passed out of my quarter, away from the grubby whores and pimps, onto the Gran Vía. I watched the traffic go by in a haze: bright buses filled with hot, frustrated passengers; three-wheeled tin vans put-putting back and forth; identical old couples walking arm in arm. I felt cut off from it all. The images were obstacles, things to avoid or go round. People, cars, trees, buildings: nothing had any reality. Just a dream-scape passing in front of me. Occasionally a luxury car would flash by – one that might interest Jesús – potential targets to be swooped upon.

'No problem with that one. Piece of cake. He hasn't even got an immobiliser. Switch the fuses and we're there.' The thoughts of a car-thief were racing inside me.

We carried on down to Cibeles and up the Castellana: Jesús's preferred hunting ground. But this time he carried on further, pacing solidly up the boulevard towards the more modern part of the city, with its glistening tower blocks, expensive houses, and the possibility of even richer pickings. I followed reluctantly, yet obediently, in the oppressive night heat.

There was always a switch when the moment arrived – from simply walking, to hunting. Jesús's body movements would change; one moment an ordinary man moving forwards, the next an animal, a leopard, shoulders hunched, head lowered, feet arched, stalking over the ground as though ready to pounce at any second. Anyone else watching might not have noticed anything beyond a look of menace in his eyes. But it was dark, there was no-one around, and it was my job to keep it that way.

He disappeared under the bonnet of a car, fiddling

with the fuse wires, and with a muffled click, the central locking opened. Sitting in the driver's seat, he brought out a steel hammer – one of the few tools he carried with him; he never had time for too much gadgetry – and smashed down on the freshly exposed steering lock, freeing the wheel. Then a simple connection of the right wires, and we were off on another drive, soaring through the sparkling night city like birds.

We raced down the Castellana – wide, open, tree-lined and free. Returning to it now was a sort of home-coming. The car we had picked up was a Mercedes soft-top, and taking down the roof, the air rushed over us like cool water, fresh on our damp, salty skin. I looked around. The car was plush and comfortable. I tried the seatbelt on for size.

Jesús had begun another monologue. The kick he got from driving was more important than the money. These were just going to end up as toys for rich Arabs, as far as he was concerned. There was just time for him to enjoy them briefly before they disappeared for good and became another unsolved case on the police records. And the high he got seemed to unlock something.

'Bottom of that road's the bullring. You like bull-fighting? *Olé! Toro! Toro!*' He took his hands from the steering wheel and, making two horns with his fingers, he jabbed at me, ducking his fingers down at my chest. We were driving very fast.

'Bullfight – guy got gored. Lived, of course: stitched him up and he was all right, no problem. Bull wasn't. Got it in the neck. Ended up on the bullfighter's table that night. Ha! Fuckers. Serves 'em right. Live like kings. In the fields, lots of food, as many cows as they can handle. Until they end up in a fucking great ring. Go mad. *Chalao*. I shit on the mother who gave birth to her. Course, there's the others, spiking it. You know . . . It doesn't stop, just doesn't stop, blood everywhere. Pain. And she's waving the *muleta*, the red cape, at you, forcing you to run, can't give up, no, you can't, see, she's got you hooked, there, in the ring. Nowhere else you can go. And you're running at her, but you're thinking, I should be running away from all this, not running into it. But there's just nowhere to run to, so you keep running into her, and she keeps stabbing you, prodding you, waving that great red thing in your face, and like a fool you keep going. That's the bull's fault. Keeps going. Other animals would give up, but the bull keeps going, never gives up, until he runs himself onto the sword up there, and . . .'

It was swerving to avoid the other car that did it. He pulled hard on the wheel, braked, and we went into a spin, flying across the road, hitting the kerb, and smashing sideways into a lamppost.

The lamp went out, the other car sped away, and we were left alone in the deserted street.

I lifted my head. Everything was silent. I'd blacked out for a few moments and my face was half-buried in an air bag, sharp pains shooting across my chest where the seatbelt had cut in. The driver's seat next to me was empty. Jesús had disappeared.

'Jesús!' I called. There was no answer. Bastard, I thought, as a fuzzy, crackling pain began wrapping itself around my skull. He's probably run off and left me here.

I got out of the car shakily and checked myself.

247

Everything seemed OK. Just dizzy, and a sense of being somewhere else, as though watching myself and everything around me on some faraway screen. The car was a mess, a great dent in the side where the lamppost had hit, glass scattered and glistening over the tyre-marks etched into the road. From somewhere came the urgent thought: weren't you supposed to run away from smashed-up cars in case they suddenly blew up? That was what happened in films. For a moment I was gripped by the certainty that the car was about to explode, taking me with it. I ran and dived dramatically onto the grass, landing heavily on my bruised ribs. Scrambling along the ground, I kept as low as possible. The blast, I reasoned, might at least go over my head.

I didn't get far. Only a few yards on, I stumbled across a body. It was Jesús, lying on his back. Pale, eyes closed.

'Jesús! Fuck it! You all right?'

There was no reply. I felt around his neck, trying to find a pulse. He was breathing. There were no signs of any cuts or serious damage, but his eyes remained shut and he appeared to be in pain.

'Jesús. Wake up.' I slapped him around the face. Another tip from the cinema. Still he didn't stir.

'Come on. Wake up.' I tried again. A bit harder this time. Nothing. I lifted my head. Two or three whining sirens in the distance were getting closer. Please, not the police. Not the police, dear God.

'JESÚS!' He was out cold.

I stood up to get a better view. It looked like an ambulance, but the police wouldn't be far behind. I began calculating how far I would need to carry him to be safe. How far could I go without being spotted, though?

The ambulance pulled up as I was caught by a moment's indecision, and the medics tumbled out to look for us. A man ran up with a blanket and hauled me away from Jesús.

'Here, this way. You need to sit down. We'll get you in the ambulance.'

I shook him off. 'I'm staying here with him.'

'You're injured. Come on. Get in the ambulance.'

I stood still. The most important thing was taking care of Jesús. They already had a blanket around him and were fetching a stretcher. There was noise, people shouting. One of the medics went to get more blankets. The stretcher got caught on one of the bars in the ambulance and for a moment they struggled to get it out, shouting at one another angrily.

Come on, Jesús. Wake up, for God's sake. We've got to get out of here.

But he was still unmoving, still unconscious.

Another medic shouted at me as he ran past.

'You still here? Get inside the . . .'

'Are the police coming?'

'Of course. Be here any second.'

I had to do something, but racing around Madrid in an ambulance trying to escape from the police did not seem very practical. There would be the medics to deal with first, and there were three of them . . .

I stepped over towards Jesús as they were about to put him on the stretcher.

'Wait!' I leaned over his body and whispered in his ear.

'Jesús,' I said gently, 'wake up now.' He didn't move. The ambulancemen moved to push me out of the way.

'Wake up now, Jesús. They're expecting the police.'

At the mention of the hated word, he opened his

249

eyes, looked at me for a second and sat bolt upright.

'Watch it, man,' the medic said. 'You've just had an accident. The ambulance is here, we're going to take you to the hospital. You'll be fine, but . . .'

Jesús was already on his feet.

'No, I'm OK.' He was leaning heavily on my arm.

The ambulanceman ignored him.

'Right. If you just come over here, we'll get you in the . . .'

'No. I told you. I'm fine.'

More blue lights were flashing in the street ahead. I squeezed Jesús's wrist.

'You're not. You've had an accident. Now get inside the ambulance.'

'We'll be off,' I said. The lights were getting closer. We turned to get away. The medic grabbed my shoulders and pulled me back with a jerk.

There was no choice.

'Go!' I shouted to Jesús. Mustering as much strength as I could, I spun on the ball of my foot and punched the medic in the stomach. He gave out a low, wounded groan and folded in half, falling to the floor like a deflated balloon. For a moment, I looked at him, surprised at my own strength. It felt terrible as he lay there, face screwed up with shock. But there was no time for sympathy: the other two were bearing down on me and the police were arriving. Turning, I ran as fast as I could. Jesús was sprinting ahead, all weakness and injury melting away as he cut off the main road and headed for one of the sidestreets that wound round the back of the Cortes, the parliament. I followed, the medics coming up behind; I just hoped they hadn't had time to tell the police what was going on.

Carrying on up the slope, our legs began to tire. We had to be careful: just one street away, police and guards were stationed, watching over the parliament building, and they would be only too happy to intercede in the far more exciting job of pursuing a Gypsy car-thief and his mate.

Jesús, slowing at a junction to decide which way to go, turning right; me running behind him, feet barely touching the pavement, flying past streetlamps, parked cars, dirty doorways.

Think fast. We couldn't get away just by running. Once the police at the crash site worked out what was going on they would radio out for help, meaning an ever increasing number of pursuers ringing us in like hounds. The streets were deserted and poorly lit, thank God, and the medics were only half-hearted in their attempts to catch us, happy to leave the job of hunting us down to the police. A pair of feet echoed in the streets behind us, pounding the paving-stones with heavy, awkward steps. The man called back to his colleagues to ask if they could see us. But he was alone: there was no reply, and his steps became slower and stiffer as he ran from junction to junction trying to see which way we'd gone. I was more worried about the police at the Cortes, though. With all the noise, one of them might come out and snoop around, just to see what was going on.

Jesús was panting and beginning to hobble. I should have been amazed he was even upright at all, but we were on the run, sweating heavily, our minds focused entirely on escape. Catching up with him, I placed his arm over my shoulder and helped him move faster, my eyes moving over the scene ahead for any way out. There were no walls to hide behind, no alleyways with fire-escapes to climb up and away, no gardens we could sneak into. For a moment I thought that Jesús could break into another car and we could just drive away, but we didn't have the time, and he was weakening. And there was always the chance of getting stopped.

More shouting from behind. I didn't dare look back. Jesús was leaning more and more on my arm. Ahead was another road. We swerved to the right, heading for the Alcalá, the main avenue leading to the Puerta del Sol and the heart of the city. If we were fast enough, and with a bit of luck . . . It was late, though. I must have been mad, but it was our only chance.

Out on the empty main road, a white car with a green light on its roof appeared a hundred yards away. I looked around; no police, but oh God it was moving so slowly. Come to us, come to us. That's right. He'd seen us now, and was speeding up. Sticking my arm out, I let go of Jesús. For a second he staggered, then righted himself. One final effort.

The door closed, the light went out and the taxi gently pulled away. Hold on Jesús, hold on. Just till we get past Sol and away from here. The driver was already suspicious – Jesús a Gypsy and me a foreigner. It didn't quite fit, somehow. I could see him trying to get a view of us in his mirror. That's it, head down on the back of the seat, Jesús, sleep a little. Just a heavy night, that's all. We'll get you sorted. Away from here, away from them, away from all this. Away, and down the Calle Mayor, away from the centre, away from the boulevards and avenues and tight, narrow streets. No more. Not tonight. It's finished. Gone.

* * *

'Listen, son. This is the last opportunity you'll have to see him. You can't miss it.'

Eduardo had called from Alicante. We hadn't spoken for months. He was coming up to Madrid for the weekend and wanted me to meet him at the bull-ring. It was a chance to see his favourite *matador* – the Alicantino, Jose-María Manzanares – in action.

'He's a great bloke. Gave me my first interview at the paper. Meet me at the main entrance at five.'

Las Ventas is one of the finest, and, Madrileños like to think, the most prestigious bullrings in the world. It is a megalithic brick monument to neo-Moorish architecture, built shortly before the Civil War, and squats, as in many Roman towns, on the edge of the centre next to the modern equivalent of the city walls, the ring-road.

I was struck by its size, hazy and soft-edged in the late afternoon sun. The red horseshoe arches, row after row, storey after storey, reminded me of pictures I had seen of the mosque at Córdoba, hitting a forgotten, aesthetic nerve and something of the romance that had first drawn me to Spain.

The area around the entrance threw me into child-hood fantasies of ancient Rome: hat-sellers, drink-sellers, roasted nuts, fans. And then more contemporary equivalents: plastic models of *toreros* and – I shuddered – flamenco dancers; or bullfighting posters on which tourists could have their name printed below those of some of the greats. Although how the sequence '*Jesulín de Ubrique, El Cordobés y Richard Docker*' was supposed to sound authentic, I could never work out.

I milled about for a while, warmed by the friendly atmosphere. The only hat big enough for my head was a dull, brown straw thing with a black ribbon, more suited to a 60-year-old. I looked up at the unforgiving sun, then handed over the money. A small price to pay for not looking like a lobster.

Eduardo was by the ticket office.

'*Hombre!*' He greeted me warmly and embraced me with a kiss for each cheek. I winced with the pain of my bruised ribs.

'Christ! Look how thin you are. They not feeding you properly here in the capital?'

He handed me a ticket.

'Here. We're sitting in *sol* – the sunny area. Where the men sit. *Sombra*, the shady area, is only for poofs. And aficionados.'

'What about *sol y sombra*?'

'That's for people who still haven't made up their minds.' I laughed. It was good to see him again.

We passed through the towering gate and headed up the stairs to find our seats. Great, wide corridors circled the outside of the ring, and were occupied by their own army of drink-sellers, snacks-sellers, and men renting cushions to sit on.

'Get yourself one of these,' Eduardo said. 'What with your head complaining about the sun, you don't want your arse moaning about the hard stone.'

He handed me a cushion.

The corridors were shady and cool, and we stayed there for a few minutes, knocking back iced beers before facing the intense heat and light of the ring itself. Old men with flat, wide-brimmed hats walked arm in arm discussing past fights, manicured ladies in silk blouses, family groups, men with their sons, young lads in training shoes, a group of four middle-aged housewives. It was a gentle scene.

'I have some good news for you, son. Your guitar teacher — your *former* guitar teacher — has left Alicante. Went soon after you did. No-one knows where, but he's gone, and that's the most important thing.'

I paused. It had been a long time since I had thought of Juan.

'Did he . . . ?'

'Spill the beans? No, I don't think so. At least, there's no indication that he did. My sources tell me everything is still normal at the school. No major break-up, no rows in the broom cupboard.'

He laughed, and slapped me on the back.

'It's history, son. You can't still be thinking about her. Thought you would have slept your way round half of Madrid by now.'

But I knew Lola. She was capable of hiding anything behind her school exterior.

We finished our drinks and headed towards the entrance. Four men stood idly in the shade, their heads crowned with the all-important cap, which, combined with the whistles hanging from their necks, marked them out as 'officials', and men to be reckoned with. We handed over our tickets and a short, deformed man with a high, baby-like voice and sunglasses that almost covered his face took us through a short tunnel and out into the ring.

The glare was fantastic, and it took a few seconds for my eyes to adjust. Only half the seats were taken and the arena was empty, except for two white framing circles. The size of the ring created a sense of awe, and despite the echoing chatter, there was a cathedral-like quality to it as the words lifted up and were blown away by the sun and wind. Even from up here I could smell the sand. But there was something else, too. A smell, not of death, but of the expectation of death, I thought: a momentary presentiment of the ghastly, tremendous events that were to come in the next two hours.

We were shown to our seats, opposite the white royal box.

'So, tell me everything. I tried to call you a few weeks ago, but some mad woman on the other end of the phone said you'd gone on a world tour.'

I laughed. 'Yes, that's Carlota, my landlady. You probably caught her at the wrong moment.'

'Well, what's it all about?'

I hesitated, not sure where to begin, trying to relate my current life to a past one. I was hungry for conversation, real conversation, a chance simply to tell someone what I was doing. And so I began: the tour, Carlos, La Andonda, Juanito, the donkey. I told him about the endless gigs, the night in Benidorm, my new guitar, and knife-throwing. And he sat patiently, quietly absorbing this deluge of scattered stories, thoughts and feelings.

The brass band – three old men with trumpets and drums – announced the opening parade had begun: men on horseback in black costumes with white scarves; thick-set men dressed in red holding wooden sticks; portly *picadores* with pointed spears in leather armour on tank-like horses. Then, the *toreros* themselves: *subalternos*, *banderilleros* and the stars of the spectacle, the three *matadores*, in their *trajes de luces*, 'suits of light', that were red, blue, gold and white, with shiny studs and tassels. The most experienced *torero* entered on the left, the second oldest on the right, and the youngest in the middle. They bowed to the president of the fight, sitting at his balcony in a sombre suit like a little dictator, then trooped out into the circle surrounding the sand, protected by thick wooden barricades – the *burladeros*.

The first part of the fight – the *tercio de varas* – began, and the bull came racing out of its stall: over half a tonne of thrashing flesh concentrated into two, fine, lethal points rising from its head. There was a gasp from the crowd as it rushed out into the sand, the pain of the rosette pinned on its shoulders already producing the initial rage necessary for a good fight. The *subalternos* waved their purple and yellow capes at it as it charged wildly around the arena, and the onlookers assessed its capabilities.

'Not a good bull,' Eduardo said. It looked fairly impressive to me.

'Why do you say that?'

'He's running too hard, too soon. He'll tire himself out.'

The others in the crowd seemed to agree, and whistling had already begun. Soon it was filling the entire bullring, nothing like the music and carnival atmosphere I had expected.

'You've got to understand, son, this is Las Ventas,' Eduardo shouted above the din. 'Not like any other bullring. You go anywhere else and people want to have a good time. Here, everyone takes pride in being the most exacting audience in the world. If they don't like what they see . . .' and he made a 'thumbs down' motion.

'So why are they whistling?' The noise was piercing.

'They want the president to change the bull for another one.'

'Will he?'

'Doubt it. It would have to be really bad. Too much money, honour, at stake, that sort of thing.' He grinned. 'It's a racket. Besides, this is Las Ventas. They always whistle. It's part of the spectacle.'

But the complaining had only just begun. The *picadores* appeared on their heavily padded horses. Two of them came striding out and sat, waiting for the bull to charge at them. They then thrust their long pikes into its shoulders to create a deep, bloody wound. And the whistling began again, almost as soon as they had started.

'What's the problem now?'

'They want the president to declare this section over, so they don't wound the bull too much, so it doesn't get too weak for when the *matador* comes on.'

'I see,' I said, confused. 'Why have this section at all, then?'

'Tradition,' he said.

Blood was pouring down the bull's back from the growing wound in its shoulders.

'Course, because they're such a critical lot round here, the greatest accolade a *matador* can have is to be hailed as a triumph in Las Ventas.'

'What happens then?'

'They lift him up on their shoulders and take him out by the gate as a hero.'

'No whistling?'

'None.'

'Thank God for that.'

The *banderilleros* came on, with their brightly coloured, harpoon-pointed sticks – *banderillas* – to ram into the bull's back. It was the most Minoan part of the show, with great acrobatic skill required to run at the animal, plant the sticks elegantly, and with a single, dart-like movement, into its flesh, then escape unharmed. The first attempt failed, both *banderillas* falling to the ground. The crowd remained silent, not even deigning to whistle; it was still early and there was a sense that things had yet to warm up. The second attempt was more successful, one of the fighters passing within inches of the horns to land home his red and yellow spear. The atmosphere changed at once and the applause rang out just as quickly as the whistles had filled the air only moments before. Great shouts of '*olé*' came from the people around us. The stress came on the second syllable, I noticed, unlike flamenco.

With the wave of the president's handkerchief and a blast from the band, the arena emptied and the steaming bull was left alone, panting, its tongue hanging carelessly from its mouth. Manzanares, the star performer, came striding out, sword and red cape tucked neatly under one arm, his hat – *montera* – raised in salute to the applauding crowd. Then he casually tossed it into the air behind him, and it landed face down.

'If it lands the other way, it's bad luck for the *matador*,' Eduardo filled me in. 'They say some of them weigh it down specially, like a gambler's dice, so that the hat always lands as they want it to.'

I wanted to ask him if Manzanares himself did this, but there was no time. The cheering turned into concentrated silence as the *matador* went through the first passes. He stood firm on the ground, chest pushed out, chin hooked in, his bottom lip contorted downwards in a vicious frown, tempting the bull with flicks of the cape, drawing it in like a cat might play with a mouse.

There were gasps, cheers, whistling, applause from

the crowd. I couldn't understand why one minute he had their approval and the next, derision.

'Sometimes it's the bull they're complaining about, sometimes it's him. If he draws the cape too low, the bull will run itself into the ground. Too high, and the animal loses momentum by charging upwards. Sometimes it's a mixture of things. And sometimes . . .' he shrugged his shoulders, all the time his eyes fixed like a falcon on the drama below. 'But just look at the man – grace, passion. He's a genius.'

It was time for the kill. The *matador* was handed his *estoque* – sword – from behind the barricade and stood over the exhausted bull ready to strike, enticing it to lower its head once more, opening up the vertebrae for the entry of the blade straight into its lungs. Manzanares waited. The bull didn't move, saliva now dripping from its mouth uncontrollably. A solitary whistle came from the stands, then bull and man both charged simultaneously, and the sword was plunged two feet into the black mass in a single thrust.

The crowd leapt to its feet. The bull fell onto its hind legs, still thrashing with his horns at the *toreros* as they gathered around waving their cloaks in its face, until a man with a dagger finished it off with an un-ceremonious stab in the back of the neck.

Manzanares stood over the dead animal majestic-ally, then saluted the crowd. With another cheer, the place turned white as people pulled out handkerchiefs and waved them frantically at the president, while the stocky men in red appeared with horses and dragged the bull's corpse away, leaving a thick, red streak in the sand. Manzanares picked up his *montera* and saluted the crowd once more. But the whistling had begun again: the president was taking his time, and the audience wanted to see their hero honoured.

'He may get one,' Eduardo said. 'But no more, I think. Not today.'

The handkerchiefs fluttered on, and the whistling and abuse soared into the sky.

'Come on, you son of a whore!' a man with a rasping voice called from behind us.

The president finally conceded, lifting his own handkerchief once to grant one ear to the *matador*. The handkerchief waving stopped, the ear was severed and handed to the *matador*, who then paraded it around the arena as a trophy of the kill.

'He killed it well. That's why he got the ear,' Eduardo said. 'Course, if he'd done really well, he would have got the other one as well. And even the tail.' He lifted his eyebrows. 'Makes excellent soup.'

Two uneventful fights later, we passed back into the cool of the corridor for the interval, and drank more beer. I had an odd sense of elation.

'There's a lot of drugs knocking about with this lot as well,' I said hurriedly.

'I can tell. You don't get that thin from dieting.'

I looked down at the clothes hanging from my body.

'Cocaine, mostly.'

'Goes with the territory.'

'Yes, I suppose it does.

We ordered two more beers.

I still hadn't mentioned Jesús. I simply didn't know how to describe him. If he was a friend, he was like no other I had ever had.

It was time to go back into the arena. A man with a bucket and a voice like a lawnmower was pacing up and down trying to attract custom.

'*Coca, cerveza, Fanta Limón! Coca, cerveza, Fanta Limón!*'

The fourth bull came on: Manzanares' second. This time, the passes went better. There was a greater sensuality, a feeling that the *matador* was caressing the animal, like a lover. The way he moved over it, with the energy of the crowd concentrated on him, and his struggle – the inevitability of death – seemed to meet a profound need in us all. But the kill went wrong, the sword failed to enter the bull properly the first time, and he had to repeat, clumsily finishing it off with a spike. Nonetheless, the applause was energetic, and the great Manzanares received a standing ovation as he left, this time earless.

'He's a master,' Eduardo enthused. 'If he were a *flamenco*, I'd say he had *duende*.'

An hour later, we passed out through the main gate. The spectators mingled and slowly dispersed in a cloud of cigar smoke, the evening sun cooling after the intensity of the arena. The feeling of elation was still with me, like a great tension had been removed from my body. Limbs supple, head cleared. The others felt it too – people were smiling, with open faces, as though the blood ritual had somehow emptied us of our own need for violence, and we were free to be human again.

We walked up the Alcalá, found a bar and ordered brandies.

'Anything else you want to tell me about this lot?' Eduardo asked.

I said nothing. It was better he didn't know. I could guess what he would say, anyway. What any 'sensible' person would want to tell me. But he was sharp, and could tell there was more to the story than I had let on.

'Listen son, you've got to realise that flamenco is yours, it's mine. It belongs to everyone.'

'What do you mean?'

'I mean you have to decide what it means for you, Jason. You can't just keep on taking it off the shelf, already prepared by other people. You have to discover your own flamenco.'

It was Friday night when I headed over to Carlos's flat for what was to be the last time. I realised immediately that something was wrong. The children were not there, no games on the stairwell, no shouting from women in clattering kitchens. Only muffled sounds.

María-José greeted me with tears at the door.

'What is it?'

She wouldn't say, but pushed me through into the main room, where I saw Carlos sitting in the middle of the floor, his back against a chair, eyes swollen, face pale. The rest of the room was crowded with half-hidden eyes, hands brought up to ward off the pain, cigarette smoke circling the bodies like a protecting veil. And the sound of women wailing.

Carlos looked up.

'Hello, my friend,' he choked. And he beckoned me to join him. I knelt at his side.

'Carlos, what's up?'

He stared at me through thick, hairy eyebrows. 'Jesús,' he said. 'Jesús.'

I felt a hand on my shoulder. It was Juanito. In the corner there was screaming, and the sound of someone hitting something slowly, rhythmically. I looked up. La Andonda was beating her head against the wall.

I stood up, shaky on my feet, and turned to Juanito.

'There's nothing left of poor Jesús,' he said. 'He left us this morning.'

I stumbled past him, unhearing, heading for the balcony. I wanted air.

'How did it happen?' I said weakly, to no-one, to everyone. There was no reply.

'For God's sake, how did it happen?' I began shouting uncontrollably. 'How did it happen? How did it . . .'

I was caught in the arms of Javier.

'Come with me,' he said as I sobbed. And he led me out onto the balcony.

'We've lost him,' he said, stroking my hair. 'We've lost our beautiful Jesús.'

I couldn't say anything. The wailing from inside was getting louder.

'How . . .'

'He had an accident. A car accident, at the Plaza de Lima, just outside the Bernabeu. It was quick. He didn't suffer, you know. He didn't suffer.'

Jesús and I hadn't been out together since the night we escaped in a taxi a couple of weeks before. I had the impression Jesús was beginning to see me as bad luck. But it could have been me in that car.

I don't know how long I was there, my face on Javier's chest, his hand on my head, swaying gently from side to side as the tears fell and fell. The time was punctuated by the rise and fall of the screams from inside, like waves of grief overcoming us and then ebbing away. In my mind, I was driving with him, driving down boulevards, country roads, car-lined streets, the lights flashing over his tied-back hair, his close-set eyes, the slightly flattened nose. But there was no sound from him.

'Our beautiful Jesús, our beautiful Jesús.'

'More beautiful than even you know, Jason,' Javier said. 'It's his mother . . . his mother. I don't know what she'll do. She relied on him for money.' And I felt his own tears splash down onto mine.

A fog of grief seemed to have overtaken us all. The banging had stopped, but no-one was moving. It seemed only now, now that he was dead, that I could begin to feel something of what Jesús had meant to me. Not an ordinary friend. He was both more and less than that.

It was black, and Javier's hand moved rhythmically on my head. Yet at the back of my mind, something was nagging me. Something we had to remember, the main reason why I had come round that night.

I stood up straight.

'Oh Christ! The gig!'

We were due to be playing that night. I pulled away from Javier and ran inside.

'Carlos! The gig! We're supposed to be there.'

He looked up at me uncomprehending, still slouched on the floor against the chair.

'The concert. Tonight.'

The understanding came slowly back into his eyes.

'Fuck! *Churumbel*, you're right.' He crawled onto his knees then lifted himself up onto his feet. He was confused for a second, unsure what to do. Was he Carlos grieving for his lost friend, or Carlos the head of this group? He looked at a clock on the wall, then decided.

'*Venga!* Come on!' He clapped his hands. The wailing stuttered for a moment, then stopped.

'In honour of our dear *compare*, we are all going to Restaurante Alegrías, now. ALL OF US!'

Like a slow, unruly army, everyone began picking themselves up, the sound of chairs pushed back, coughing, a nose being blown. The order was un-questioned, quietly conceded as the best thing, the only thing, to do.

We left the flat: Juanito, La Andonda, Javier, Antonio, María-José, her two daughters and their friends, a couple of neighbours, all led by Carlos. We squeezed into a couple of cars, and headed over the ring-road into the centre of the city.

It was late, and the bar was already emptying. A group of Japanese businessmen in suits were standing in the doorway on their way out.

'Good job they're going,' Carlos said. 'Don't want any Chinkies around tonight.'

We trooped in, pushing the Orientals aside, and passed into the main area. The stage was empty – the last group had finished some time ago, and the manager was waiting for us, furious.

'Just where the hell have you . . . ?'

Carlos swept past him with a flick of the hand, and we took the direct route to the stage, walking through the tables and chairs where the audience were sitting rather than passing down the side. A fat German tourist proved difficult to push past, obstinately refus-ing to pull his chair in any further, until Carlos bent down and with both hands lifted the edge of the man's seat and sent him flying to the floor. He then walked over the man's glasses where they had fallen from his face. We all followed in a line as the German sprawled about like a fly on its back, unable to right itself.

The house lights went down as we clambered up onto the platform, and just three spotlights focused on the area where we stood. Carlos called over to Antonio and spoke lightly in his ear, then we all pushed back to the edge in a semi-circle, facing the audience, leaving Carlos alone in the centre.

Antonio began to play. We all knew at once. It was a *Taranta* – slow, mournful, painful. Antonio played the first chords, stroking gently on the strings, then finished, and Carlos was left to sing on his own:

> *Carretera, carretera,*
> *llévame por caría*
> *a las minas del Romero,*
> *que acaban de asesinar*
> *al hermanico que mas quiero.*

> For pity's sake, road,
> show me the way to the Romero mines,
> for they have just killed
> the brother I loved most.

We stood still around him, motionless, the song entering us and holding us down like a thick, heavy blanket of sorrow. His voice became a piercing, bloody scream, tears flowing from his eyes onto the floor. This time the expression on his face was real. My skin tingled. La Andonda was holding my hand tightly, leaning on me every few seconds as she swayed, unable to support her own weight with the grief. The audience was silent and still. Even the German had stopped his muttering. All minds were concentrated on Carlos, and the pain echoing from inside him. And it was not simply to marvel at how well he expressed his feelings – it was because he brought the same grief, the same sorrow out in every person there. His pain was their pain. And our pain.

We left after one song. There was nothing more to be done. The manager quietly handed over the fee. I wondered if anyone had told him, but it hardly seemed necessary. He would have been able to tell anyway.

We gathered outside for a moment in the black street, no-one knowing quite what to do. La Andonda was still holding on to me, as though ready to collapse. Carlos came over and spoke softly in my ear.

'Listen, *churumbel*. It's over. We're leaving here, going to Barcelona. I've got a cousin there.'

He gave me a handful of notes.

'Take this. You'll need it. But I tell you: get out of Madrid. This is a bad city, a bad city, I tell you.'

He pressed my hand and placed his thick, hairy arm around my shoulders with a resigned grin.

'It's for the best.'

He took La Andonda's hand and led her away to the cars.

'Wait!' I pulled out the knife from my pocket and handed it to her. She took it, kissed me and then handed it back.

'Keep it,' she said.

The others followed behind, dragging their feet on the tarmac. I didn't know if they realised I was no longer amongst them, but there were no goodbyes.

And they drove off, leaving me alone, standing in the street with my guitar, waving blindly at the red tail-lights, before I turned away and headed home.

chapter TEN

Por Granaína

Tierra que baña el Genil
viva Graná la sultana;
y bendita sea la mañana
en que yo te conocí
con tu carita tan gitana.

Long live Granada, the Moorish queen,
a land watered by the River Genil:
and bless the morning I first saw you
with your Gypsy face.

'*No. Tengo guitarristas hasta aquí!* I'm up to my ears with guitarists.'

Another rejection, at the last school but one on my list. Perhaps I was a bit ambitious calling at the Escuela Mariquilla, the best flamenco dance centre in the city, but it had been the same story everywhere. No-one needed another guitarist – the place was awash with them. Still, I pushed on. I was searching for something, and had an intuition that here, in Granada, despite the tacky image of flamenco the city pushed at the hordes of tourists, I might find what I was looking for.

The air was thick with sweet-smelling aromatic flowers – jasmine by day and *galán de noche* by night. Deep blue morning glories climbed the whitewashed walls, while every street was lined with cypress and plane trees, and here and there, an old stone fountain like a wedding cake stacked three or four storeys high. The city reminded me of Pedro's garden back in Alicante, and his prediction that one day I would come to the Alhambra and the Generalife. This was his

270

inspiration, I could see it now: the world of the old-school Arabists, Miguel Asín Palacios and Emilio García Gómez; a slightly old-fashioned, heavy city, where manners long forgotten in the rest of democratised Spain still counted. A Granadino would either dismiss you or respect you in an instant based on hazy, universally recognised factors such as *calidad* – whether or not you were a person of 'quality'.

This was not the light, thin air of Madrid, though, despite being near the mountains. It was dry – so dry that often I had to breathe through my mouth to protect the inside of my nose – but it was dense, like blood: suffocating. The patron saint of the city was the Virgin of Distress, weeping over the body of her recently crucified son. Images of her distraught face – wrapped in powerful dark cloth, beneath a gold crown three times the size of her head – were everywhere, on posters and postcards. It was said that more people had been killed here during the Civil War than anywhere else in Spain. The dead seemed to have left something of themselves behind to torment their killers, the city that betrayed them. Even now, with a deep sense of loss and bewilderment following Jesús's death, I always tried to keep in mind the Spanish proverb: *Dios aprieta pero no ahoga* – God tightens the noose but doesn't strangle you. In Granada, despite the beauty of the city, there were people who, from the expression on their faces, seemed to be in a perpetual state of mourning, forever focused on some inexplicable pain.

I walked down the Gran Vía, lined with its brooding, muscular, old banks. On one side the Albaicín – the old Moorish quarter – sloped upwards to face the Alhambra across the River Darro, and on the other, spread the more modern, European city, still bearing signs of the Arab past in the winding cobbled streets that slowly straightened out the further from the old town you walked. I was looking for the last school on my list, a list scribbled down after a frustrating investigation at the tourist office. No-one seemed to understand I wanted to play, not have lessons.

'*Soy tocaor.*'

'You want guitar lessons?'

'No. I'm looking for dance schools who might need a guitarist.'

'Here. Try this man. He teaches at . . .'

Finally I had extracted some names from a wad of pamphlets, most of them places catering for tourists in the Gypsy caves up in Sacromonte.

I heard it before I saw it. The unmistakable sounds of a flamenco dance class issuing from heavily barred open windows.

'*Vamos!* From the beginning!'

Tak tak-a tak tak. The heels of what sounded to be up to twenty shoes were pounding a wooden floor.

I passed through an open doorway into a dark, musty hall with a large Moroccan-style glass lantern hanging by a thick chain from the ceiling. An elderly man was sweeping the floor: white hair, balding, with loose trousers and braces hitched over his white shirt. I stopped and watched. There was something engaging about him, something about the way he was sweeping, how he held himself, was engrossed completely in his task. It took all his concentration, yet he was also absolutely aware of everything around him, as though he had eyes in the back of his head. He had poise and presence. He knew I was there. Yet he had something to complete first, and I would have to wait.

He bent down with a dustpan, collected the grit he had been sweeping, placed it into a bin, put his broom in a little wooden booth standing against one of the walls, and then turned to me. Everything in its own good time.

'*Dígame Usted*. What can I do for you, sir?'

The polite form was becoming so rare in Spain I had almost forgotten what it sounded like. Even in shops, especially if the assistant was young, the *tú* form was normal.

'I wanted to visit the school,' I said. 'I play the guitar . . . I thought they might want a guitarist.'

The sense of calm and centredness about the man made me slightly self-conscious at first. He had probably guessed what I was there for, carrying the guitar over my shoulder, but he waited patiently for me to finish, neither judging nor second-guessing me.

'You'll want to speak to Juana,' he said. 'Come with me.'

We walked through a wooden door and up the stairs.

'You're English, aren't you,' he said. 'I can tell from the accent.'

The comment smarted a little. Despite looking very foreign, I always tried to speak Spanish as well as I could so that at least I might not *sound* like an outsider.

'Yes,' I said. 'Perhaps that's something I should work on a bit more.'

'No! Absolutely not! That is you. That is who you are.'

He walked on ahead as his words registered inside me. He was right. I had always been seeking acceptance; I might not feel so English any more, but no matter how long I stayed, or who I was with, I would never really be Spanish, or a Gypsy, or any of the things I had aspired to be. I was always something else, always on the outside. It was a hard thing to take on board, but at the same time, as I thought it through, I realised there was something liberating in this as well: an outsider might never be fully accepted, but he was free to be different, perhaps free to make something more of himself. Wasn't that what had attracted me to flamenco, after all – the promise that it might release something in me and make me freer in some way?

A number of girls were emerging from the main dance class, hair tied back with clips, faces shiny with exertion. The old man pointed.

'That's her,' he said. And he left.

I went in, squeezing past the dancers. The classroom was small, with windows on one side, a wall of mirrors, a couple of posters at the back, and an empty wooden floor, beaten and cracked from years of crashing heels. In the corner sat a man in his thirties leaning over a guitar. Juana had her back to me, a silver fish hairclip pinning her hair at the back of her head, large shoulders. I waited for them to finish talking.

'*Hola*,' she said, turning round. The guitarist was packing up and leaving.

She did not look like a dancer. For one thing, she was overweight, but it was the thick, hard fat of an active middle-aged woman. Her eyes were jet-black, like her hair, and her skin was unusually pale.

'Juana?'

'Yes.' She had a deep, businesslike voice.

'I was speaking with the man downstairs . . .'

'Señor Emilio.'

'Yes. He said I should talk to you about . . .'

'Oh, you're learning the guitar. Well, you're welcome to come and sit in. You should talk with Luis.' She pointed to the door and the guitarist who was just leaving.

'Actually, I was thinking more of playing *for* the classes.'

'We don't need anyone right now,' she said. 'And even if we did, I couldn't pay much. This is a small school. You should try the Escuela Mariquilla. They . . .'

'I already have. They said the same thing.'

'Or there are plenty of places in the Albaicín, Sacromonte, round there. You should try the *tablaos*. Some of them do classes for foreigners . . .'

I shook my head.

'I'm sorry. I can't offer you anything. But you're welcome, as I said, to come and play with us.'

I thanked her and turned to leave. She thrust out a thick, heavy arm to shake my hand. It seemed unusual, but I took it, and she held my hand for a moment.

'Have you been playing for long?'

'I just did a tour with a group from Madrid.'

'How long for?' She was still holding my hand.

'A couple of months.'

'Good.' She let go. 'Keep it up. You'll thank yourself one day for all the hard work.'

I headed for the door.

'Did you dance?' she called behind me.

'Sorry?'

'Did you dance, ever, when you were in Madrid?'

'No. I only played.'

'We'll have to get you up on your feet, then.' She smiled and turned her back on me, as if to show me the interview had come to an end.

I stepped out and walked downstairs, through the hallway, with its distinctive musty smell.

'See you again!' Emilio called out from his wooden booth.

'Yes. See you again,' I said, unsure if I ever would.

I sat in the dark of the cheap hotel room, tired and depressed. The combination of grief, loneliness and the sudden collapse of my highly stimulated life had burnt me out. I had fled Madrid in a rage. Months of living on my nerves and little sleep began to burst out in petty squabbles with station assistants, arguments with other passengers, and a general short temper with everyone.

I knew, from the moment of Jesús's death and our last gig, the nonchalant farewell, that I had been cast out, rejected. All my suspicions about the group began to ring true. I felt I had been some sort of joke for them, an adornment to appeal to their foreign audiences. They would never have taken me on otherwise. How else could I explain the speed of the ending? Jesús had gone and I was of no use to anyone any more. In an attempt to console myself, I imagined that the group had disbanded altogether. Carlos would probably start selling second-hand clothes on street markets again. But I was stung, disillusioned and alone once more.

Like any foreigner I had fallen for a romanticised image of the Gypsy: free, passionate, alive, anti-establishment. But a kind of Orientalism applied to Gypsies, in much the same way as westerners had a distorted image of people from the Middle East. In my own experience Carlos and the Gypsy members of the band had been suspicious, proud, hierarchical, generous, tribal – free from some of the concerns and

276

worries of the *payos* surrounding them, perhaps, but not free in the real sense of the word. Different walls, different bars on the windows, but imprisoned, none the less.

Even at this point, though, low as I was, I knew I would stay in Spain, at least for a little longer. I had made the choice to come and learn flamenco and this alone was enough to keep me going, despite the thick, inner turmoil that now threatened to smother me. What I needed was rest. And so I slept, seeking refuge in unconsciousness.

The following morning I forced myself to get up and go out, breaking the routine of depression, and convinced that with some degree of effort I might see a new chink of light. This was Granada, and it was time I experienced it.

I had arrived in a dream-state, not really knowing why I had chosen this most emblematic of Andalusian cities. I had wanted to leave Madrid – was never really happy there. I always felt it failed to be the great European capital it aspired to be, its beauty all locked away in museums while pimps ruled the streets. But where to go? The name Granada rang loudly in my mind. At first I ignored it, but when, after several days, I found the idea still haunting me – still biting me on the arse, as Eduardo would have said – I decided to follow my instincts and caught the train, still unclear as to what I would do, or what I expected to find.

Granada has its own strong flamenco tradition. Home to the *Granaína palo*, and the *Zambra* – played by the Sacromonte Gypsies – it is also where the great experimental singer Enrique Morente lived. Known for his encyclopedic knowledge of the *cante*, he was vilified by conservative *flamencos* for his innovations, such as singing with a heavy metal band as his backing group in the masterpiece recording *Omega*.

'This music is not a museum piece,' he always said. 'Flamenco can be understood, even without being inside the flamenco world, by anyone who knows how to listen.'

I admired his free spirit – a typical flamenco quality – and his refusal to enter the political-style arguments and factional fighting amongst the aficionado grandees.

Lorca was also a draw to Granada, the city that destroyed him. Perhaps the only person to have come close to producing in words something of the feeling of flamenco, he became its patron saint, a martyr and a hero. There were songs about him, poems of his set to music, a constant stream of dedications – as though the flamenco community was aware of what it owed him, yet remained frustrated in its attempts to repay the debt. He and Manuel de Falla had virtually revived the form in their *Concurso de Cante Jondo* in 1922, at a time when flamenco was passing through one of its periodic descents into popularisation and stagnation.

More than anything, though, there was something in his poetry:

> *Oye, hijo mío, el silencio.*
> *Es un silencio ondulado,*
> *un silencio,*
> *donde resbalan valles y ecos*
> *y que inclina las frentes*
> *hacia el suelo.*

Listen, my son, to the silence.
It is a silence of waves,
a silence
where valleys and echoes slip past,
which turns faces
towards the ground.

And then there was something about the Alhambra. The Red Palace, a jewel above the city, cloaked in the deep green of cypress trees, set against the snowy mountains of the Sierra Nevada and the intense blue Andalusian sky. They said it had even inspired the Taj Mahal. Pedro had talked of it with a lilt in his voice, as though remembering a lover: it seemed to have that effect on people. In my own mind, it had become a unique concentration point, an axis between Europe and Africa, western Christianity and Islam; an artistic powerhouse where two worlds were pressed into one. Beautiful, but almost suffocating at times. Lorca had complained of feeling stifled by Granada. And I knew, almost as soon as I arrived, that my time here would be short. A few months maybe, not more. It felt like being in a pressure cooker.

I climbed the hill – the Cuesta de Gomérez – past austere guitar-makers and bright T-shirt shops, through the Pomegranate Gate and up the steep, green avenue to the palace, feet slipping on the loose gravel path. Young Germans with fluff-moustaches and broad shoulders powered past me as I struggled my way up, unfit after months of doing little but sitting around. Professional guitarists, I often noticed, had strangely atrophied bodies, usually slightly pear-shaped or knock-kneed from dedicated practice. In the hotel, I'd caught sight of my profile in the mirror; head low, tight neck, hips rocking forwards, arched back. I swore to reverse it and pushed myself harder up the slope.

The Nasrid Palace, with its Patio of Myrtles and the Patio of Lions, was exquisite, and made me realise that I had been living blind. Here was colour, form, balance; a labyrinth of designs and geometric patterns. The sound of water everywhere; row upon row of fine, needle-like columns; wooden ceilings like star-speckled, upturned boats.

Something was bothering me, though. It was different to the palace I had seen in picture books. Something about the intricate design work itself. I had imagined it to be made of stone, but crafted so finely as to look like paper, or lace. This was not stone that ran beneath my fingers, however, it was stucco, and had the look of a cheap modern replica. Surely, I thought entering the Patio del Mexuar, the original had been replaced. But no, this was the original, as I discovered the same effect throughout the royal palace. It was clumsy, thick, and lacked the grace I had expected from the photos.

I sat down at the far end of the Patio of Myrtles in one of the throne-like leather chairs, looking across to the Hall of the Ambassadors and an arcade of seven ornate arches perched on fine white columns. The circular marble fountains were silent and the image was clearly and calmly reflected in the pool of water stretching out ahead of me like a sheet of glass, peppered every once in a while by sparrows breaking out from the cover of the bushes and speeding into the sky. It was beautiful, one of the most beautiful buildings I had ever seen. But it was a joy tinged with disappointment. Or perhaps it was just my melancholy speaking. I glanced up, and saw a design I had often seen repeated around the building. Arabic writing, the motto of the Nasrids: *Wa la ghalib illa Allah*, no conqueror but God. It was everywhere, like the refrain of a poem. Pedro had once said the Alhambra was the largest book of poetry in the world. I missed him now. His cheerful, romantic slant on life would have been welcome.

I ran the words through my head again and again. They felt comfortable, comforting. 'No conqueror but God, no conqueror but God', a rhythmic phrase that seemed to calm something in me. And gradually, as the tourist groups passed by like schools of fish, I began to understand something. The stucco work, which seemed temporary or makeshift, had been deliberately crafted that way. The decorations had the power to take you somewhere else, even make you forget the physical world. Yet one day this would all crumble and disappear. The builders had wanted us to remember that. Nothing was permanent, not this place, nor its beauty, nor the people gazing at it. For a few minutes I allowed myself to explore the thought. Everything I had started since coming to Spain seemed to have come to a sudden and unexpected ending. The relationship with Lola, and now the group. I was incapable of building anything, always seeming to take the wrong path as I sought understanding and meaning. *Duende*, whatever it might be, was as elusive now as it had ever been.

Everything would come to an end, even, one day, my interest in flamenco. At first I was shocked at the thought. But for a moment, it was strangely clear, as if a space had opened within me. Flamenco had become an obsession, a way of defining myself by what I did. It gave me identity. Perhaps it was time for another approach.

*   *   *

The next day I decided to return with my guitar. The still, serene beauty of the Alhambra had acted upon me like a balm and the surroundings might give me inspiration.

I found a secluded stone bench in the Generalife – *jannat al-arif*, the gardens of knowing. Irises, marigolds and roses, vibrant and powerful even now in autumn, splashed bright colours amid the fountains and myrtle bushes. Opposite, on the other side of the River Darro, stood the Albaicín, all white and green with terracotta roofs. I took the guitar out of the case and looked around to see if anyone was watching. It was foolish to think I wouldn't attract some attention – a blond foreigner playing flamenco in the gardens of the Alhambra – but I wanted to be un-observed at the beginning at least.

I started by playing an *Alegría*, fingers missing the strings for a few moments before settling into the familiar rhythm. Within a few minutes I had focused on the music, and the plants, trees, late summer flowers and Albaicín began disappearing from view.

'*Di di di tran tran tran.*' I hummed to myself the nonsense words usually sung in an *Alegría*. People said they had been improvised one night by the singer Ignacio Espeleta when he forgot the lyrics he was supposed to sing, and ever since had been in-corporated as a standard opening for the *palo*.

A few people walked past, some hovering to hear a *falseta* before moving on. They were mostly foreign – Japanese, French, Germans, an English couple – but I was more concerned about one of the gardeners trying to throw me out. I wasn't clear what their policy was about people using the place for music practice. But an hour, then two hours passed and still no-one had complained. I felt the experience begin to lift me in the way I had hoped.

The sun was quite low, drawing long shadows across the pathway, when I packed the guitar away. The instrument had responded well to Granada, with its dry, Madrid-like air, and I was happy with my playing. Looking up, I could see the reddening light brushing the roofs of the ancient Arab town across the valley. I might go and look for a bar there later, perhaps meet some new people.

There was a sound behind me and I realised I was not alone. A woman came forward and stood close by, looking at me, and wanting to say something. I fiddled with the guitar case hoping that she would walk on, but she waited for me to finish and eventually I looked up, beaten by her patience.

'*Tú. Muy bien*,' she said in a thick English accent. An old, open, round face, smiling with crooked teeth; she must have been in her seventies at least.

'*Gracias*. Thank you.'

'Of course, you're English. I thought so.'

It felt good to talk to another English person again. At that moment, she was a link to a home that seemed more distant than ever. And I warmed to the uncharacteristically relaxed way in which she had started speaking to me. But there was a sudden awkwardness between us, as though something was going wrong, as though it wasn't part of the script that this should be happening. And so we fell into a strange silence for a moment, not sure what to say to one another.

'Have you been listening for long?' I said.

'Yes, for some time now. How long have you been

playing flamenco?' There was a flash in her crystal-blue eyes that betrayed a much younger spirit inside her aging body.

'A couple of years.'

'Oh really? As long as that?' She laughed. 'It looked as though the guitar was playing you,' she added. 'Not the other way round, if you see what I mean. Ha ha!' And she turned away, pacing down the slope towards the palace. I stared after her in a rage. How dare she say such a thing! What did she know about playing the guitar?

'But, of course, I don't know anything about playing the guitar,' she said suddenly, over her shoulder as she walked away. 'Please don't be offended.'

I watched as she headed down the slope. A young Spanish man sitting on a wall stood up as she approached, handed her a document case, and they continued together towards the exit, hand in hand.

I walked out of the Alhambra grounds and back into the city, annoyed and confused. What on earth had she meant? 'The guitar was playing me'? It was a senseless thing to say, and it gnawed away at me as I thought up all kinds of witty put-downs that would have been far more useful had I been able to think of them at the time. I returned to the hotel full of anger and threw the guitar down onto the bed.

'There. I've had enough of being played today,' I said and walked out into the evening streets.

The *paseo*, the evening stroll, was in full swing. People walking amid the low-flying bats, dressed in elegant, colourful clothes, bronzed skin showing under pinks, blues, whites, reds. Women linked arms, stopping to look at shoes in shop windows, while the men hailed one another loudly, voices echoing up the high, narrow streets into the cooling air. Groups of teenagers circled the squares on bicycles. One boy on a small moped with a high-pitched screaming engine gave rides to each girl in turn, up and down the hill, while the other boys looked on with envy. There was something earthy about the people here: thicker features, shorter bodies.

I walked to the far end of the Plaza Nueva by the Church of Santa Ana and sat on the wall overlooking the trickling Darro, people passing to and fro. It was a crossover time. The first seats at the open air cafés and restaurants were being taken for evening drinks and Granada's famously large *tapas*, tourists looking for somewhere to eat, while many locals were still leaving work and heading home.

Lazing in the gentle sunset atmosphere of the square, I caught sight of a priest on my left. A fairly ordinary priest, I thought, dressed in the usual brown robes, with his hands clasped piously behind his back, clutching some sort of small parcel. I thought nothing of it, and let my eyes drift across the square to the other side. A young man with long, dark, greasy hair had set off walking from one of the bars at exactly the same moment as the priest, and looked as though he was about to cross his path a few feet ahead of him. But instead he slowed down, circled, and very deliberately walked in such a way as to pass inches behind the priest, only a few yards from where I sat. It seemed like odd behaviour, first to make such a detour, and secondly to do so in order to brush so closely to a man of the cloth. Perhaps he was hoping for some of the priest's holiness to rub off, I joked to myself. But as I kept my eyes on the man, and then looked back at the priest, I noticed something: the small parcel that had previously been in the priest's hand had been passed to the man who was nervously, if not unprofessionally, looking around to see if anyone had noticed. There could be no doubt now what the parcel was. I had seen this before, but never with a priest.

The young man walked to the other side of the square. Fascinated, I was still watching him as he hovered by the doorway to a small building. He gave another quick glance to right and left, then caught my eye. He stopped and we looked at one another for a moment. He knew I had seen him. I tried to pretend not to notice and turned away, looking down the square at what now seemed to be dangerously thinning crowds. But it was too late, and from the corner of my eye, I could see him walking towards me. Fear streamed into my veins as I tried to work out what to do. There were fewer people at this end of the square. He could quite simply push me backwards into the river and I would never be seen again. Nobody would know. They were all too busy drinking, eyeing up the skirt, rushing home with the ingredients for dinner. I did not want to run, or even walk away. That would betray me, and I thought even now I might be able to convince him otherwise.

He came and sat down on the wall beside me. Very close, almost touching. He smelt strongly of nicotine mixed with adrenaline, a taut, sinewy type of energy circling his skin. One blow to the neck and I would be easily and efficiently dispensed with. I began to rue my earlier decision not to run. What the hell had I been thinking? Of course I should have run. This man did not want to talk, he wanted to kill me.

He was holding something. A knife, a lock-knife that

he had produced from his trouser pocket. He opened it out with a jerk and began rasping the blade against his thumb, never looking at me, his eyes fixed on the square ahead. I was unable to move for fear, and some morbid part of my mind began imagining the sensation of the blade passing through my ribs. There was so much to do with death in this city. It was almost appropriate that I should meet my own end in such a place, now that my flamenco journey seemed to be drawing to a close. Flamenco and death. They seemed to fit well together. I could understand the blood-curdling cry of the singer – *el llanto* – why it moved people so, how it seemed to come from the earth itself, and drew you back, like clay, to some sense of your-self, and the anguish of a naked inner being that has been ripped away from an unknown source. Somewhere inside me, I could feel that I was already falling, already hitting the water, already passing away. It was a calm and silent feeling.

The man was still drawing the knife across his fingers. It would come now, I told myself.

But in the same moment, as the thought raced across my mind, I realised that I was safe, that he wasn't going to harm me at all. This was a threat, nothing more. I had seen La Andonda doing something similar: playing with the knife when she was annoyed just to let you know she had it there, cleaning the dirt from under her fingernails, or, like now, rasping the blade with her thumb. If this man had wanted to kill me, I would never have seen anything. He would simply have stabbed me as quickly and as silently as he could.

'She says it's all right,' he drawled in a thick Andalusian accent. I wasn't sure if I had heard him right and it took me a moment to work out what he had said. It didn't make sense. But I slowly understood that my life was being spared. I kept my unseeing eyes fixed on the square ahead as he flicked the blade back inside its wooden handle, thrust the weapon into his pocket, and smoothly stood up to leave.

I opened my mouth to say something, grateful that he had decided not to kill me, but nothing came out.

'Beautiful square, beautiful city. You must cover your eyes.'

The young man walked away. Not to the door where he had headed before, but up the hill, into the labyrinth of the Albaicín.

I dragged myself to the nearest seat at one of the outdoor cafés, slumped down, and ordered the hardest liquor I could think of. I looked up at the Alhambra, still there. 'No conqueror but God.'

Half an hour later, drinking whisky with a shaky hand, I noticed a familiar face only a few tables away. It was the English woman who had spoken to me in the Generalife. She hadn't seen me. I turned my back and continued drinking.

Then, as I was calling the waiter back for a fourth time, I glanced over again. She was still there, sitting with a man. Not the one I had seen her with earlier, but someone else, older and more aggressive. He leaned towards her as though intent on her hearing his every word. I watched them talking for a while. They were arguing. The man seemed to want her to do something, but she refused. Then, without warning, he got up and walked away, knocking the chair over as he left.

I decided I should go and talk to her, picking up the chair that lay on its side.

She smiled, bright blue eyes, short white hair, as I sat down beside her. She seemed completely unaffected by what had just happened.

'Oh, I'm so glad you came over,' she said before I could ask if she was all right. 'I wanted to apologise for earlier on. It was terribly rude of me. I shouldn't have said such a thing.'

I paused to answer, slowed by the earlier shock and the whisky.

'This afternoon, in the Generalife,' she added, as if to clarify. 'Have I pronounced it right? Khe-ne-ra-lee-fay. I haven't been in Granada for very long. Is that how you say it?' Her voice was high and chirpy.

'Yes,' I said, still trying to catch up with her. 'Yes, that's right.'

'I'm afraid I've been getting terribly lost ... and receiving some very strange looks. I haven't quite got used to the '*kh*' sound. *Khuh*,' she said. 'Can you say it for me?'

Her pronunciation was fine, but I felt obliged.

'*Khuh*,' I said.

'*Khuh*,' she repeated, perfectly, but with emphasis, as though pretending to be a learner. 'You see, I can't do it as well as you. But then you're better at languages than I am.'

It was hard to tell whether she did this kind of thing for effect, or if she really had noticed my level of proficiency.

'Have you noticed how the Spanish are obsessed with pork and ham? I can't seem to sit down without someone offering me ham this, or ham that. See, even here on the menu, pigs' ears. Some friends gave me some, said it was a delicacy, so of course I felt I could hardly refuse. But they were awful. Ha, ha!' and she pulled a face, the wrinkles around her mouth and eyes creasing more deeply.

'I met a very interesting man the other day, just as I was unloading my car. You know, I could tell, there was a connection of sorts.' She gave a knowing look. She seemed to have no trouble meeting men in this foreign place.

'He was a middle-aged man. He told me a friend of his had done a painting of the crucifixion in a church, with people waving their hands and pleading.' She pulled a face. 'So I asked him, "Is your friend a very *emotional* man?" And he said, "Yes, I suppose he is." But he didn't understand what I was talking about, really.

'He said he worked in some business, but I didn't catch his name. Anyway, he was married, with four children,' she added disappointedly. 'Maybe I'll bump into him some day.' And she gave me a look as if to say such a thing was more than likely to happen and had often happened to her before.

'When did you arrive in Granada?' I asked. I assumed she was here on some sort of tour, or package deal, to see the sights of Andalusia.

'Oh, two days ago. I drove down from Surrey.'

'Surrey?!'

'Yes, Surrey. It's a perfectly respectable place you know. I almost didn't make it. I went round a roundabout the wrong way in France – just outside Paris – and a policeman stopped me (he was very good looking). I told him in my best French that it was all very confusing, and I was terribly sorry, but I'd been in England for the past eighteen years, and had forgotten how to drive on the other side. He leaned over and said "Are you looking for your coffin, *madame*?" in his husky, deep voice, and waved me on. "*Allez, madame*".'

'But why did you come here? Why did you leave?'

She paused. 'My work in England had finished. So I thought I might as well do nothing in Spain instead of idling about in England. So I brought what I could fit in the car and drove here. I never take more than a car-load wherever I go; it gives you a wonderful opportunity to shed so many possessions. Don't you find? You must have discovered that on your travels.'

Her words acted like a trigger, and in moments I found I had opened up to her, won over by her humour and eccentricity, and had begun the story of how I had come to Spain. She sat and listened silently. I told her things I had not told anyone, not even Eduardo. But she made me feel comfortable, and the words came like a stream. Flamenco, I said. Flamenco was what had really brought me here.

'Yes, there's nothing like an obsession to stop us from thinking about what we should really be paying attention to,' she said. I didn't understand, but her words found an echo with my train of thought the previous day in the Alhambra.

By the time we finished talking, it was gone midnight. We had been there for four hours, swapping stories and anecdotes. Grace – I didn't discover her name until some three or four days later – was a master storyteller, the product of an age before television, when entertaining through tales was a normal, necessary activity.

'I must go,' she said at last. 'Shall we meet here again tomorrow at the same time?'

I agreed.

She stood up, we kissed each other on the cheeks,

and she walked away. As she did so, a man stood up from one of the other tables and walked over to join her. They said a few words and then walked off together, hand in hand.

It was the man with the knife.

The conversation had lifted me, but I was confused by Grace's odd behaviour. How did she know the man with the knife? Was she dealing drugs? Perhaps it wasn't drugs at all that had been in the parcel. Maybe the man sitting on the wall was only trying to be friendly. I wasn't sure any more. In fact, I wasn't sure of anything.

But in a more positive state of mind, I decided the next day to go back to Juana's dance school, just to get back into flamenco again. I had slept well, and wanted to maintain the momentum. Playing with dancers and another guitarist would be ideal for this mild, sunny day. It was early, but I had seen the list of classes pinned on the wall. There was a two-hour morning lesson twice a week.

I walked into the hall. Emilio, the doorman, was sipping coffee in his wooden booth. He waved as I passed by, the thin grey moustache above his lip lifting and curling at the corners.

'*Buenos días,*' I called.

'*Buenos días, señor!*'

Inside the school it was quiet. Only a handful of adult students, dark hair swept back in the traditional way.

'*Ay!* Thank God!' It was Juana.

'Hello. I thought I might join you today, if that's . . .'

'Thank God you're here!'

'What?'

'You know *Guajiras*?' she asked. It was one of the 'return ticket' *palos*: songs and rhythms that had come back to Spain from Latin America and been absorbed into flamenco, like the *Rumba* and *Colombianas*. With a slow, twelve-beat rhythm that gradually got faster through the piece, *Guajiras* – originally from Cuba – usually had a light, lyrical feel to them and were wonderful to watch when danced well.

'Yes.'

'Good. Then play. We need you.'

'But what about . . . Isn't the other guitarist coming?'

'Luis? No he can't come. Won't be here for some time,' she said pushing me towards the chair, urging me to begin.

'Come on!' She clapped her hands to gather the girls and start the lesson. They stood in a line in front of the mirror.

'But what happened to him?'

'His girlfriend kicked him down the stairs and he broke something,' she said without turning round. 'Put him hospital! *Leche!*'

'No more questions, now,' she ordered. 'Play!'

chapter ELEVEN

Por Guajira

El río Guadalquivir
tiene la barba granate.
Ay dos ríos de Granada
Ay uno nieve y otro sangre.

The River Guadalquivir
has a pomegranate beard.
Two rivers in Granada
one of snow, the other of blood.

F. García Lorca

*L*uis's injuries were worse than we realised. His girl-friend was the national Tae Kwon Do champion. Multiple fractures meant he would be out of action for at least six months.

'Whatever you do,' he whispered in my ear when we went to visit him at the hospital, 'take my advice: never, and I mean never, go out with a martial artist. Stick to dancers, they're not half as dangerous, believe me.'

In Luis's absence, I became the full-time school guitarist, playing at the two morning classes, along with evening sessions that stretched from five in the afternoon to ten at night. The students were of all ages, from girls of seven to elderly ladies just taking it up for the first time. The majority were women between the ages of sixteen and twenty-five. Some looked like Moors; black-haired, dark-skinned. Others were blondes or red-heads; you could imagine their ancestors with helmets and shields with great crosses on them cleaning the land of heresy. Now they were all dancing together, upright, heads held high. More like a ballet class, I thought. But Juana was professional, and it felt good to be there when she was teaching. There was much for me to learn. Despite my time in Carlos's group, I still lacked confidence playing with dancers, and the classes gave me the opportunity to hammer out the *compás* for each *palo* again and again. It was easy to become distracted or change to something else when practising on my own, but here I had to repeat monotonously, always concentrating on Juana and the dancers, speeding up with them or slowing down depending on the pace she set, watching for the signs of a coming *llamada*, the signal that another section of the dance was about to begin. Difficult at first, eventually it became routine, like everything.

The classes were very technical, with great emphasis placed on the *zapateo*, or footwork, and the position of the hands. But there was a spirit here, or flamenco quality, as well.

'Relax your legs,' Juana would order the students. 'But from here,' she drew a line at the level of her groin, 'everything has to flow upwards, *hacia arriba*.'

Then she would order me to stop playing for a moment and sing the *palo* herself as she directed the class, hammering out the beats and off-beats with her heels.

Some of the girls in the classes were very *flamenca* too: confident and sassy, they often made up for what they lacked technically with a playful, flirtatious look in their eye. Others were more graceful and gave the impression of being real dancers. Then there were the very middle-class ones who did it as a hobby: short bobbed hair, sweat bands and pink cardigans against the cold. Some of them danced well, but never with any love, never flamenco.

Grace and I usually met in the afternoons, or once my classes had ended in the evenings, and we would spend our time chatting and exploring the city together: buying dried herbs from the spice sellers behind the cathedral – *flor de azafrán* for depression and migraines, *fucus* for losing weight – or pretending to bargain with Moroccan traders selling tourist tack in the bazaar, walking away once we'd beaten them down to their lowest price. She talked constantly, hardly allowing me to say a word, and any questions I had about her – particularly about some of her male friends – never had any light shed on them. There were some things you just couldn't ask a woman of her age.

We both had flats in the Realejo district – perhaps the most authentically Granadan area, with its half-broken houses, whitewashed walls and dirty, stepped streets at the foot of the Alhambra. The Albaicín, the more celebrated Moorish quarter of the city, had been taken over by Moroccan tea-houses, terrace restaurants serving heavy, oily food that you chose from pictures on a plastic card, and further on, in the Sacromonte area, Gypsy caves offering a night of sangría, gazpacho and 'genuine flamenco shows' – transport to and from your hotel included.

One night we went to a gig – partly out of curiosity and partly for fun. We sat in the open air listening to a *cantaora* who sang like she was chewing gum, and watching a twelve-year-old girl in a red and white polka-dot dress dance around a minute stage, contorting her face into a look of hate and aggression. It was clear she was being taught by a man, with graceless, masculine hand movements. At one point, a group of drunken *flamencos* passing in the street outside climbed up onto the railings to get a closer look, laughing and shouting abuse. '*Viva Jerez!*' one cried. But his sarcastic reference to one of the genuine centres of flamenco went over the heads of the mainly foreign audience.

'*Anda, tomar por culo.* Bugger it,' said a bored-looking Spanish woman to her husband at the next table. 'Let's go back to the hotel.' He made her wait until the end of the song, and they left.

It was impossible for flamenco to exist in such self-conscious circumstances. I remembered the story of La Niña de los Peines, who was spurred on to give the greatest performances of her life – so Lorca said – when one night a bored aficionado in the crowd shouted '*Viva Paris!*', as though to say 'Enough of what you sing for the tourists. Give us the real thing!' *Duende*, I was beginning to realise, could not be produced on demand. It needed something else – perhaps something from outside – and could only exist in a special, fleeting moment, as though the performers were channels for some power that came from beyond themselves.

There was a lightness about Grace, something I could not quite put my finger on. It was impossible to pigeonhole her. No sooner had I thought I understood her, than she would act in completely the opposite way. Scatty one minute, then sharp and acute the next. Or friendly, then distant, although these periods would never last very long. Moody? I wasn't sure. Sometimes she gave me the feeling there was some hidden agenda.

She would tell me folk-stories from all over the world. Or simply select interesting events from her own life. Even everyday occurrences seemed to act as a kind of launching-pad for her.

'There were some crickets on the wall in my flat,' she said one afternoon, knocking back her glass of Alhambra beer. 'I kept looking up at them and there they were, always in the same place. And then about twice a day they would just start making this horrible sound, for up to an hour – a high, screaming sound, not like any crickets I've heard before. And then just as suddenly, they would stop. The next day, it would be the same again. I left the windows open, and tried everything, but they just wouldn't go away – always the same thing. Anyway, I was getting quite annoyed by this point, so I called my neighbour in and I said, here, can you please help me to get rid of these crickets? They're making such a noise. And you know what he said? He said: "Those aren't crickets, it's a smoke alarm. I was wondering why you never turned it off." Well, he was quite nice about it, and switched the thing off for me. The black things were just marks on the wall, it seemed.'

'So they're not making the racket any more?'

'No, no. It's stopped. But it's funny how we mistake one thing for another.'

Carmen came to the youngsters' class in the early evening, when the teenage girls poured in, sucking sweets and filling the corridors with brightly coloured rucksacks and high-pitched chatter. Juana would often go easier on them than the older ones. She felt their lives were already regimented enough by school and homework, and wanted flamenco to be fun for them. But with Carmen she was different. Carmen was an intense girl. While the others treaded carefully, as though afraid of their own power, there was a surety about her footwork, a contact with the earth, as though she had roots descending beneath the floorboards and into the ground. She looked much like the other girls in the class – tied-back brown hair, brown eyes, soft, thick features – but there was something that set her apart: a playfulness and flexibility of expression, changing from happiness to surprise and despair as each movement demanded, as though she were dancing with everything she had, every part of her body and mind. It gave her a gravitas, a maturity, and a sensuality that were lacking in her classmates. The problem was her technical weaknesses. She'd started relatively late, aged fifteen, and had only been dancing at the school for just over a year. It was frustrating for her, but there was something in her movements that captured the eye, and I found myself watching her whenever I could during the lessons that she attended.

Juana did not give her more attention – if anything, it was less – but I could tell whenever she did direct a comment at her, there was a seriousness in her voice that was missing when she addressed the others.

'Watch how I move, Carmen.'

And Carmen seemed to respond, increasing her efforts until she mastered the new technique, a faint smile forming momentarily on her mouth in triumph before she got caught up in the next sequence.

Then one night after class, when the winds seemed to come off the mountains and a chill lay on the city for the first time, Juana said she wanted to start giving Carmen special lessons, once, twice a week. It would mean working later.

'Can you manage it?' she asked.

'Yes, of course. It's a pleasure to play when she's dancing.'

'We have to work on that girl,' she said.

The first class was the worst I ever attended.

'No! Like this. Again . . . Again . . . Again. Arms up! Don't let them drop. Fingers! *Use* your hands, don't wave them at me!'

We were working on a *Bulería*. Too complicated and fast, I thought. The poor girl danced, and moved, and danced, and stomped the floor till she was dropping from exhaustion.

'Hold your head up, girl! Now, come on! To the right, to the left, to the . . . No! Like this. Here, like this. Again! Softly, now. Look at me! Hands like doves. Lift your waist. Here, lift, up, more. Hands! Again. *Un, dos, TRES* . . .'

Her long legs began to flop onto the floor uncontrollably as the same step was repeated and repeated ten, twenty times or more. And the graceful little dancer I had seen previously began to look disjointed and artless.

'Chin up! Arms like the wings of an eagle. Come on! Believe in what you're doing. Separate your hips from your waist. Breasts out. More! Like bull's horns. *SIETE OCHO nueve DIEZ*. Relax!'

At one point I thought Carmen was going to stop: the point when the inevitable sense of rebellion was reached, the point when she might call out, 'No more!' But it passed rapidly, swamped by yet more commands, more demonstrations, more reprimands. And she simply kept going, tired, exhausted, sweating from every pore, unable now to complain or question what she was being put through.

After an hour and a half that felt much, much longer, she left, and was barely able to pick up her bag. It was late, and she left without changing.

Juana could see I was disturbed.

'You must understand: I'm teaching her body,' she said. 'More than her mind, I'm teaching her body.'

Winter meant Grace and I had to look for new bars to hang out in, warming ourselves away from the icy air that blew off the Sierra Nevada. We'd often meet in old men's drinking holes in the more hidden parts of the Albaicín, near where a deaf pensioner with jam-jar glasses used to cut my hair. They were the kind of places where the only cigarettes that were sold were black-tobacco Ducados. Or we'd have a drink at a big, barn-like bar off the Gran Vía that had Moorish arches, old, oak barrels of sherry and homemade vermouth made with vanilla and cinnamon, and enormous faded posters announcing the 1928 Corpus festival.

One day, feeling lazy, we went to one of the tourist cafés that lined the edge of the Plaza Bib-Rambla. The waiters wore stained white shirts and black bow ties, standing in the doorway when business was quiet like menacing bouncers. It was late on a Sunday afternoon after a heavy lunch at Chikito's – Grace paid; I couldn't afford such a high-class restaurant. We were both knocking back glasses of rum and drawing on thin, dark brown cigars. For someone in her seventies, I was amazed at how much Grace could drink. Her round face was pink with an alcoholic flush, and her short white hair, bobbing just above a pair of long silver and turquoise earrings, looked distinctly ruffled.

'I was pausing to open the door downstairs,' she said, 'when I caught sight of an elderly chap behind me doing odd things in front of my car. I looked round and saw him perform a complicated hand gesture near the licence plate and then walk off. "What are you doing to my car?" I said. "Nothing, nothing," he assured me. "I always do this to English cars for good luck."

'It transpired that someone had told him at a petrol station many years ago that English cars could bring good fortune. "As you can see I'm sixty-seven years old and I didn't touch your car at all." He was right there. Not sure if he was right in the head though. I thought about telling him that my car had been broken into three times in its checkered career, but he'd walked away by this point. I always knew Spain was a richly primitive Third World country in disguise.'

'Can one learn to tell stories?' I asked.

'Oh, yes. I should think so. But what do you mean?'

'Well, do you find people just have a natural talent, or can you develop it, learn storytelling techniques?'

'You must learn to relax. That's very important. It's important not to worry about getting it wrong, or falling flat. You learn, and hopefully do it better next time. Or the time after that, or the next. Just keep going. Practice is all important. And you can always improve.'

My mind turned to the gruelling lessons with Carmen as Grace began another anecdote about her travels. Only half-listening, I heard the words 'Bangkok', 'masseur', 'wedding'.

'You married him?' I asked as she paused for breath.

'Oh heavens, no. Why on earth would I want to do a thing like that?'

She lifted her glass to finish off her drink. On her finger was a thick silver ring, enormous really, with a large reddish-brown stone inset, and Arabic writing. The waiter placed another couple of full glasses beside us.

'But you should try it,' she said.

'What?'

'Telling stories. Try telling me a story. Now. From your life. Or it could be anything. Just try.'

'Grace,' I asked, 'what did you mean when you said that thing about the guitar – in the Generalife, that it was playing me?'

'It's about who's in control,' she said. 'Excuse me.' And she got up to find the loo.

I looked around the café. Some of the waiters were watching our table suspiciously. A young man and an old woman slowly getting drunk together. They didn't like it. It wasn't normal. I turned my eyes away, and silently cursed the rigidity of it all, the deeply conservative seam running through this country.

'Did you know,' Grace said when she returned, helping herself to another cigar, 'Gypsies spit at someone who has something that they covet. It's to ward off the Evil Eye. They believe envy brings on the Evil Eye, so they spit to deal with the envy. You can't envy someone you've just spat at.'

I was dubious. I had never come across anything like this.

'Another drink?' she asked.

'Yes. Go on then.'

But we didn't have to call the waiter. He was already upon us, standing over the table like a crow.

'We're closed,' he said, in broken, angry English. 'You must go.'

I looked at him startled. We had been to this bar before, and it had often stayed open well into the night. The man was obviously lying. I replied in Spanish.

'*Pero, qué dice?* You never close this . . .'

'You must go!' he repeated in English, the blood rushing to his face.

I sat still, refusing to budge, but Grace was already on her feet, moving out from the table. She put her coat on, pulled her bag from the bench, and then, very determinedly, turned to face the waiter.

'Could you tell me where I can find the bus station,' she asked, her voice steady, not a hint of the litres of booze she had drunk that afternoon. 'You see, I have to travel to Málaga to meet some friends, and I wasn't sure if there was a train, or another way of getting there. I would like to arrive before it gets too late.'

'Yes, of course, *señora*,' the waiter said, and began giving directions. I watched the conversation out of the corner of my eye, still furious at the man. But within moments he was smiling, and from being rude and confrontational, had suddenly become friendly and helpful. By the time we were walking out the door, he was positively overflowing with good humour. I still wasn't quite sure how it had happened.

'It's much more difficult to be angry towards someone you've helped out in some way,' Grace said. 'Goodbye.' She kissed me on the cheeks and turned to go. 'I have to catch that bus,' she said. And she strode off confidently towards the corner where a man with a beard and a trilby hat was waiting for her. She slipped her arm through his and they disappeared.

Some time in December, I received a phone call from Alicante. It was Lola.

'Hello, *guiri*.'

Her voice was frothy.

'We're going down to the Sierra Nevada to do some skiing, and I thought I might pop into Granada to see you. God knows why.'

'Of course. But . . . how did you know where I was?'

'Oh, I asked your journalist friend. He told me you'd run away from Madrid. We've become quite friendly.'

Eduardo had told me nothing. I didn't even know he'd met her. I might have felt betrayed, but I was curious.

A week later we were sitting opposite one another in a bar in the Albaicín.

'Why did you come here, for the love of God? I mean, why not Guadalajara, or Oviedo, or Cáceres, or some other happening town? It's dead here. The only flamenco here is what they put on for tourists. You know what that's like. Horrendous!' She articulated the word slowly and lovingly.

I couldn't explain. So much had happened since we split up. And there were things I didn't want her to know.

'Just a whim,' I said.

'A whim, eh?' She looked me hard in the eye, then down at the table. 'You seem to do quite a lot in your life on a whim.'

The reference was clear. I was being made to feel responsible.

'Look, I . . .'

She held up her hand to stop me. 'Don't talk about it! It's finished.' And her wide, full mouth forced itself into a resigned smile.

There was a pause, until we both started talking at once, and then stopped.

'No. You go ahead, *guiri,*' she insisted.

Her persistent use of the word annoyed me, but I carried on.

'Did you come here with a group of friends, that was what I was about to ask you.'

'Eh?'

'You said "we" were coming skiing.'

'Oh! No, I came with Vicente and the kids.'

It hit me like a train. With her husband? After everything, all the talk of leaving him?

'We often come here in the winter.'

I remembered the lunch at their flat, and the mild, tame woman serving food dutifully and politely. They had been an ordinary couple that afternoon.

'I take it things are OK between you two,' I said, forcing the words out. A hundred barriers were falling down across the table between us.

'Oh yes. Yes.'

'I'm glad.' I fell into a closed silence as I realised she had used me as a plaything, a distraction from the real relationship in her life. For all their unsuitability, she and Vicente were strongly tied to one another, by the school, their children, and their need for sex. What she sought were lovers, and only when her sexual needs were being satisfied by someone – myself, Juan, who knows how many others – could she ever contemplate leaving her husband. In the end, though, for all her talk of flamenco and her free spirit, she didn't have the courage to do it. She would be with him for ever.

'And you,' she said. 'Got any girlfriends? Any nice Granadinas here for you? You didn't choose well coming here, *guiri*. They're all ugly as sin down here.'

'No.'

'What – no they're not ugly, or no you don't have a girlfriend?' She leaned forward. 'Have I hurt your feelings? Have you got a little Conchita tucked away here somewhere?'

I had barely looked at another woman since we split up, and felt, even now, that I might never love again with such intensity. It had been the most romantic and passionate experience in my life, and the emptiness I had felt when the relationship ended had only been filled by pushing myself to a drug-charged extreme that had left me feeling dry and barren. My friend had died, and others who I had counted as friends had cast me out. Apart from Grace and the dance classes, I was lost, barely recovering from the emotional highs and lows of the past two years, looking back on Alicante as the best of times, a period I could remind myself of to soothe my melancholy. Yet here she was, mocking me, mocking our relationship, mocking what for me had been a life-changing experience as though it were nothing, and had meant nothing to her. I wanted to get up and leave. A quiet inner voice inside urged me to stay.

'Actually, I've got three on the go at the moment.'

'Three!' She laughed at the joke. 'You *are* keeping yourself busy!'

'Yes. It's the blond hair, you see. Makes me stick out in a crowd.'

She laughed again. But had nothing else to say.

'So how's everyone else?' I asked. I wasn't interested, but it was worth saying.

'Fine. Pilar gets madder by the day, and Rafael is still as boring as ever. But I don't see them as much any more.'

'And Juan?' He was the only one I wanted to hear about.

She looked intensely at the tablecloth, and drew her nail forcefully across the grooves of the weave.

'He left,' she said finally. 'Shortly after you . . .' She sighed. 'I don't know where he went.' She looked up, and I nodded. Then her head bent forward again.

'He left a note. Said he was sorry.'

We chatted for a little longer about inconsequential things, until finally unable to stand it any more, she looked at her watch and announced she was leaving.

'I told Vicente I was coming down to do some shopping.'

Even now she had to lie.

We kissed each other goodbye, with a squeeze on the arms just to register something between us, even if it did now belong to the past. And she walked away, among the dark, narrow streets, her hips still swaying musically under her dress, and her dark red hair blowing gently off her face.

'I met up with an old lover the other day,' I said.

Grace's eyes lit up.

'Oh really? Tell me.'

'She wanted me to feel guilty,' I said. 'She was making me feel guilty, even though there was no reason. So eventually I decided I wasn't going to feel guilty, or angry or anything else I didn't want to. And it sort of worked. At least I was able to see it happening.'

'Yes,' she said, knocking back her glass of red wine. 'We often congratulate ourselves on things we observe. But what about all the gaps in between? What's happening then, between our observations, I wonder.'

'El Niño Ricardo told me once how he sent his son to learn guitar with the father of Paco de Lucía.'

Despite being a doorman, Emilio loved to talk about people in the flamenco world, most of whom he appeared to have met. I suspected he might be a member of the *Peña Platería*, Granada's secretive flamenco club, which employed a closed-door policy to outsiders.

'Antonio had it right – the kids had to practise all day every day. It's like a job, just like anything else. Anyway, Ricardo knew there was little life left in him, so he sent his son to Antonio Sánchez, told him to teach the kid what he knew. And you know what? The kid came back after a month saying he couldn't take the pace. Good player, but without the slog, he was no better than anyone else. That's what makes Paco so great: he stuck at it, worked at it.'

He knew I loved to hear these insider tales, and would simply carry on, like most Granadinos when they were on a roll.

'I met Sabicas when he came back to Spain.'

Sabicas, the great flamenco guitarist, autodidact and almost mythical character, was in exile for most of the Franco dictatorship, living in New York and Mexico, only returning to Spain for visits towards the end of his life.

'Everyone was waiting to hear him live. But, you know, flamenco is in the air round here. You live for too long cut off from that and it shows, no matter how good you are.

'So he went back to New York, and he was dying there, so he went to the *peña* they have for aficionados – used to go a lot. And everyone's playing, so he decides to join in – he always liked to show off, Sabicas. But he played badly. Everyone knew, but they didn't say anything, because he's Sabicas. But he knew, and he went home annoyed and locked himself in the house and practised and practised without coming out. A whole week. Then the next week he goes back to the *peña* and plays the best gig of his life. Everyone was amazed. Someone even recorded it on video. But you know what? That night he went home and the next morning he left feet first.'

I felt more at ease at the dance school now. Juana treated me as one of the crowd – I could tell by the way she corrected me if I made a mistake: less harsh, more playful. And in addition to his flamenco tales, Emilio would give me late-night tutorials on local recipes, or the flowers and wildlife of the Sierra Nevada. His impression of an eagle soaring through the valleys looking for food was particularly memorable, as he pounced on his broomstick pretending it was a snake.

Meanwhile Juana drove Carmen on and on. I would sit in, playing as ordered, often spending the whole session going over the same passage again and again, my fingers clicking into a kind of hypnotic rhythm as they went through the same movements a hundred, two hundred times. For Carmen, though, it was more difficult. She was being drilled and Juana never slackened the pressure. No encouragement, no words of praise. She seemed to want to grind the girl down, as though engaged in some war of attrition. Obsessive perfectionism, I thought, but I had already been warned not to make any comments.

My discomfort with Juana's methods increased, however, as I saw the raw, spirited girl begin to change. The quality we had all praised her for, her energy and maturity, was ebbing away. Hammered by a barrage of instructions, she quivered with fatigue, her face often straining and hard now, no longer breathing life into her movements as she once had done. And whereas before it had flowed, naturally and easily, too much concentration was now creating a tension that left her dancing dry and lifeless.

I watched it all from my corner. Sometimes I put more life into my playing, just to try to spur her on when the pressure seemed to be getting too much. I wanted to see that spark she had when I'd first seen her, and thought perhaps by giving something to her with the music, I might help draw it out. Even just a chink, to see that it was still there, and might still be brought out of her again.

'*Compás! Compás!*' Juana would shout, and I knew she wanted me there as a musical metronome. Keep the rhythm. Nothing else required.

In desperation I tried to catch Carmen's eye, to smile at her, or give her a signal of some sort. But battered into submission as she was, she stared ahead faithfully at the mirror, eyes unmoving, only too aware of the watchful gaze of Juana. Any drop in attention would be seriously criticised. And then, after the class, she would simply pick up her bag wearily and head straight out without a word, her hair flattened down, stooping under the weight of her own body. To me, Juana began to take on the appearance of a sadistic school mistress, secretly taking pleasure in the destruction of her pupil.

'I want her to audition for the Conservatory in Madrid,' she said one evening after another drubbing of her student.

'The Conservatory?' I asked. 'She's a flamenco dancer, not a ballerina.'

'She is a dancer,' she countered. 'She could be a great dancer. She has potential. It is up to me to prepare her.'

'But the Conservatory? Why not the Amor de Dios school? That would be far more . . .'

'Dancing is dancing. If she works hard enough she will be able to pick it up. Other *flamencos* have gone on to classical dance and come back to flamenco. It is never lost.'

I shook my head.

'Hey! Listen to me!' She raised her powerful voice to a shout. 'You don't know what it has been like in this country for flamenco. For years they have laughed at us. No-one takes us seriously. But now we can prove to them we are every bit as good as the rest of them. They cannot simply treat us as old-fashioned folklore any more. Amusing, yes. Good for the tourists, the odd performance before the king, just to remind him that we're still here. Those days are finished. We are serious dancers, as good as the best of them. Good enough to go to the best schools and turn the laughter back in their faces.'

'And you . . .'

'Look at Joaquín Cortés,' she said. 'He's just the beginning. A *flamenco* who trained in classical dance, and now fills the biggest theatres in the world. That's us, that's what we're doing here.'

I *had* looked at Joaquín Cortés. He was everywhere with his trademark naked torso – on TV, in magazines, doing world tours, filling the gossip columns with his private life. But as his status grew, his spirit seemed to diminish, and I felt he spent more of his time on stage demanding the adoration of his audience rather than winning it with his genius. That was not flamenco, at least not in my mind. Not the stardom of Joaquín, nor the strict discipline of Juana. I loved flamenco because there was something free about it, something ineffable. A spirit that could not easily be defined, captured or possessed. For me, Joaquín Cortés had lost whatever *duende* he may have had, and Juana was quickly forcing it to flee from Carmen by driving her too hard, not giving her the time or space really to dance from within. There were other options, other avenues for a promising young dancer. But it was pointless saying anything. Juana would simply not have heard.

One evening Juana was called away halfway through the class, and for the first time, I found myself alone in the studio with Carmen. She was tired, as usual, and took the opportunity of the unexpected break to crouch down and catch her breath.

'How's it going?' I asked.

'Worn out.' She lifted her head.

'How're you finding the lessons?'

'Hard.' She looked down again at the floor.

'You enjoy it?'

She tossed her head from side to side to show doubt. 'Yeah.' Then hesitated before continuing, 'It's a lot of work.'

From the corridor came the sound of Juana speaking loudly to someone on the phone in the office. Her powerful voice was echoing into the bare studio. She would be finishing soon, and I wanted to make contact. There would be no other chance. Time to try again.

'Juana told me you want to try for the Conservatory in Madrid.'

'Yes, that's right.' She lifted her head again and looked up.

'Do you want to go to Madrid?'

'Oh yes!' There was a hint of a spark in the tired face.

'Why?'

'I don't want to stay here. It's dead. There's no life. *No mola aquí.* Granada's the pits.'

'But where would you stay?'

'Oh, my aunt lives there. *Es muy maja.* She's cool. Goes out all the time. She says she'll show me everything when I get there.'

'What do you want to see?'

'Oh, you know, the usual stuff. I've been to the Prado and the Thyssen museum and all that. But she said she'll take me out at weekends to all the bars and stuff. She said I can get a moped as well. Then I can go everywhere on my own.'

'Can't you do that now?'

'Yeah. Well . . . it's different. There's just nowhere to go. And then there's homework, and things to do at home.'

She looked back at the floor, her back arched over, face red with exertion.

'I used to live in Madrid,' I said.

'Really? Where?'

'Off the Gran Vía.'

'Wow! You must know it all. I really can't wait to go. I've got to get out of here. Granada's a dump.'

From the corridor, we could hear Juana's conversation coming to an end. There was something else I wanted to say.

'Granada's not that bad,' I said.

'What? You haven't had to live here since you were born. I tell you, it's . . .'

'No, really, listen to me.' I could hear Juana putting down the phone and her footsteps pounding our way. 'Listen, I found out yesterday: Paco de Lucía is giving a concert here in May.'

Her face lit up in surprise.

'Really?'

The footsteps were getting louder. We both glanced to the door – only seconds left.

'He's coming with El Grilo. El Grilo's going to be dancing.'

Tall, powerful, and with a very male and very

graceful style of dancing, El Grilo was a great, possibly one of the greatest, living male flamenco dancers. Along with Antonio Canales, Javier Latorre and Adrián Galía, he had been part of a group of young dancers who had dominated the flamenco scene in Madrid in the late 1980s and early 90s. Carmen's eyes opened wide when I mentioned his name, and she laughed.

'You want to come? I'll take you,' I said quickly, as Juana entered the studio. We returned to our places, but not before Carmen had turned to face me quickly and flashed me an enormous pink grin of excitement.

'What did you do?' Juana asked after Carmen had gone. There was a faint smile on her mouth. The lesson had continued as usual on her return, the same barrage, the same incessant criticism, but there was a small change: just a hint of defiance in the girl.

chapter TWELVE

Por Seguiríya

Escondida en su concha
vive la perla
y al fondo de los mares
bajan por ella . . .
No olvides nunca
que lo que mucho vale
mucho se busca.

Hidden in its shell
lies the pearl
and they dive to the bottom of the sea
in search of it . . .
Never forget,
things of great value
are greatly sought after.

Grace picked me up in a battered old Seat.

'Come along!' she sang out from the street. 'We've got a wedding to go to.'

I got dressed and hurried down. She never ceased to surprise me. Whose wedding?

The car was no more than a tin-can on wheels, filthy inside and out, with cigarette butts and scraps of old magazines decorating the floor in the gaps between the yawning holes beneath our feet. We put-putted through town. It was amazing to think she had driven this all the way from England.

'Great car,' I said.

'What?' she cried above the din of the engine. I looked down at the grey asphalt, flying past like sandpaper.

'I said I suppose you and this car have been through a lot together.'

'What are you talking about?'

'Didn't you drive this down from England?'

'What, this? You must be mad!'

I was mad? She was the one driving it.

'I got rid of my old car some months ago,' she said after a pause. 'A Frenchman bought it off me. Said he wanted it for some tax dodge or other.'

For a woman who lived on what she could fit into the back of a car, she had sold this key item off with surprising alacrity, I thought. But then, that was Grace all over. Nothing, not even her nomadism, was fixed. She travelled light in all senses of the word, to the extent that even the travelling itself could be jettisoned at any moment. She needed no reminding of who she was. There was only ever today. The problem was, I wasn't sure how long today was going to last: Grace was a hopeless driver.

I had always felt safe when Jesús was driving, despite the smashes. Grace, though, was a 70-year-old woman with dodgy eyesight.

'Oh! I know him,' she said cheerfully, looking in the rear-view mirror at the man she had just forced off his bicycle. I wondered if the last time they met she had knocked him sideways as well.

'Look out!' A schoolboy laden down with bags almost became her next victim. We swerved, banked the kerb and brought down part of a vegetable-seller's stall. Pomegranates rolled everywhere.

'Don't worry,' she said as we got back into the car having cleaned up the mess and paid off the shop-keeper. 'I'd seen him.'

At times she seemed to realise that her driving was less than orthodox, and let out a chuckle, like a schoolgirl caught peeping into the boys' changing rooms. Keep calm, I had to tell myself. This woman drove all the way from England. She's probably driven all over the world.

'I've had much worse cars than this, of course,'

she said. 'I once had one in Sri Lanka with no brakes.'

'What! How the hell did you stop a car without brakes?'

'Oh, we just used to hit the kerb and then stick our feet out the door and slow it down that way.'

I sank further into my seat and began concentrating on the world outside to try to take my mind off such insignificant worries as life, death and emergency surgery. But Granada was relatively small, and before long the city gave way to thirsty-looking, white, wrinkled rocks and an enormous straw-coloured landscape as we headed out into the countryside. Fewer things here to collide with, I thought, as long as she can keep on the road. But as soon as we were in the country, her driving improved.

It felt good to escape into the air and space after the closed atmosphere of the city. Yet even here, in springtime, there was a heaviness that rose up from the earth and touched everything – the rocks, the trees, even the air. The land defined all, giving a sense of place, of self, yet also acting as a prison and a cage. Why had Lorca come back here? Returning to a city which had made him, yet which would also claim him, like a sacrificial animal. There seemed an inevitability about his death. It was part of being a Granadino.

The car pushed on up the crumbling roads, and my thoughts turned once again to Jesús.

'When it's time to go, it's time to go,' I muttered, half to myself.

'There it is.' We had reached the top of a hill and descended to a modern, square-blockish village.

'Whose wedding is this, anyway?' I asked.

'I told you already.'

I was sure she hadn't mentioned a thing.

She parked at the top of a steep hill near an isolated church. Scores of cars were parked chaotically, half-blocking the roads, sticking out at awkward angles, taking up the space of two or three other vehicles. There was a familiar feel to it. I caught a glimpse of some of the number plates: Málaga, Seville, Cádiz, Madrid, Barcelona. Whoever was getting married had friends all over the country.

We walked up to the church. People were standing outside the entrance, some passing through to get inside, others milling about chatting. There was a formality and sense of chaos about the group that I recognised. Gypsies. I felt a rush of joy. A Gypsy wedding! And it was suddenly comforting to be back amongst them. After months in Granada, away from Madrid, mourning the loss of my friend, this was where I wanted to be.

We joined the crowd, greeted by a few suspicious looks. As two blonds, we stood out. But the bride – no more than seventeen – quickly appeared, draped in white chiffon, and clinging to her father's arm. She lowered her head modestly and the crowd gathered round her like bees, while her father grinned, his gold teeth shining from behind thin, cracked lips and a weather-worn face. From his waistcoat hung a gold watchchain, while more gold adorned his wrists. On his forearm was a primitive-looking tattoo: *Nací para sufrir* – Born to suffer.

Father and daughter pushed their way through, stopping to talk briefly with uncles, cousins, grand-mothers and nephews. Everyone shouted and sang at once, a great wave of energy and enthusiasm. I looked for Grace – we had been separated in the scrum. She was near the bride, talking to a Gypsy man who was treating her as an important guest, leaning his face towards hers to hear what she was saying above the spiralling din. She smiled and turned away, clapping her hands with the rhythm now pulsating around the bride and her father as they slowly edged their way towards the church doors.

The little building was overflowing, people cramming in the door, and jumping up and down to see above the other heads in front. Grace had disappeared again. I copied some of the young boys and climbed up the pillars in the doorway, hanging on with one hand and leaning out over the crowd to catch a glimpse of the altar. Grace was at the front, being given one of the best positions by the father of the groom. Both mothers were standing on either side, waiting for the ceremony to finish. But the singing started before they had even got halfway through. It was only a religious formality anyway.

The priest braved it out, straining to make his voice heard. Meanwhile the congregation shouted, slapped one another on the back, and swapped stories. The guitars began playing *Alboreás* – the special Gypsy wedding *palo* with a droning, *Alegría*-style rhythm – the clapping began, and the whole church exploded into an impromptu flamenco concert. The poor priest began to look disturbed, sweating heavily, blood pressure rising dangerously under the strain of his collar and heavy robes as the cries of '*Ole! Ole! Ole!*' drowned him out. But moments later the ceremony had ended, the couple left under a hail of rice, and a white dove was released into the air. It flew frantically up above the trees to get away from the madness.

'For her purity,' one of the boys said, pointing up

at the bird and grinning. Virginity was all important.

The mass headed down the hill into the village, where a local restaurant was waiting with cold prawns in mayonnaise and *jamón Serrano*. The patio had been covered over with a white awning, and long tables laden with wine, beer and bread waited underneath. Everyone made straight for the drinks before sitting down on benches to nibble at the food, still shouting and singing. There was no seating plan as far as I could tell, but the natural Gypsy hierarchy asserted itself. The families of the couple, the elders, the strongmen – they could all be made out by the way they were treated, how the others behaved towards them. It was there in the posture, the tilt of the head, the shape of the shoulders.

But as I listened to the violent din of voices all talking at once, I noticed people were beginning to scream: the women first, then the men. We all turned to see what was going on. Some at the back stood up on the tables to get a better look and the young boys rushed forward. A mountain goat was standing by the main table, bleating loudly and chewing the tablecloth. The bride screamed and threw herself into the arms of her husband, but he was as frightened as she was. For a moment everyone was still, before the goat, tiring of the tablecloth and doubtless noticing the huge amount of food on the tables, jumped up and started tucking into the three-tiered wedding cake. Everyone fell back in shock, and when one of the braver types tried to shoo it away, he was met with a threatening show of teeth and a kick from the animal's powerful hind legs.

'Fetch a stick!' came the cry. The restaurant owner came out from the kitchen with a broom.

'A broom! A broom! Come on Pedro. Charge!' The

cries of encouragement came from all sides. A small, overweight man stood at the side, nostrils flaring, the broom in both hands like a Roman infantryman, pointing it at the goat, which was quickly ruining the biggest event in the village all year. He thrust his weapon forward tentatively, but to little effect. The animal was moving on from the cake to the ham and prawns.

'*Venga, Pedro!*'

The bride was beginning to cry. The restaurant-owner gathered himself, then with a shout dropped the broom, ran at the beast and, with a great swing, punched it as hard as he could on the chin. The goat stumbled sideways, gave a startled yelp and leapt nimbly from the table and onto the ground. With a couple of bounds, it was out of the restaurant and running indignantly down the hill, shaking the remaining crumbs of food from its beard. Pedro, however, was not so nimble, and before he could stop himself, he had landed face down in the garlic mushrooms. Everyone was too shocked to say anything for a second. Then a cry of '*Olé! Pedro!*' rang out from the back, and the poor man, realising it was his moment, stood up to take a bow before the cheering crowd.

'Drinks are free!' he spluttered above the cries of congratulations, and with the grin of the all-conquering warrior, he headed back into the kitchen.

'What about the other one?' the girl next to me said under her breath as we all sat down again. 'There's more than one with horns at that table.'

Her friend sucked her teeth and one of the women started handing out food noisily, trying to drown out talk of the bride's alleged infidelity.

A queue was now forming: the couple were sitting

on a dais, like kings, and each person was passing by, congratulating them, and handing over amounts of money. Grace and I joined the back of the line.

'Best day of your life,' I said to the groom as we reached him, and I looked in the direction of his new wife. He looked solemn for a minute, then laughed.

'*A que sí!* Too right!'

The money-giving ceremony lasted an hour and a half. Everyone wanted to make sure their contribution was the one the couple would remember. And with the cash came promises of favours, best wishes for their future children, gifts, embraces, anecdotes, offers of work. When it was all over, the bride was approached by an elderly woman I had noticed earlier. There was something striking about her, an air of importance, accentuated by the vast number of gold and beaded necklaces resting on her chest. But she had remained in the background, and didn't seem to be a member of either of the families.

'That woman there,' Grace said. 'That woman is brought especially to examine the purity of the bride. They call her an *ajuntaora*.'

The bride looked ill, and was quickly led out of sight into a private room. A few glances were exchanged but everything continued as normal.

Barely five minutes had passed, though, when a woman on the other side of the table began tutting.

'Shouldn't take this long,' she said. Her neighbours agreed.

'They should be out by now.'

'Never takes this long.'

The women looked concerned; the men, serious.

The anxiety appeared to have reached the main table, where the groom was sitting, pale-lipped, eyes tight like a fist. The bride's family were beginning to flap like birds.

'Too long, too long now. I always said it.'

Someone was sent to find out what was going on. The groom stood up sharply, chair flying out from beneath his legs. His brother ran round and grabbed him by the shoulders.

'Wait!' he shouted. 'Wait!'

But the bride's family were also beginning to stand up, arms hanging by their sides, breathing quickly. Then that smell. I recognised it from the bullfight. The portentous smell of blood, the smell that tells you it will soon be spilled here.

We were all on our feet, the pitch of voices rising higher and higher. The bride's father was trying to calm things down. He smiled and made steadying gestures with his hands, but sweat dripped from his temples, and his hands were shaking. Just now, I thought, the flick of a knife, and all would be lost. Hands began to reach round, behind backs, into pockets. Something had to be done, but I felt a hand on my arm pressing down. I looked and saw the thick silver ring on Grace's finger. Don't do anything, it said. Just watch, observe.

At that moment the old woman came running out of the restaurant clutching a white handkerchief and raised it high for everyone to see, screaming at the top of her lungs. We leaned forward: the cloth was embroidered with a red rose in each corner and in the middle there was a dark, yellow stain. The groom's family stared hard for a second, and then an almighty cheer went up, more out of relief than joy. The two fathers embraced each other like brothers and people sat back into their seats, smiles and grins replacing the angry scowls of a moment earlier. The bride was brought forward looking paler than when she had gone inside, and was swamped with well-wishers, lifting her up in the air and dancing with her, parading triumphantly out into the street. Car horns sounded, the men threw off their jackets, tearing at their shirts in ecstasy, until they stood naked from the waist up, waving their arms and shouting like lunatics.

The music started: two guitarists beating out more *Alboreás*. The women took turns to dance in a frenzy, some in pairs, each trying to outdo the other.

I began clapping to the rhythm, letting myself feel, once more taken away by the joy, the all-embracing energy of a flamenco *juerga*. My face was flushed and an uncontrollable smile forced its way onto my lips. Standing there, tapping my foot, letting myself get drunk on it all. I was aware of a space next to me and then I turned. Grace had gone. I expected she had found herself another companion. But then I spun round the other way and looked up. She was standing outside on a slope by the road on her own, her head clearly visible above the others, looking me directly in the eye.

'Too noisy in there for you?' I asked as I walked up to her.

'I have to go back to Granada. You can stay if you want. I'm sure you'll be able to get a lift from somebody.'

It had the makings of a party that would last at least three days. I would be lucky if I got out of there before the end of the week. I looked back at the crowd – the groom's brother was standing on a chair pouring wine into the father-in-law's mouth as he lay on the ground. Only a few moments before they had been close to killing one another. I turned back round and looked again at Grace. There was no question about her intention, it just seemed odd timing – just as it was all starting.

'No, no. I'll come with you,' I said reluctantly, and we headed up to the car.

The music was still audible through the open windows as we headed out of the village, and didn't fade completely until we had passed over the hill and into the next valley. Grace was quiet. I slumped back into the seat, a swift hangover, brought on by the heat and sudden tearing away from it all, descending on me like a damp cloth. I dozed for a while, and woke up once more under the streetlights of the city.

'They're a funny lot, aren't they?' Grace said as she dropped me off. 'Such an *emotional* people.' There was something about the way she said it.

'Yes,' I said automatically. 'I suppose you're right.'

I climbed the stairs in the dark, opened the door and threw myself down on the sofa, trying to work out what she meant, my thoughts passing over the day's events in chaotic detail. The noise of the city at night was dull by comparison.

'Deep song always sings in the night,' Lorca had written. 'It knows neither morning nor evening, mountains nor plains. It has nothing but the night, a wide night steeped in stars. Nothing else matters.'

It was the credo of the *flamenco*: a rejection of the mundane, the ordinary, the life of the everyday man, embracing, rather, an extreme world – extreme passions, extreme feelings, the extremes of life and death. And it was a way of life I had wanted to believe in, had been intoxicated by – its excitement, its danger, the affirmation it gave that you were different, and alive.

But I was beginning to have doubts. For over two years I had done little but listen to music, think about music, play music. There was so much music I barely spent a moment without some tune, some rhythm playing itself out in my mind. First thing in the morning, as I was having a shower, over lunch, walking in the street, or when I tried to go to sleep – this was the worst. There were times when I would spend hours trying in vain to switch my head off, fingers on my left hand involuntarily twitching as an idea for a *falseta* or a variation on a *compás* would play itself out over and over again.

I had begun to listen to less music in general, though. Whereas it had always been there in the background – a cassette player or the radio – now I began to crave silence. Just the thought of hearing music would make me feel nauseous, like being offered a rich creamy pudding at the end of a heavy, greasy meal. I had overdosed, was suffering from music fatigue, and wanted nothing more than to hear the natural sounds around me with no artistic interference.

Grace had something to do with it. There was a calmness about her, despite – or perhaps because of – her eccentricity, which seemed to rub off on me. She was right about the Gypsies at the wedding: they *were* very emotional, probably over-emotional. Just as I myself was. I was beginning to see that now. Stifled by the academically-oriented life I had been leading in England, I had thrown myself to emotional extremes with Lola and then with Carlos and Jesús. Now I found myself seeking some sort of balance: neither the madness of what I had lived in Alicante and Madrid, nor a return to the passionless life I had led beforehand.

I didn't want to reject what I had done; I knew that something in me had been allowed to develop in Spain, although exactly what that was was hard to define. Perhaps a greater emotional awareness. As a child, I had absorbed the qualities and attitudes of my surroundings, making unconscious choices about who I was, based on the values of the world within which I was growing up. But this left areas untouched or underdeveloped, and these needed their own space in which to grow. So I had come to Spain and learned flamenco, free from the restrictions of an English personality, exploring parts of myself that would otherwise have remained dormant, absorbing a new set of values and norms. Spain had allowed my emotions to breathe and be expressed, perhaps even to excess. But they were visible, out in the open. England had frozen them, pretended they didn't exist.

As for *duende*, I was beginning to see it less in terms of the ecstatic emotional state I had viewed it as before, or a half-glimpsed vision of beauty I was constantly trying to recapture, and now perceived it as more of a subtle phenomenon. It could mean different things to different people. Certainly it existed – I had felt it as a palpable force, even as an independent spirit of sorts – but I wondered if the quality of what each individual felt depended on what he or she brought to the experience. For Juan, it had been love. But that had been Juan all over: fossilised in the state of jilted lover, forever defined by what he had failed to resolve in his inner life. For Jesús, *duende* had been life on the edge, until he finally pushed it too far and was killed by it. For myself, I was no longer sure.

'Every man and every artist, whether he is Nietzsche

or Cézanne, climbs each step in the tower of his perfection by fighting his *duende*, not his angel, as has been said, or his muse. The distinction is fundamental.'

But Lorca appeared to be certain about what *duende* was. For him, the muse and the angel came from without; *duende* came from 'the blood'.

If *duende* were to be approached at all, it could only be done so obliquely. I had been down at least two wrong avenues in my search, and viewed Juana's teaching approach as antithetical to cultivating *duende*. Discipline, yes, but you had to be allowed to breathe. Perhaps, I thought, I would have to start looking for answers away from the world of flamenco. Or perhaps, even, my search had never really been for *duende* after all.

Getting hold of tickets for the Paco de Lucía concert was more of a challenge than I had expected. The notice in the paper was so small it was as good as lost in the smudged newsprint. And when I asked where the 'Casa Cultural' was, no-one had a clue. I went back to the Tourist Office. The girl was as helpful as when I had first gone there.

'I don't know where it is,' she said.

'But how else am I going to find out if you can't tell me?'

She shrugged her shoulders.

'I don't know. I only tell people what I read in the brochures. You could try the Corte Inglés,' she called as I stepped out into the street.

The Corte Inglés? That was a department store. I was none the wiser. But I had nothing to lose from trying.

The cool air-conditioning hit me like a wall of

plastic as I walked in. A melancholic salesgirl was standing by the lipstick counter.

'Oh yes,' she said when I asked her, as though this was her real job, not selling make-up after all. 'Top floor.'

The top floor sold suitcases and jockstraps.

The jockstrap salesman also welcomed the question as though it were the most normal thing in the world and pointed me to a counter in the far corner hidden by a row of naked mannequins.

'It's gone twelve o'clock,' the woman behind the desk said. 'We can't sell any more tickets now.' I looked at the clock: it was ten past twelve.

'Surely ten minutes . . .'

'Too late. They're mostly sold out anyway.'

How? Had several thousand other people already followed the same labyrinthine route? I began to suspect a conspiracy.

'Look, there must be some other way.'

'Try Juan Carlos's newspaper kiosk. He might have some left. But not before three, mind.'

I slid down the escalators armed with this vital piece of information. Only one problem: who was Juan Carlos and where the hell was his kiosk? I went back to the lipstick girl.

'Just one more thing. I don't suppose you know where Juan Carlos's kiosk is?'

She pointed across the road. 'Just there. Enjoy the concert.' Why hadn't she sent me there in the first place?

Juan Carlos was about to close.

'Come back after three,' he grunted, trying to pull down the metal shutter.

'I just want some tickets for the Paco concert,' I said hopefully.

334

'Yeah? Like flamenco then, do you?'

I sometimes forgot how foreign I looked.

'Come on then.' He beckoned me forward. 'Here, I've got some good seats left in the middle. I was keeping them for someone else, but he said he'd be back before lunch and he hasn't shown up. You can have them.'

I handed over the cash and the tickets were slipped into my hand.

'Where is the Casa Cultural, anyway?' I asked.

'Eh?'

'The place where the concert's happening.'

'Don't know what you're talking about. He's playing up in the Generalife.'

Luis returned to the school in late April, more than ready to pick up the guitar again.

'Tell you what,' he whispered, 'that illness lark wasn't so bad.' He nudged me in the ribs. 'There's nothing she wouldn't do for me. Know what I mean?' He winked knowingly. 'Any time, day or night. Fantastic!'

I carried on playing for Carmen at the late-night special classes, but Luis's natural place was that of principal guitarist, so I fell back to accompanying him in the main lessons. Not that it involved very much – in effect we were providing two metronomes for the dancers instead of one. Occasionally there would be a bit of interchange between us – an echoing *rasgueo*, for example – but, for the most part we simply kept *compás*. He was totally concentrated on the dancers and Juana, and less interested in making music. It was clear that my time at the studio was coming to an end.

A week later, after everyone had gone, I told Juana I was leaving. A resigned smile formed on her large, powerful face. She knew it was coming. It probably saved her the trouble of telling me herself.

'Thank you,' she said, kissing me on both cheeks, and walked away. She didn't like goodbyes.

I walked out of the empty studio, through the hallway, and found Emilio. He was sitting in his booth, writing.

'Remember to watch the animals,' he said. 'Study them – how they move, how they hunt, how they live. They have wisdom.'

I made to leave.

'Wait!' he called. He held his hand out as if to halt me in my tracks. There was something fluttering overhead, a shadow in the sky. I couldn't make it out. It looked like a leaf. Then it slowly came down, circled around once more and landed on his arm. It was a butterfly.

'*Colias croceus*,' he said. 'They only come down to the city at this time of year. Not often, though. Less and less now – the pollution and everything. But they only land on you if you are very, very still. They frighten easily.'

I looked and saw its yellow wings gently opening and closing as it rested on his cotton sleeve. Emilio was concentrating on the creature on his arm, but I felt he was gazing directly at me.

'There she goes.' The butterfly took off and flew out into the street. 'It's just like *duende*,' he said.

We both followed it for a moment as it fluttered above the cars in the road, until it lifted on a breath of wind and disappeared into the bright air.

Grace and I sat under the inadequate shade of a parasol at a café in the Albaicín near the Mirador San Nicolás, trying unsuccessfully to stay cool and ignore the argument developing among a group of German tourists at the next table.

'This heat is too much,' she said. 'I think I should be heading north somewhere. Morocco, possibly.'

'That's south.'

'The Arabs are very good at building cool houses,' she went on. 'When I lived in Tangiers I never used to feel the heat. Isn't that interesting?' And she turned her sparkling blue eyes towards me.

'I've heard that igloos can be very warm and comfortable,' I said.

'Yes. I suppose that's similar. But I don't think I'd like it up there. Igloos or no igloos. And I don't find Eskimo men attractive.' She sipped her cold beer, and we fell back into silence, too exhausted to talk much more.

The waiter came and suggested we try the local dish – Sacromonte-style tortilla. He rattled off the ingredients and I agreed, without listening too carefully. I hadn't heard of it before and wondered what it would be like.

'I gave up my job at the school.'

'But what about your guitar? What about flamenco? I thought you'd made your life here.' She paused. 'Or do you find it doesn't satisfy you as it once did?'

'I love flamenco. It's . . .'

She waited while I tried to figure out what I wanted to say.

'I want flamenco to be a *part* of my life. Not *be* my life.'

She nodded.

'Most of the *flamencos* I've known do it because they think it makes them free – on the edge, away from the mainstream. But they're not. They create their own

337

rules, their own restrictions. And they think the charm, the power of flamenco can only exist within flamenco itself. Nowhere else.'

'I knew an old Gypsy woman once who told me very authoritatively that Bach's music has *duende*.'

We had never talked about *duende* before.

'Personally I've only experienced it a handful of times,' she said. 'But on each occasion it was in very different circumstances. Not all of them musical, either. But you already know all of this by now, of course. You must have had plenty of *duende* experiences.'

As ever, she was one step ahead. The understanding she assumed I had was only just forming in my mind.

'I've been so obsessed with flamenco, trying to live a real flamenco life – whatever that is . . .'

The waiter bringing the food cut me off, and our attention was diverted to lunch.

'What did you say this was?' Grace asked with a smirk on her lips.

'It's some special local dish. It's got all sorts in it.'

She dipped her fork into it hesitantly. I had to admit, there was something strange about the smell. We pushed on, forcing it down through sheer hunger.

'Do you think it's off?' she laughed, pulling a face.

'Can't be. I've been here before. Food's always pretty good.' I had to admit, though, this was awful. I tried to remember what the waiter had told me it had in it. Peas, was it? Beans? I couldn't remember. And then there was something else. Ah, yes.

'I know what's making it taste funny,' I said. 'Brains. It's got sheep's brains in it.'

Our stomachs both churned simultaneously. Grace put her fork down.

'I think I've had enough for now, thanks. Do you think you might order some more water?'

We tried to wash the offending taste away; brains and heat just didn't go well together. For another two hours we sat at the table, slowly trying to digest, drinking steadily, unable to move or even think through sheer discomfort.

'Do you think we should go somewhere else?' Grace asked. Her face was pale and she suddenly looked her age, as though a light inside her had been turned off. 'We've been here for quite some time without ordering anything.'

'No, it's all right,' I grunted. 'They won't mind.'

The afternoon wore on. Children were coming out from the school nearby. I shifted in my seat to gauge the state of my guts. Not so bad this time. Perhaps there was light at the end of the tunnel.

'I've got an idea,' I said. Grace looked as if she were asleep in her chair. 'Let's drive up to the Sierra Nevada.'

There was still no movement from her and her face was quite pasty now. I leaned over to feel her hand. Perhaps . . .

'What a good idea!' she cried, opening her eyes wide. She sat up, knocked back her water and was on her feet in seconds, the colour rushing back to her cheeks.

'Here,' she said, handing me the keys. 'You drive.'

I was hoping she'd say that.

We sped away from the city, heading for the mountains. Within minutes the heaviness seemed to lift as we started climbing, and the air blowing in through the windows became cooler.

The road was lined with pine trees, isolated wooden

huts with logs stacked against the outer walls for winter, and roadside cafés with chalet-like roofs. Like the Alps, but without the rain.

'They do a lot of skiing here in the winter, apparently,' Grace said. 'The king comes here. I wouldn't mind seeing him in his skiing outfit.'

Every so often we could spot Mulhacén ahead, the mountain covered in snow above the green trees and ash-grey rock.

'Are we going all the way up there?' she asked.

'I hope so. Unless we get snowed in, of course.'

'Snowed in? In June? What a silly thing to say.'

'A friend told me there are eagles up here,' I said.

'How exciting!'

The road wound on, and the air became steadily lighter and thinner.

'I've been thinking about a line of Lorca's,' I said. 'He says: "*A mí se me importa poco que un pájaro pase de un alamo a otro*".'

'Oh.'

'He doesn't care about little things,' I explained, 'about whether a bird flies from one tree to another. The only things that matter to him are big events. Life, death, blood, passion. But he's wrong. There's as much life in a bird, or an insect for that matter. You miss so much if you only concentrate on the dramatic.'

'What do you mean?' she asked.

'Well ... imagine there are lots of different sounds, some loud, some soft, some in between. If you can only hear the loud ones, you're missing all the other ones, you're not getting the whole picture. And they might be more interesting, more subtle. More important, even.'

'I see,' she said. 'And how can you learn to hear the softer sounds?'

'I don't know. Developing other interests, perhaps. I've thought of little else but guitars and flamenco for the past couple of years, trying to learn as fast as I could. It's made me feel lop-sided.'

'Yes, I've always thought it's very important to have more than one pole in life.'

We continued up the mountain. She wasn't going to give me any easy answers.

Twenty minutes later we reached the Sierra Nevada ski resort, and the end of the road. The place was deserted. Just a few other cars, and a barrier preventing us from driving on to the radio transmitter further up the slope. We pulled over and stepped out of the car. The air was crisp and cold, such a change from Granada. A few yards ahead of us lay the snow, and we instinctively walked towards it. It was hard, crunchy, off-white.

'Come on,' said Grace. 'We can reach those rocks over there.'

We scrambled over, slipping on the ice beneath our feet.

'If I'd known it was going to be like this, I wouldn't have worn this flimsy little dress,' she said.

A few slips later, and having carried her piggyback across the roughest part of the rocks, we were standing together on a promontory looking back down into the valley we had driven up. It looked dark down there: the shadows were beginning to lengthen as the sun dipped lower towards the horizon.

'It's strange,' she said. 'It looks blue.'

I stared down and then up towards the brilliant, azure sky. Such a rich, deep colour. So close, it seemed, and yet still out of reach.

'I feel this is a time for thinking about the need to

love and the need to be loved,' she said. 'Yes, that's it. It's been swirling around inside me for a while, but it's only now that it has become clear like this. I'm very interested in love at the moment.

'Relationships can come to you at any time, when you least expect them, or when you're not thinking about them, but about other things, and they can grow, from somewhere you didn't expect them to come from.

'It's funny, because I've lived many thousands of years more than you – ha, ha – yet it's only now that it came to me: "This is what you should be thinking about." Of course, that's today. Tomorrow it may be something completely different.'

I stood still for a while, transfixed by it all. She had the ability to say exactly the right thing at exactly the right moment, connecting with something in me.

'Over there,' she said gently. 'An eagle.'

I turned to where she was pointing. The eagle was gliding slowly and effortlessly, circling below us over the vast open space of the valley. We watched it, following its path up and over the crest of the mountain, one minute stationary, the next swooping down, turning and rising again as it came closer towards us. It was magnificent. Calm and alert, searching the valley floor for possible prey, it had presence; a total mastery of the area beneath its gaze as though the land were part of itself. 'Watch the animals,' Emilio had said.

Grace began to walk away, shivering, while I remained for a minute more. It was so peaceful up here; it felt as though any separation between myself and the surroundings was beginning to blur. The eagle turned once more and I followed it down the slope, circling in the dark blue shadows, then up over the hill till it reached the golden outcrop in the distance and disappeared.

Something hit the back of my head. It was cold, hard and wet. I turned and saw Grace with an innocent look on her face, hands behind her back.

'Don't look at me,' she said. 'I didn't do anything.'

The snowball was melting and dripping down the back of my shirt. Then she pulled out another two and sent them flying in my direction. I ducked down, to dodge them, scooped up some snow of my own and prepared to launch a counter-attack.

Carmen and I were accompanied by Luis and his kick-boxing girlfriend.

'I wouldn't miss this if I were dead,' he said emphatically as we walked round the back of the Alhambra. 'I tell you, sex on tap is great, but it doesn't beat being able to listen to Paco.'

It seemed things weren't so great with his girlfriend again.

'She just seems to think I'm some sort of punch-bag. And I told her: a bit of rough, no problem. But at the right moment. I mean look,' he showed me the bruises on his arms, 'I can't carry on like this. Martial arts and flamenco, they just don't mix.'

Carmen, meanwhile, was skipping ahead, urging us to hurry up. The news had just come through of her acceptance at the Conservatory.

'All thanks to Juana,' she said. 'I'm finally getting out of this place.'

We found our seats and settled down under the clear night sky. The open auditorium was set in beautiful gardens, with the thick, sweet scent of *galán de noche* blowing over our heads like liquor fumes. There was the usual noise and excitement, cigarette smoke and bronzed limbs. But I needed a pee.

'You can't go now! He's about to come on,' Luis cried.

'Back in a tick.'

I made my way out of the auditorium, onto the gravel path, and started looking for the loo. There were people everywhere, guards and ticket collectors, long tables serving as makeshift bars, but I couldn't find the toilet. In the rush, I decided there was nothing for it but to go behind a tree. I cut through a gap in the hedges and started heading cross-country. After a few minutes I found what looked like a suitable spot, pulled down my fly and relaxed. No-one would see me there, I was certain. But trying to urinate as fast as I could, I heard a rustle nearby. Someone else had had the same idea. I looked up and saw a man with long, dark blond hair, a mournful face and an expression equally astonished as my own. It was Paco.

'*Hombre, Paco!*' I said. Here I was, in the Generalife, pissing next to the greatest guitarist of all time.

'*Hola*,' he said nervously.

'No toilets backstage?'

'This is backstage.'

'Oh. Sorry. It's just I couldn't find . . .'

'Don't worry. Neither could I. Everyone gets nervous just before going on, and all the toilets were taken. I couldn't wait.'

We both finished at the same time and zipped ourselves up.

'Nice meeting you,' I said.

'And you.' He smiled, turning to leave.

'Good luck tonight.'

'Thanks for coming.' And he shook my hand.

I watched as he walked away. He looked uncomfortable on his feet. Too much sitting down practising, probably. Then I looked down at my hand. This was one handshake that would definitely be washed away. I knew exactly where his hand had been before it touched mine.

I was back in my seat just as Paco came onto the stage. He looked different up there, dressed in his traditional white shirt and black waistcoat. The guitar on his lap changed him, somehow. More powerful, more presence.

'You almost missed him,' Carmen hissed.

The concert started with a *Taranta*. Paco sat alone on stage, gradually drawing the audience into the concert as they settled down, and the hum of voices in the hot, perfumed air of the garden fell silent.

For the following piece more members of the band appeared, and the concert moved up a gear. But something happened when El Grilo – the tall, powerful-looking dancer with greased-back black hair – arrived. Previously playing percussion on the sidelines, he threw himself onto the centre of the stage towards the end of a *Bulería* and started dancing, taking us all by surprise. The man was panther-like, commanding and graceful, and with clean, elegant movements he managed to mesmerise the audience. There was absolute joy in the way he danced; unaffected, playful, almost childlike.

The hairs began to lift along the back of my neck and arms, an electric energy passed through the audience. He had it, he had *duende*: holding us all down in our seats and seizing our attention. And we watched him, his tall, dark animal-like form hammering the floor with immense speed, sweat flying from his head, arms thrust out at his side. A moment of near-madness descended upon us for a second, and then, just as quickly, flew away, leaving a hollow, joyous echo.

His performance inspired the other players. Paco, I could see, had been coasting along until then. But now he had something to play for, to play against, as did the other members of the band, and they all responded with more energy, greater passion. It produced a spark, each one trying to improve on the other, while the audience sat back in pure enjoyment, music flowing over and into us, like the scent of flowers. Paco's playing was sublime.

'I wonder if I could play like that one day,' I asked myself.

'Twenty years of practice, eight hours a day,' said Luis. 'That's what it takes to play like that.'

'You need genius for that,' Carmen added.

'She's right. The girl's right.'

Genius and obsessive discipline. It felt like a tall order. Would I ever be able to produce *duende*?

I was finding other things.

epilogue

*T*ak taka-taka. Tak taka-taka. Tak taka-taka. TAK.

I am woken from my siesta by the rippling of heels against the wooden floor in the next room. The space in the bed beside me is empty. Stretching up above my head, I open the windows to the sunny January air and allow the late afternoon sounds of Gypsy sweet-sellers and mopeds drown out the sharpness of her shoes. My head is still heavy from the rice and *verdejo* wine of lunchtime and I need five minutes more.

The firecrackers start in the street below; a great thundering crescendo that echoes around the *fin de siècle* apartment blocks. I am used to it by now – back in Valencia, the pyrotechnical capital of Spain – but it once sounded to me like the beginning of a battle. Echoes of the Civil War.

I get up and go to help Salud prepare for tonight's gig, although she would never ask me to. Her nervous tension fills the corridor and cannot be ignored. We're running late, as always. A quick massage of her hands and feet and it will be time to go. Her bag is already prepared: red dress, tights, towel, make-up, a comb for her hair, and shoes. She wears Gallardo shoes for dancing. Coral, the other main make, never last her very long, she says. She has been dancing flamenco for half her life.

After five years away, I have returned, as I always thought I would. Back on the eastern coast, a flamenco connection once again. But different this time – another turn in the cycle. I am still fascinated by Spain, perhaps the *only* country, as Hemingway suggested. It is a labyrinth-like land, a place only partially influenced by the mechanical world, it seems. I always have the sense that, on turning any corner, or entering any village here, I might pass unexpectedly into an ancient, fairytale world where earth spirits still reign. Or meet an old man with simple phrases of wisdom that are passed down from generation to generation. Fates and *duendes*, song and blood rituals: this was the land from which flamenco was born and to which it still belongs.